Handloom Weavers in Ulster's Linen Industry, 1815–1914

Handloom Weavers in Ulster's Linen Industry, 1815–1914

Kevin J. James

FOUR COURTS PRESS

This book was set in 10.5 on 13 Times for
FOUR COURTS PRESS LTD
7 Malpas Street, Dublin 8, Ireland
email: info@four-courts-press.ie
http://www.four-courts-press.ie
and in North America by
FOUR COURTS PRESS
c/o ISBS, 920 N.E. 58th Avenue, Suite 300, Portland, OR 97213.

ISBN (10-digit) 1–84682–001–4
ISBN (13-digit) 978–1–84682–001–4

A catalogue record for this title
is available from the British Library.

Printed in Great Britain
by Athenæum Press Ltd, Gateshead, Tyne & Wear.

Contents

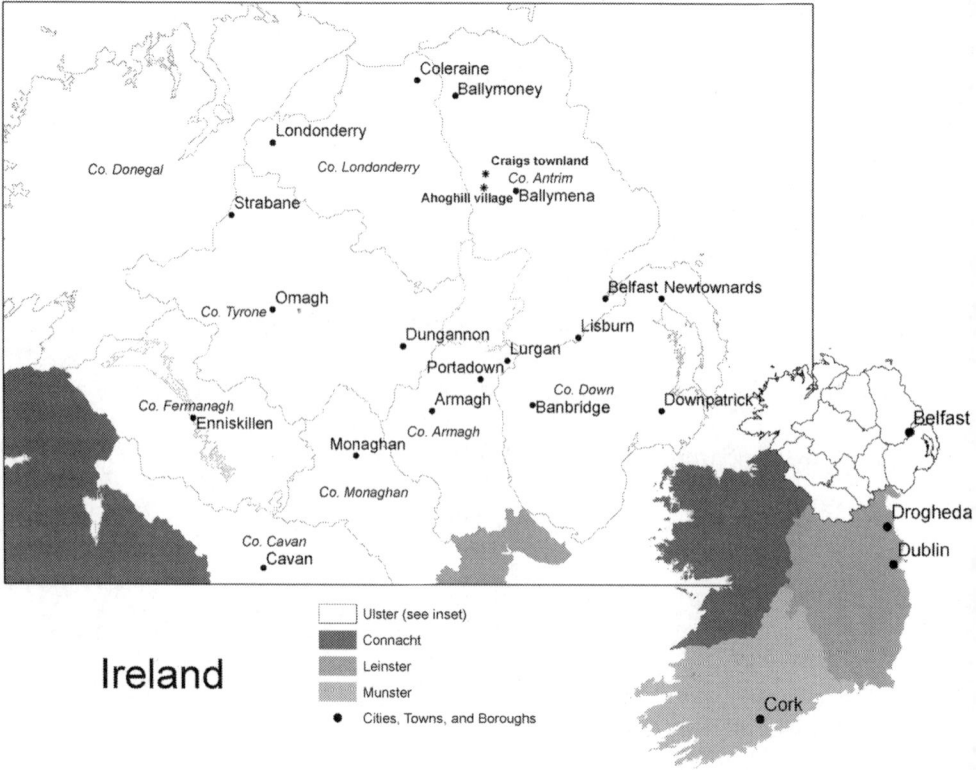

Co. Donegal

Coleraine
Ballymoney

Londonderry

Co. Londonderry

Craigs townland
Co. Antrim

Ahoghill village Ballymena

Strabane

Omagh
Co. Tyrone

Dungannon

Lurgan

Lisburn

Belfast Newtownards

Portadown

Co. Down

Armagh

Banbridge

Downpatrick

Co. Fermanagh
Enniskillen

Co. Armagh

Monaghan

Co. Monaghan

Co. Cavan
Cavan

Belfast

Drogheda

Dublin

Cork

Ireland

Ulster (see inset)

Connacht

Leinster

Munster

Cities, Towns, and Boroughs

*Selected linen markets in Ireland and Ulster,
including the principal places to which this study refers.*

Acknowledgments

This book began as a PhD thesis in the Department of Economic and Social History at the University of Edinburgh. I am grateful for the support of my advisors, Professor R.J. Morris and Professor Graeme Morton (now a colleague at the University of Guelph). I have also benefited from the advice of Dr Andy Bielenberg, Brenda Collins, Dr W.H. Crawford, Dr David Dickson, Dr Trevor Griffiths, Professor Maria Luddy, Professor Ged Martin, Dr P.E. O'Connor and Dr Peter Solar. Dr Colin Coates, Roger Hamill, Dr Janice Holmes, Dr Billy Kelly, Martin, Moira and Sarah Laidlaw, Dr Éamonn Ó Ciardha, David Scott and Grace Owens offered hospitality and friendship during my three years of study and travel in Scotland and Ireland. The Commonwealth Scholarship Plan and the Social Sciences and Humanities Research Council of Canada provided generous support for my doctoral studies. Research in Ireland in 1998 was funded by the Justin Arbuthnott Fund. Subsequent financial support was provided to me by the Department of History at the University of Guelph, whose spirit of collegiality and mutual support I appreciate; I also owe a debt of gratitude to the many fine students of History I have had the pleasure to teach at the University of Guelph. I am grateful to Four Courts Press for support of this publication and to Michael Adams, Martin Fanning and Aoife Walsh for shepherding the manuscript to monograph. Joshua MacFadyen offered his cartographic expertise to create the map in this book, and Justin Dell assisted in reviewing the final draft.

I also wish to acknowledge and thank the editors of two journals, *Textile History* and *Saothar*, in which earlier research related to this project appeared as 'The hand-loom in Ulster's post-Famine linen industry: the limits of mechanization in textiles' "factory age"', *Textile History* 35, 2 (2004), 178–91 and 'Merchants, manufacturers and the Ballymena handloom weavers: market conflict in the Ulster brown linen trade, 1873', *Saothar* 27 (2002), 19–29.

I especially wish to thank my parents, Joseph and Jane Marie James, my brother Michael, my wife Monica, and our son Charles Ansley Theodor, who was born as revisions to the manuscript were completed.

This book is dedicated to my maternal grandmother, Helen M.N. McNab, who encouraged my interest in history.

'An Antrim Hand-Loom Weaver'.
In *Some Irish industries* (Dublin: *The Irish Homestead,* 1897), p. 68.
Courtesy of the National Library of Ireland.

'Girl Weaving Cambric in Country Home'.
Sketched by Paul Rénouard. In *Some historical notes on linen, ancient and modern* (Belfast: Robinson & Cleaver, n.d.), p. 80.

Introduction

As the twentieth century turned in Ireland, the sound of the linen handloom fly shuttle echoed in cottages and workshops in Cos. Antrim, Armagh and Down, although the din of the steam-loom in Ulster had become much louder during the previous fifty years. Between the end of the Famine and the beginning of the Great War, the powerloom made inroads into branches of the Irish linen industry which had once remained beyond its application. Yet its advance was not universal. Linen weavers remained at the handloom half a century after the first, hesitant experiments with new steam-powered weaving technology. This study aims to integrate them within the history of rural Irish labour. It explores contexts in which handloom weaving continued in Ireland's northern province — the seat of the linen industry — after the mid-nineteenth century, and examines relationships between gender, status and skill in the Irish linen trade. Textile workers in Ireland encountered new technologies, and experienced organizational change, in diverse ways. Gender, understood here as the social theorizing and organization of sexual difference, was central to these encounters.[1] Yet its influence over rural hand production remains obscure.[2] The linen trade was marked by sexual divisions of labour, around which handloom 'skill' was also constructed and contested. When male linen weavers invoked their 'historic' monopoly over craft skill as the twentieth century turned, for instance, they articulating a defence of historic craft identities and claims to expertise as they encountered a changing commercial climate. The handloom 'skill' over which they claimed proprietorship was a protean category subject to intensive gendering and to revision as the structure of the trade and the workforce changed. This study charts those changes, focusing on encounters between labour, technology and hand production.

As the scale of linen hand production diminished, there was a parallel re-evaluation of handloom skill through which some work was elevated as exemplars of traditional craftsmanship. In Ireland's late-nineteenth-century handloom trade struggles over the definition of weaving expertise were linked to cultural politics that glorified selected peasant handicraft traditions. They had strong ties to discourses of Irish nationalism and 'Celticism'. Thus the handloom weaver had an

---

1 See S.O. Rose (1993) and (1992); S.O. Rose & L.L. Frader (1996); N.G. Osterud (1986); C.E. Morgan (2001); A. Clark (1995). For a discussion of craft identities in the pottery industry in later-nineteenth-century Britain, see C. Buckley (1989).   **2** By contrast, studies of non-factory manufacture in the urban apparel and textile trades pay close attention to sexual segregation of work and gendered work identities in both domestic and workshop settings: B. Taylor (1983); K. Honeyman (2000a).

iconic status in the turbulent cultural politics of the late-nineteenth century — and male weavers appropriated the mantle of the Celtic revival to buttress their claims to special standing as practitioners of a traditional craft. But handloom weavers were more than a vestigial craft labour force after 1850. The workforce remained large through the 1870s, its structural features were changing, and the handloom was firmly integrated within the commercial linen trade — and mass textile manufacture — in Ireland. [3] As females entered the handloom workforce in large numbers in the 1830s and 1840s, the trade became stratified by sex. Similarly, as the fate of various handloom branches differed through the 1860s, 70s, 80s and 90s, weavers had divergent experiences of industrialization.[4]

The long-neglected female weaver was a particularly pivotal figure in these decades. No marginal participant in rural industry, she became the mainstay of the rural workforce — and, to some late-nineteenth-century observers, the harbinger of a skilled trade's decay. My effort to bring her under a scholarly lens was conceived partly in response to the ambitious research agenda for Irish women's history set by Maria Luddy in 1992 — one that called specifically on historians to expand the study of cottage industries in the nineteenth century.[5] After that piece identified fertile terrain for women's social history, a number of seminal pieces on cottage industry and female employment in rural Ireland followed — and Joanna Bourke's path-breaking paradigm extended the agenda beyond the empirical reconstruction of rural women's work to theorize the apparent decline in their paid activity.[6] Other studies of home industries have tended to focus on themes of patronage, rather than on the experience of labour.[7] Although the study of rural women's paid work in Ireland is still in its infancy, [8] the analysis of linen handloom labour is par-

3 In the economic and social history of modern Britain, the handloom workforce has been widely studied. J.H. Clapham acknowledges widespread co-extensive hand- and mechanized textile production (1963), 83–5. The structure and 'decline' of the handloom workforce has also been explored in E.P. Thompson (1963); G. Timmins (1993); J.S. Lyons (1989); D. Bythell (1969); N. Murray (1978). The cotton industry in England has generated a large literature, much of which incorporates discussions of labour: S.D. Chapman (1967); A. Howe (1984); R. Lloyd-Jones (1988); M.B. Rose (1986). Industrial organization in the wool and worsted branches, involving co-extensive mechanized and hand production in the nineteenth century, has been studied by D.T. Jenkins & K.G. Ponting (1982); P. Hudson (1986); J. Smail (1999). M. Berg (1985) emphasizes organizational diversity within many branches of the British textile trades — and offers an important corrective to interpretations of their linear development. In contrast with work on cotton in particular, most work on the British linen sector focuses on commercial themes and industrial organization and not on labour *per se*: N. Evans (1985); A.J. Durie (1979); W.G. Rimmer (1960). In Ireland the study of hand work after 1850 has focused not on weaving, but on making-up and garment work which were outgrowths of centralized production. See M. Neill (1994); B. Collins (1991) and (1988). **4** J. Gray (1993a) and (1993b); A. McKernan (1994) W.H. Crawford (1991) and (1988); M. Cullen (1990). **5** M. MacCurtain, et al. (1992). **6** J. Bourke (1999), (1994), (1993), (1991a) and (1991b); P. Sharpe and S.D. Chapman (1996); M. Neill (1994); see also B. Collins (1988) and (1991) for excellent studies that preceded Luddy's call for more work in the field. **7** J. Helland (2004a); N.G. Bowe and Elizabeth Cumming (1998); N. Harris (1992). **8** J. Bourke (1993); M. Daly (1997a) and (1981); R.M. Rhodes (1992). See also J. MacPherson (2001); M. Luddy (2000) and (1995); A. O' Dowd (1994). For the linen trade, see M. Cohen (1997a); J. Hamill (2000) and (1999).

ticularly limited — especially relative to the rich literature on factory work.[9] Research on the eighteenth-century and early-nineteenth-century handloom trade has questioned both the structural features identified by Conrad Gill in his pioneering history of the industry, and the teleology that underpinned it;[10] this in turn has nourished a research agenda on the post-Famine trade to which both W.H. Crawford and Brenda Collins have contributed, exploring relationships between the sexual profile of handloom labour, tenurial systems and household economies.[11] This analysis of handloom weaving aims to advance our understanding of relationships of labour and skill, and to establish an empirical foundation for the study of rural industrial labour. So doing, it complements growing research on the Irish textile sector, as historians of Irish industry question conventional understandings of the woollen, cotton and linen industries in Ireland's nineteenth-century economy.[12] In the linen industry, several studies have greatly expanded our knowledge of business organization in the nineteenth century.[13] Peter Solar has documented the wider commercial context within which these businesses operated,[14] and we now know much more about the wider European industry in which Ireland's linen trade operated.[15] Still, the labour history of the post-Famine linen industry is much less developed. The scale of rural hand production, the diversity of its workforces, the chronology of its growth and contraction, and its salience to broader debates surrounding the 'home industries revival' in Ireland demand that it receive a more expansive analysis.

Handloom weavers, the focus of this study, are by no means neglected in the historiography of industrial labour in the United Kingdom. Indeed, they have

---

9 For factory work, see B. Messenger (1978); J. Hamill (2000); M. Greiff (1997); M. Cohen (1997a). Non-factory paid work has been explored in B. Collins (1997), (1991) and (1988); M. Neill (1994); J. Bourke (1993); J.A. Grew (1987). See also a classic study that attempts to restore the role of women in cottage industry to prominence: E. Boyle (1971).   **10** P. Solar (1990); W.H. Crawford (1991) and (1988); J. Gray (2005).   **11** B. Collins (1997); W.H. Crawford (1993). See also E.R.R. Green (1944).   **12** See R.V. Comerford (1989), especially 379–80. E.R.R. Green's classic study (1949) emphasizes the incomplete character of factory development after 1850, but focuses largely on the preceding half-century. Recent research into Ireland's cotton and woollen industries undermines long-standing assumptions about their nineteenth-century decline. F. Geary (1989) and (1981) has led the reassessment of the Irish cotton sector. In the woollen trade, L. A. Clarkson (1989b) has led a revision of the eighteenth-century industry and A. Bielenberg (2000) has argued that domestic production was resilient in many areas through the 1840s, even as the industry contracted in some centres. He has shown how factory production substantially increased the output of woollens in the second half of the century. Its relative resilience, and indeed growth, is now emphasized in place of its contraction or displacement in the later-nineteenth century. These reinterpretations have been central to a revision of the putative 'national crises' in the nineteenth-century textile sectors — which were seen as outgrowths of Ireland's economic and political integration with Britain — the classic expression of this view being O'Brien (1921). See D.S. Johnson & L. Kennedy (1991), especially 21–7. L.M. Cullen (1972) also remarks on the 'national crisis' in textiles in the 1820s, but emphasizes that the linen sector's experience was one of regional crisis as production became concentrated in Ulster (106–8, 124).   **13** F. Geary (2005); E.J. Boyle (1997); P. Ollerenshaw (1997).   **14** P. Solar (1990) and (2005).   **15** B. Collins & P. Ollerenshaw (2003).

been central to debates on the impact of new technology and organizational systems, the displacement of craft skill, and the 'proletarianization' of the workforce ever since E.P. Thompson's magisterial study of Britain's cotton weavers — to him the pre-eminent exemplars of the tragedy of craft erosion.[16] In Thompson's analysis, the participation of 'secondary' workers in the trade affirmed weaving's declining status even before the death knell sounded for cotton hand production.[17] While economic and social historians have identified many nuances in the experience of these weavers, challenging Thompson's periodization by emphasizing diverse regional and sectoral experiences,[18] and gender historians have openly challenged the putatively obvious correspondence between female participation in the labour force and processes of deskilling, the handloom weaver remains an emotive emblem of the ravages of Britain's Industrial Revolution. Structural interpretations of the Irish linen trade informed by Marxist theory, the most famous of which is Peter Gibbon's synthesis of social and economic relations in the nineteenth century,[19] largely endorse Thompson's analysis. More recently, the Irish linen trade has been brought under the lens of historical sociology, and used to test precepts of proto-industrial, world-systems and gender theory.[20] These studies have largely been confined to the period before mechanization, or to the powerloom factory; an analysis of hand work's coexistence with mechanized production can help to bridge these literatures and deepen our understanding of the relationships between 'traditional' production and skill in the Factory Age.

CRAFT, SKILL AND HAND WORK

Hand production occupies a famously ambiguous place in British industrialization — as the exemplar of a craft mode of production whose displacement many anticipated, yet whose stubborn persistence they observed (and often lamented) in almost all sections of industry. Commentators as divergent in their assessments of industrialization as Andrew Ure[21] and Karl Marx[22] believed that manufacture passed through discrete organizational stages towards centralized, mechanized production. While their analyses of the implications of these changes diverged, both men regarded the factory as the apotheosis of industrial capitalism. Yet the factory itself — distinguished here from the workshop by its adoption of mechanical motive power — was only one form of industrial organization. From cotton to

---

16 E.P. Thompson (1963). In the historiography of British industrialization, this thesis stretches back to J.L. & B. Hammond (1919).   17 G. Timmons (1993), 10; J.S. Lyons (1989), 47.   18 G. Timmins (1993); J.S. Lyons (1989); D. Bythell (1969).   19 P. Gibbon (1975).   20 J. Gray (2005), (1999) and (1993c); D. O'Hearn (1997a); Cohen (1997a).   21 A. Ure, *The philosophy of manufactures* (1861)   22 Karl Marx, *Capital: a critique of political economy* (1906).

linen to silk to wool, almost no branch of textile production operated using steam power exclusively in the mid-nineteenth century, despite its pioneering role in Britain's and Ireland's industrial expansion.[23] Indeed, hand production often intensified with the adoption of new technologies of mass production. The narrative of hand production's contraction is thus far from a corollary to factory industrialization.[24] The factory has nonetheless become the primary arena in which industrial relations of class and gender are studied. The concepts of 'labour aristocracy'[25] and 'sexual segregation',[26] for instance, offer explications of the fissures, internal divisions, and conflicts within the 'working class' that focus on factory labour. They have contributed to a complex picture of a hierarchical, segregated and heterogeneous industrial working class that highlights the extent of its stratification. They can also offer valuable lessons to students of Irish cottage industry.

Several frameworks for the study of sexual segregation in the industrial workplace provide insight into the handloom trade. Some historians of industrialization theorize the origins of differential male and female earnings and their occupational segregation with reference to divergent levels of output and productivity, seeing the 'wage gap' as an outgrowth of unequal male and female 'human capital'.[27] In its crudest formulation, this theory presupposes a neutral labour market and unconstrained, rational choices about labour allocation.[28] Most historians have criticized this approach. They identify important cultural constraints placed on women's participation in paid labour markets. Many European and North American women's historians in the 1970s sought to formulate a theory of labour-force stratification premised on the influence of deeply-embedded cultural assumptions about men, women and work. Central to their theorizing were questions about how wider gender relations influenced the demarcation of 'men's' and 'women's' work, and how sexual divisions projected ideologies of men's and women's innate social difference onto the workplace. The concept of 'sex-typing', whereby tasks and work were assigned according to a putative 'natural' correspondence between their intellectual and physical requirements and corresponding attributes of each sex, was foregrounded in the sociology of work.[29] Scholars also questioned the concept of human capital as a value-free construct.[30] Instead, they focused on interwoven cultural relations of gender and authority in the construction of expertise.[31] The tension between class- and gender-based explanations of labour-force stratification

23 R. Samuel (1977); C. Sabel & J. Zeitlin (1985).   **24** D. Bythell (1978); J.A. Schmiechen (1984); J. Lown (1990); J. Rendall (1990); P. Sharpe & S.D. Chapman (1996).   **25** For the classic discussion of 'labour aristocracy', see J. Foster (1974); R.Q. Gray (1976); G. McLennan (1981); H.F. Moorhouse (1978). A critique of this theory appears in C. More (1995).   **26** For an excellent discussion of this theme see C.E. Morgan, in 'Introductory essay — gender in labour history', in Morgan (2001), 1–20.   **27** J. Burnette (1997); J. Mincer & S. Polachek (1974).   **28** See S. Walby (1988).   **29** See J.A. Matthaei (1982).   **30** F. Blau & C. Jusenius (1976); P. England (1982).   **31** See S. Alexander (1983); V. Beechey (1979).

led to a number of ambitious syntheses, especially by historians seeking to elaborate a theory of gender compatible with Marxist interpretations of industrial capitalism's development. Heidi Hartmann's 'dual systems' theory[32] proposed that the cultural context within which industrial labour was structured influenced the demarcation of men's and women's roles in the division of labour, their access to skills and status, and their earnings. While historians emphasize that 'patriarchy' was not unique to the period of industrial capitalism,[33] and debate its meaning, their emphasis on cultural ideology in the production and reproduction of sexual segregation has led them to question how such categories as human capital and skill are developed and used, especially in relation to technologies of production.

GENDER AND SKILL

Skill lies at the heart of workforce stratification and of claims to intellectual and social authority, yet as a category it has been subjected to limited scrutiny.[34] Gender historians have tended to reject the gender-neutral conceptualization of skill that equates it with an objective set of competences and abilities. This formulation underpinned Marxist interpretations of capitalism, which charted the relationship of capital to labour through phases in which skill was progressively eroded — in some cases inaugurating new sexual divisions within the workforce. The related concept of 'deskilling', by which labour's expertise diminished through mechanization, lay at the core of the analysis of the technological displacement of craft skill.[35] From a largely gender-blind perspective, skill has been portrayed as an objective set of competences displaced by technology in the development of industrial capitalism. In more recent years, scholars have questioned this understanding of skill, and have focused on ways in which it was constructed and reconstructed; the conflation of female labour with skills displacement has been seen as a product of cultural ideologies of gender. Skill is now widely treated as a protean category embedded within them.[36] The 'social construction of skill', as mapped out by A. Phillips and B. Taylor, provides a rubric under which many scholars have explored how skill is created and contested as a category denoting intellectual, technical and social authority.[37] Industrial textile workforces — in the factory, at the machine, but also in the home engaged in hand production — provide a focus for these investigations.

32 H. Hartmann (1976) and (1979). **33** S.O. Rose (1988); M. Berg (1985). Early, classic studies of customary wage differentials include I. Pinchbeck (1930) and A. Clark (1919). **34** C. Cockburn (1983); W. Lazonick (1979); S.O. Rose (1986); C. Buckley (1989); M.J. Prus (1990). See also S.P. Vallas (1990), 379, and the issue of *Work and Occupations* 17, 4 (1990) devoted to exploring the category of 'skill'. **35** H. Braverman (1974). **36** The pioneering work in this research direction was A. Phillips & B. Taylor (1980); see also J. Parr (1988). B. Littlewood (2004) provides an overview of the sociology of skill in ch. 3, 'Divisions of labour', 41–75. **37** C. Cockburn (1983); B. Taylor & A. Phillips (1980); C. F. Sabel (1982). See also J. Rule (1987); D.

The mill and factory have been primary sites of research into the cultural and social negotiation of skill during industrialization.[38] Yet historians have shown these processes to be neither unique to factory production, nor indeed to the Factory Age. Let us take the domestic mode of linen production in Ireland, which was no expression of inter-familial egalitarianism, but in fact a hierarchical system in which tasks were assigned by sex and age. Household members co-operated in manufacture, but relations between them were markedly uneven.[39] Adult men tended to maintain control over looms and authority over production. Women spun yarn and children were assigned various ancillary tasks. The payment for the products of domestic work — expressed in a remittance to the male weaver (when there was one in the household) — was largely seen as his property.[40] Historians have debated the extent to which factory production disrupted these relationships; did the introduction of independent wages, for instance, grant female workers greater autonomy?[41] Several scholars have cast doubt on this proposition, noting that females' industrial earnings were consistently lower than those of males, and that female workers were received into workshops and factories in subordinate positions of status and authority, even if their numbers were much greater than those of male factory workers.[42] Indeed, males frequently made claims to craft control and authority in the workplace as a strategy to exclude females from high-paid, high-status work and to strengthen sexual segregation and gender hierarchies in industry.[43] The apparent threat of displacement by 'unskilled' female workers led to the formulation and assertion of the male breadwinner and the family wage. It also led to fierce contests over the operation and command of new technologies.

While technological displacement of male craft control was often seen as a precursor to the sexual reassignment of labour, social contexts in which technology was created and received presents a much more complex picture of the relationship between gender, skill and technology. The adoption of the self-acting cotton-spinning mule, for instance, gave birth to a new set of practices that reconstructed

Simonton (1998), 264–6; G. de Groot & M. Schrover (1995), especially 'General introduction', by the editors, 1–16. **38** Indeed, such important historical concepts as the construction of industrial skill, the development of labour and capital strategies within the workplace, internal divisions within the working class, paternalism and 'dual systems' theory all have as their locus the dynamics of industrial capitalism as played out on the factory floor. See P. Joyce (1991); C.E. Morgan (2001); J. Humphries (1991). **39** See S. O. Rose (1987); M. O'Dowd (2005), 138–40. **40** J. Gray (1993a). **41** A good discussion of the 'pessimists' and 'optimists' positions on women's status during industrialization may be found in J. Thomas (1988). **42** K. Honeyman (2000b), 51–94; J. Lown (1990); D. Valenze (1995). An excellent analysis of the relationship between new technologies of production and the gendering of labour in a range of textile trades can be found in M. Berg (1987). **43** The role of male-dominated labour groups in defining an exclusive, male proprietorship over industrial 'skill' is one of the most debated questions in labour history. See M. Brown & P. Philips (1986); W. Seccombe (1986). See also C.E. Morgan (2001), 19–43 for an extensive discussion of how the rhetoric and ideology of 'separate spheres' influenced strategies to obtain legislative 'protection' for women in textile factories through the Factory Acts.

industrial skill and legitimatized male authority over new technology in cotton mills. William Lazonick suggests that the mule became an instrument around which claims to 'natural' masculine authority were crafted. No longer premised on physical strength, men claimed 'mastery of the machine' as a natural extension of their social authority. This evaluation of skill was premised upon a demarcation between skills associated with the operation of technology and those associated with managing and implementing it (what Steven Vallas has referred to as a distinction between 'conception' and 'execution').[44] In her analysis of how industrial skill was reconstructed, Mary Freifeld argues that the mule's operation required a set of technical competences to which males had privileged access. It remained associated with male labour and skill because women were deprived of such training — reflecting durable cultural barriers to their skills acquisition.[45] While the adoption of new machinery often initiated a reconstruction of industrial skill, this study underlines that the relationships between gender and traditional instruments of production were also unstable.

STUDYING A 'HIDDEN WORKFORCE': SOURCES AND PROBLEMS

This book uses a case study of the mid-Antrim shirting trade as the focus for an analysis of work, gender and technology. The sources upon which it draws include contemporary published commentaries, observations of key figures in the industry, trade periodicals and data from British Parliamentary Papers. It also makes extensive use of church and census returns in an effort to expand the empirical base for the study of the handloom workforce. Each of these sources demands separate consideration. Contemporary documents surveying conditions in the industry, written by observers and participants in the trade, offer insight into discourses on technological and social change. However, this study shows that such perspectives were anchored by wider assumptions about industrialization premised upon the linen trade's anticipated mechanization. Many documents also give expression to particular interests and privilege their perspectives. The famous reports of the assistant handloom commissioners in the 1830s, for instance, were influenced by views of industrial and commercial development that held that the weaving trade's reorganization was a necessary adjustment to new economic and industrial imperatives. These assumptions framed their investigations and their commentaries on districts through which they passed. Treated as records that do not simply document conditions in the trade, but constitute and organize understandings of labour, technology and industry, they provide a window onto ideologies of work, gender and industrialization.[46]

---

44 S. Vallas (1990), 381.   **45** M. Freifeld (1986).   **46** P. Richards (1979). The volumes of data

I must also comment on the census. Its limits, especially for investigating patterns of women's work, paid and unpaid, are well documented,[47] but it is used extensively in this study. The census embodied the various values of policymakers, enumerators and participants. Gaps in the enumeration of women's work were expressions of wider contemporary assumptions about productive labour: their protean character was signaled by continually revised instructions to enumerators as to whose work was to be recorded, and how it was to be done. The organization and undertaking of this expansive social survey was also an act that constituted and gave meaning to social and spatial categories — carving the population into discrete territorial units, and soliciting specific information about them in a heavily mediated encounter between the state and the surveyed. Because ideologies of gender and authority shaped the census from its inception, and because the survey devolved considerable authority to the 'social' head of the household responsible for completing the nominal census forms, the resulting data must be approached with an appreciation of its underlying structure. The census enumerators did not survey female and juvenile labour as comprehensively as that of males. This weakness has important consequences for documenting women's work.[48] Yet this study underlines how attention to the content of these records, including 'empty' sections of the manuscript census forms, can advance our understanding of labour force structures and ideologies of work and gender. Close scrutiny of weavers in mid-Antrim reveals that they did not have a uniform encounter with commercial and industrial change. Their experiences reveal nuances that continue to undermine long-standing assumptions about experiences at the handloom in the industrial age.

that were collected by government and trade bodies, especially regarding linen commerce in overseas markets, must also be approached with caution. See P. Solar (2005) and (1990).   **47** There is an extensive literature on this subject. See, for instance, B. Hill (1993); E. Higgs (1990) and (1987); S. Alexander (1983); S. Horrell & J. Humphries (1995); M. Drake (1999); M. Anderson (1999); K. Honeyman (2000b), 51–94.   **48** See N. Verdon (2002).

1

The Irish linen industry in the pre-Famine era

Handloom weaving was both men's and women's work in the second half of the nineteenth century, but the profile of male and female weavers, their work, and the skill level attributed to them, often differed. In order to understand how this happened, we need to examine years that preceded steam-powered mechanization, when a sexually-mixed weaving workforce developed in Ulster's handloom trade. The increase in female weavers was paralleled by a reconstruction of sexual divisions in domestic industry and by an explicit gendering of handloom skill. The implications of both were far-reaching.

AT HOME AND AT WORK: DOMESTIC LINEN PRODUCTION

When Arthur Young conducted his tour through Ireland in 1776–8, he observed widespread linen manufacture, from coarse sets produced around Drogheda to fine cloth traded in Cos. Down and Armagh. Flax was harvested in late July and in the beginning of August, 'steeped' in water, then spread on grass for several days before being taken to scutching mills, where the fibre was separated from harder stock, then heckled, or combed, and divided between long-fibred flax and tow, suitable for coarser webs. Flax yarn was spun from these fibres and then sold in local yarn markets or woven and sold as cloth to drapers, bleachers or their agents.[1] Young also identified mixed agricultural and textile work as a feature of weaving households. Production was organized at the household level, sometimes incorporating flax cultivation, spinning and weaving. Weaving was usually the province of older, male householders (although apprenticeship to the trade began at a young age for many males). They were assisted at the loom by children who wound yarn weft, while women spun yarn and attended to a range of unpaid domestic tasks. The weaver Joseph Carson celebrated their work in verse in 1831:

> My Bess the house trims up full-tidy,
> An' wi' her wheel sits down beside me,
> While I maun make the shuttles play,
> To crack an' wile the time away ...[2]

---

1 Occasionally 'jobbers' would procure supplies in the yarn market to give to weavers in other districts, See C. Gill (1925), 38–9, 170–2. 2 In J. Hewitt (1974), 22. For excellent treatment of

Another poet, James Orr, remarked of his neighbour's household that:

> His thrifty wife and wise wee lasses span
> While the warps and queels employed anither bairn.[3]

The final web was a product of the collective labour of the household unit. Indeed, a parliamentary committee concluded in 1825 that 'one of the causes of the cheapness with which linen is produced in Ireland [is] to be found in all the different parts of the manufacturers' family taking a share from the earliest period of life in some one process or other of the manufacture'.[4] In the first years of the nineteenth century, most Irish linen weavers were also seasonal producers, combining textile production with agricultural work. The extent of their market activity varied accordingly.[5]

Some historians see the autarky of linen-manufacturing households as exceptional. Indeed, their capacity to incorporate all stages of cloth production from flax cultivation to weaving cloth may have been anomalous in the context of the European textile sector.[6] But even in early stages of the Ulster linen industry's development, few weaving households were sheltered from markets, and most spinners and weavers were active in them, buying and selling raw materials, as well as yarn and cloth: A large import trade supplied finer branches of manufacture with continental yarns, and drew weavers of fine cloth into market relations.[7] Indeed, Edward Wakefield saw spinners' and weavers' extensive participation in markets as an impediment to determining their earnings, because their *net* income was affected by costs of raw materials. Earnings, he declared, 'depend on the rise or fall of the markets'.[8] John Dubourdieu made similar comments in his *Statistical Survey of the County of Antrim*, published in 1812, in which he noted that 'where the workman weaves upon his own account, his profit depends not only on his own exertions, but on his skill, or good-fortune in purchasing his material.'[9] Regional specializations also testified to the wider penetration of market relations throughout the trade.

these sources, see D.H. Akenson & W.H. Crawford (1977) and J. Gray (1993b). **3** In J. Hewitt (1974), 22. **4** In E.J. Boyle (1977), 16–17. In 1810, Edward Wakefield attempted to quantify the earnings and costs of handloom labour, reckoning that the average weekly wage was 7s. and the average annual wage £15. Wakefield estimated that weavers working for themselves gained 10s. a web: the cost of a loom ranged from 4 to 5 guineas. He valued the unpaid work of a weaver's child attending the loom at 8 guineas per year. If the weaver's own children were not able to assist at the loom, additional costs of 13s. to 34s. half-yearly were expended in hiring children to perform these tasks (in *Royal Commission on handloom weavers*, Assistant commissioners' reports, Pt. III (Yorkshire, West Riding; Ireland) (43–II), HC 1840, vol. xxiii [hereafter '*Royal commission on handloom weavers*'], Report of C.G. Otway, 621). **5** J. Dubourdieu, *Statistical survey of the County of Antrim* (1812), 397. **6** Weavers in the British cotton industry, for instance, were more obviously dependent upon markets, rather than domestic cultivation, for raw material. See W. Mager (1993); P. Kriedte, et al. (1993). **7** C. Gill (1925), 40–1. **8** *Royal commission on handloom weavers*, Report of C.G. Otway , 621. **9** J. Dubourdieu (1812), 394.

THE GROWTH OF THE COMMERCIAL LINEN INDUSTRY

The expansion of the commercial linen trade, underpinned by domestic production, was spectacular in the eighteenth century. Its development was the result of several factors:

1 Political encouragement of the linen trade, and discouragement of other industries through measures such as the Woollen Act of 1699, which restricted the export of woollen textiles from Ireland and admitted plain linen to England without duty;[10]

2 the supply of skilled weaving labour, especially after the immigration of French Protestant weavers (most famously Louis Crommelin) following the revocation of the Edict of Nantes;[11] and

3 expanding demand, especially in the English market during the first decade of the eighteenth century, when competing continental producers were cut off from English markets.[12]

Agrarian and institutional contexts also privileged early industrial activity: Conrad Gill identified the security of Ulster's land system, which supplied household capital, as a key factor in the linen industry's development.[13] The commercial textile sector emerged as a large-scale enterprise supplying markets at home, in Britain and abroad. In 1705, it was estimated that 520,000 yards of cloth were exported from Ireland. By 1725, that number had increased to 3,864,987, driven by new demand as English markets turned away from traditional continental sources of supply.[14] An extensive linen market network was regulated by statute and superintended by state institutions. The core of these regulations developed in the first decade of the eighteenth century.[15] Between 1711 and 1828, the sector's development was placed under the government-sponsored Board of Trustees for Linen and Hempen Manufacture, which comprised leading members of the Irish political class.[16] It adopted strategies to encourage home production and promote linen exports, including subsidies for capital investment; subsidies for

---

10 C. Gill (1925), 12.   **11** *Royal commission on handloom weavers*, Report of R.M. Muggeridge, 679. An excellent overview of the debate over Crommelin's role in the development of the Irish industry is found in B. Mackey (2003).   **12** C. Gill (1925), 12. See also N.B. Harte (1973).   **13** C. Gill (1925), 23–30. Writing in 1849, C.E. Dobbs attributed the development of tenant right to the linen trade in Ulster. According to his interpretation, it was not an expression of the value of improvements effected by tenants, but rather an appraisal of the value of the land in the context of its proximity to vibrant manufacturing districts ('Some observations on the tenant right of Ulster', *Transactions of the Dublin Statistical Society*, 1 [1849]: 3–13). While he argued that it contributed to Ulster's exceptionalism, intensive linen production in the eighteenth century also took place in districts outside Ulster, as this chapter will show.   **14** H. McCall in C. Gill (1925), 10; N.B. Harte (1973). **15** C. Gill (1925), 64–5.   **16** H.D. Gribbon (1977), 77.

exports; and surveillance over production and exchange. These measures impacted local market practices in uneven ways, even though they aimed to establish
more uniform standards in the trade.

The first Trustees were bequeathed legal regulations that preceded the
Board's creation. The commercial linen trade was historically characterized by
regional specialization — a result of many factors, including the inter-generational transfer of specialist weaving skills. Merchants seeking fine shirtings,
coarse drills or cambrics could procure large quantities of relatively standardized articles in well-known local markets under such a system. Often their
trade involved an extensive network of commercial intermediaries — local
market officials, linen halls, drapers, jobbers, bleacher-merchants and agents.
The Trustees saw regulation of these actors as an early imperative. In 1719,
they began appointing lappers, or inspectors of cloth, in Ireland's many linen
markets.[17] Under successive regulations, goods were classed according to their
measurements and quality (fineness, weight and tightness of weave), often taking the names of their principal districts of manufacture. Cloth 28 yards long
and 21 inches broad, for instance, was classed as a 'Dungannon', and webs 41
yards long and 20 inches broad as 'Lurgans'.[18]

Cultures of exchange in many regional centres of linen manufacture often
operated in tension with this national system of regulation, and in some markets
the introduction of the 'seal-master' system provoked conflict between weavers,
manufacturers and merchants. For instance, it was the custom of the brown seal-
master to inspect cloth using an instrument described as a 'gallows' and to stamp
it if it conformed to legal requirements.[19] Many weavers served as brown seal-

---

17 C. Gill (1925), 67.   18 A. Moore, *Linen from the raw material to the finished product* (1914),
15. The regulatory power of the Trustees was expanded when its oversight was extended to the
bleached cloth trade and to webs made using bleached yarn by 10 Geo. 1, c. 2, s.1 (*Royal commission on handloom weavers*, Report of R.M. Muggeridge, 681). In 1763, in response to years of criticism of their failure to effectively supervise officers of the Board, and in spite of weavers' fierce
resistance, the Trustees secured a bill which received Royal Assent the following year (3 Geo III, c.
34), under which they assumed power to appoint 'seal-masters', replacing lappers in most linen markets (*Royal commission on handloom weavers*, Report of R.M. Muggeridge, 685). These powers
were augmented by 21 & 22 Geo. III, c. 35, which outlined new penalties, expanded the duties of
Board officials, and created new offices, such as that of Inspector. Inspectors served under an inspector-general and had the right, through seal-masters, to seize yarns and webs deemed unsuitable for
sale. Brown linen webs were required to have their prescribed lengths and breadths marked on an
outside fold, bearing the stamp of seal-masters. See *Select committee on the laws regulating the linen
trade of Ireland*, Report, minutes of evidence, appendices (463), HC 1825, vol. v (hereafter '*Linen
trade of Ireland*'), evidence of James Corry, 13.   19 *Linen trade of Ireland*, evidence of the marquess of Downshire, 28. By 1822, county inspectors were paid an annual salary of £40, along with
sums for travel and a commission of 6*d.* and 2*s.* for every wheel and loom, respectively, which they
inspected (*Linen trade of Ireland*, evidence of James Corry, 12). In 1822, the marquess of Downshire
reported that buyers were complaining that brown seal-masters were unable to identify fraudulent
webs, but nonetheless declared that the office of seal-master and the system of inspection over which
they presided had brought great benefit to the trade (*Linen trade of Ireland*, evidence of the marquess
of Downshire, 29).

masters; concerns about potential conflicts of interest stoked fears that weavers might unscrupulously stamp poor-quality cloth, and led to the establishment in some districts of 'sole seal-masters' — salaried individuals responsible for entire market towns. Merchants were divided over the effectiveness of this system. Weavers complained of excessive delays in inspections. Critics pointed to places such as Armagh, where on market day some 4,000 to 6,000 webs were exposed for sale, with the sole seal-master required to inspect each web.[20] In response to weavers' opposition, the sole-seal-master system was rescinded in Banbridge and throughout Cos. Armagh and Down.[21] But local reactions to regulatory systems varied widely, with some markets operating in relative harmony and others witnessing deep divisions between market actors.[22] Both weavers and merchants found faults in the seal-master regime: John Stevenson Ferguson, a linen merchant in Belfast and chairman of a local committee of the trade, preferred a regulatory system to be connected with linen manufacturers, especially in Cos. Antrim, Down and Armagh.[23] He argued that the distinction of holding a seal would be an incentive for 'respectable' weavers to advance through the trade and become manufacturers.[24] This class of traders, who organized production and sold cloth to merchants and bleachers, became increasingly central to the linen trade as the nineteenth century progressed.

By the 1820s, political opinion turned against subsidies and export bounties, which were seen as impediments to market freedom. Concerns over market surveillance were also superseded by new anxieties as the sector developed a variety of new systems of production and exchange. In the subsequent decade, open markets declined in some districts — a change which many observers regarded as salutary. Indeed, several prominent commentators heralded the open market's 'eclipse', which they viewed as advantageous to the trade, and lauded the 'rise' of the manufacturer. John Dubourdieu, for instance, lamented weavers' vulnerability in the open market, and preferred a system under which their yarn was supplied by manufacturers. To him, this was better than weavers purchasing yarn on their own accounts. Under the 'putting-out' system, in which raw materials were entrusted to weavers with whom manufacturers contracted work, Dubourdieu reckoned that good workers could earn 7s. to 8s. weekly — while the earnings of the independent weaver were much more unstable.[25] His laudatory comments

20 *Linen trade of Ireland*, evidence of the marquess of Downshire, 29.   **21** Ibid., 31.   **22** Indeed, some Ballymena linen traders demanded that capital punishment be introduced for offences committed against them, in order to deter fraud. See F.W. Smith, *The Irish linen trade hand-book and directory* (1876), 61.   **23** Ferguson also denounced a ploy practiced by some weavers of plaistering and glazing their cloths, thereby disguising the quality of their webs and rendering finishing more difficult (*Linen trade of Ireland*, evidence of John Stevenson Ferguson, 35–9). See also A. Moore (1914), 28–9, who attributes the fraudulent practices to the structure of the bounty system.   **24** *Linen trade of Ireland*, evidence of John Stevenson Ferguson, 49.   **25** *Royal commission on handloom weavers*, Report of C.G. Otway, 622.

were echoed by the parliamentary commissioners who passed through Ulster in the 1830s. As we shall see, they tended to see open markets as vestigial systems of exchange that were ill-suited to the modern textile economy.

The Board of Trustees of Linen and Hempen Manufacture was dissolved in 1828. It had attracted criticism for several years: in the wake of British-Irish union, for instance, fewer senior figures attended the Board's meetings in Dublin, and its interventionist mandate also provoked criticism from advocates of free trade.[26] But the dissolution of the Board did not signal an abolition of many of the instruments which regulated the trade. After 1828, lords lieutenant assumed powers to appoint county committees to superintend the linen trade and oversee brown seal-masters, who continued to hold office.[27] Following the Board's demise, a more elaborate legal framework also developed which regulated commercial activity and defined market relationships under the expanding putting-out system. In 1835, earlier acts were modified and extended by new legislation which focused on open-market transactions.[28] Standards of measurement for yarn and cloth sold in fairs and markets continued to be mandated by statute. The law also prescribed penalties for the fraudulent act of pasting linen, outlined procedures for settling disputes between buyers and sellers, and affirmed the right of lords lieutenant to appoint twelve-member county trade committees.

The institutional framework for market regulation changed with the dissolution of the Board of Trustees, the enactment of new statutes and the expansion of commerce outside local markets. Still, complaints about both putting-out and open-market exchanges exercised commissioners who examined the handloom trade in the 1830s.[29] In some areas, they described widespread embezzlement in markets dominated by manufacturers. They identified only a few districts in

---

26 *Linen trade of Ireland*, evidence of the marquess of Downshire, 33. See also the analysis by A.J. Durie (2003). **27** F.W. Smith (1876), 72–4. Other institutions also stepped into the breech left by the dissolution of the Board of Trustees. The Flax Improvement Society, established in 1841 (from 1846 it was known as the Royal Flax Society), focussed on the quality of flax in Ireland. This issue had bedeviled the Board of Trustees, which granted funds for the erection of scutching mills but whose local officers had no authority over the flax trade (*Linen trade of Ireland*, evidence of James Corry, 14). The secretary to the Board of Trustees, testifying before a parliamentary committee in 1822, described a number of fraudulent practices in flax markets that, in his view, necessitated more robust intervention by market authorities. They included the addition of pebbles and dirt to bundles of flax to increase their weight. The sector relied to a large extent on seed and flax imports. Annual flax yields in Ireland fluctuated widely, representing one of the most unstable inputs in the linen industry, owing to a number of factors which included: the climate, which played a key role in determining flax yields on an annual basis; the quality of (usually imported) seed used in flax cultivation; the availability of agricultural labour to assist in the planting and harvesting of the flax crop; the quality of preparation of flax, especially in the scutching process, before it was disposed of in public markets; and the availability of flax imports. **28** 5 & 6 William IV, c. 27; 3 & 4 Vic. c. 91 revised the legal framework under which the putting-out trade operated. **29** One of the men charged with surveying the Irish weavers, R.M. Muggeridge, lamented problems that attended independent-market systems. Seal-masters, he feared, could stamp a piece without carefully measuring it, often using a

which vaunted new systems of production and exchange had developed —
despite hailing their potential to advance the sector. The largest managers of capital in the trade remained the province's powerful bleachers, whose influence in
fostering technological developments in the sector accompanied their increasing
commercial power as managers of large capital in the trade.

The role of bleachers and merchants in the eighteenth-century linen industry has
been explored in research which illuminates their emergence as agents of capitalist transformation.[30] Originally working for weavers on commission, bleachers
were the linchpins of textile commerce, buying cloth, bleaching it in increasingly
mechanized and capital-intensive processes, and then selling it in home and export
markets.[31] Their bleachgreens were the premier centres of textile capitalism and
technological innovation, where new processes were applied in the later-eighteenth
century, including the use of such products in bleaching as soda ash and lime, sulphuric acid by 1770, potash in 1780 and chlorine of lime in 1795. All of these innovations drastically reduced the time required to bleach cloth, and the output of
Ireland's bleachgreens expanded rapidly.[32] Indeed, in contrast with earlier processes employed in bleachgreens, in which buttermilk was used as a souring agent and
a long period of exposure to the sun was a principal means of bleaching, the chemical advancements of the later-eighteenth century were revolutionary.[33] These
developments, and a growing investment of capital by bleachers, are estimated to
have reduced bleaching costs from 2*d.* per yard in the mid-1700s to 1½*d.* in 1809.[34]
By 1760 there were some 200 bleachgreens in regular operation in Ulster.[35] By
1787 there were over 350.[36] Their proprietors managed floating capital through bills
of exchange and an elaborate credit network that financed trade in home and international export markets.[37] In local linen markets that they dominated, bleachers
vied with drapers, many of whom were shopkeepers and small-scale merchants
unable to obtain credit on the terms enjoyed by merchant-bleachers.

The bleaching and finishing process was complex, capital- and labour-intensive,
and bleachgreens engaged large rural industrial workforces. Nineteenth-century

deputy or 'measurer'. If the piece was subsequently sold to a bleacher who found it too short, he
could seek recourse to an inspector for reimbursement, and the cost eventually fell upon the weaver,
who had sold the article in good faith. See *Royal commission on handloom weavers*, Report of R.M.
Muggeridge, 699–700.   **30** See W.H. Crawford (1980) and (1967); A. Monaghan (1963); M.
Cohen (1997a), 29–58.   **31** H.D. Gribbon (1969), 82.   **32** *Linen Trade Circular,* 6 August
1852. The newspaper reported that skilful damask weavers could earn as much as 20*s.* or more
weekly, while 'a good deal of cambric and lawn is woven by young females', who could earn
from 4*s.* 6*d.* to 9*s.* per week. Weavers working on 'ordinary makes of plain linens' earned from
5*s.* to 14*s.*   **33** C. Gill (1925), 50–1.   **34** C. Ó Gráda (1994), 283. See also William Charley,
who gives 3*d.* and 1¼*d.* as comparable values in *Flax and its products in Ireland* (1862), 103.
35 H.D. Gribbon (1977), 84–8.   **36** W. A. McCutcheon (1984), 290–3.   **37** Bleaching interests
also worked, at times uneasily, with the Trustees. They opposed the Board's early restrictions on
the bleaching end of the trade. Bleachers also criticized the Board's short-lived efforts to limit
the use of wash-boards.

observers described workers placing linen webs in large boilers with potash or bar-illa before they were transferred to washmills, where they were exposed to water, and then spread upon grass for several days before the boiling and washing processes were repeated.[38] Webs then passed through 'rub boards' and were steeped in 'rives' treated with sulphuric acid. Finally, the cloth was transferred to drying lofts. When dry, it was beetled — a process in which the cloth was finished through beating by wooden billets. Then it was 'lapped', or folded, and sent to sorting rooms for measurement and boxing. Ulster's bleachers often exported their cloth to Great Britain — and London and Liverpool in particular, from whence it was shipped to other home markets or re-exported to America and other places.[39]

Commercial links between bleachers and merchants on one hand and weaving households on the other became more complex and, in some cases, indirect in the first decades of the nineteenth century. In some districts, these years saw the rise of linen 'manufacturers' — men such as David Lindsay of Ashfield in Co. Down, who began in the trade as a draper, buying cloth from weavers and small manu-facturers on his and his father's accounts. He then had webs bleached before sell-ing them to agents and other buyers. In the late 1820s, he ceased this work and directed capital towards manufacturing, finding it to be more profitable.[40] The transition from independent linen production and open-market exchange to a putting-out system organized by manufacturers was neither sudden nor even in Ulster's markets. In mid-Antrim, for instance, some bleachers continued to par-ticipate in the marketplace at mid-century. Indeed, through the 1820s and 1830s, the diversity of systems of production in the trade was pronounced.

THE REGIONAL GEOGRAPHY OF LINEN PRODUCTION

In the second and third decades of the nineteenth century, as some markets con-tracted and others grew, the linen trade became centred on Ireland's northern province. Districts specialized in specific classes of goods, the merchant John Stevenson Ferguson remarking in 1822 that a 'person acquainted with the trade can easily tell the part of the country' in which webs were produced.[41] Histori-cally, most of these places had been in Ulster, but there were other regions of commercial linen production in Ireland. As late as the 1820s, for instance, Ardee in Co. Louth had an active market in 6°° to 10°° webs,[42] and Drogheda was known for its specialization in coarse cloth. Connacht also had an extensive linen

38 Mr & Mrs C. Hall, *Ireland: its scenery and character, &c.* vol. 3 (1843), 94–6.   **39** *Linen trade of Ireland*, evidence of Carey McClellan, 73.   **40** *Royal commission on handloom weavers*, Report of C.G. Otway, 639.   **41** *Linen trade of Ireland*, evidence of John Stevenson Ferguson, 51.   **42** This measurement, used throughout this study, identifies the number of splits, each holding one or more warp threads, in a standard measurement of 40 inches. Five splits are called a 'hundred', and the higher this count, the finer the cloth. See A.S. Moore (1914), 60.

trade,[43] mostly in goods not exceeding a count of 12°°, and the markets of Munster specialized in coarse bed-ticks, settings and dowlas.[44] Indeed, Ireland's southern province had an especially famous industry: in 1822, Peter Besnard estimated that thousands of weavers resided in south Cork, producing mainly coarse cloth and specializing in webs styled after German platilla cloth.[45] Still, Ulster dominated Ireland's commercial linen trade, and this dominance grew as the industry became concentrated in eastern areas of the province.

Some of the most extensive accounts of Ulster's linen markets, which attest to this intensive geographic specialization, come from the records of John Greer, the Linen Board's inspector-general for Ulster in 1784, and from James Corry, secretary to the Board, who recorded details of his 1816 tour of the province's markets. Both Greer and Corry described an industry in which specialized production was pronounced. Greer wrote that Armagh, one of the principal markets of the trade, was the 'first market of the province' in the trade of 9°° to 11°° linen cloths. In 1816, half-bleached linens of low sets for home consumption formed the bulk of the cloth sold in its market, valued at around 9*d*. per yard for sets from 7°° to 8°°.[46] Outside this market, with its dominant trade in coarser cloth, Co. Armagh's markets varied in specializations. Lurgan was known for coarse linens as well as lawns and diapers produced for domestic markets. The coarser cloth was used for linings, and higher sets for printed pocket handkerchiefs and children's wear. The production of fine lawns and cambrics became Lurgan's niche as the century progressed, and handloom weavers continued to work there even as the twentieth century turned. In other areas of the 'Linen Triangle',[47] market specialization was equally pronounced. Banbridge's niche in 1816, for instance, was in fine, high-value linens, of sets from 13°° to 17°°, sold in a brown state and then bleached in Down and Antrim for export to American, West Indian and British markets. Downpatrick's market saw a significant trade in yard-wide brown webs of sets ranging from 6°° to 17°°. Belfast was known for the finest yard-wide linens, but its linen production was still dwarfed by cotton.[48] Lisburn, famous for fine yard-wide cloth destined for both foreign and home markets, was also known for lawns of the highest quality. Its specialization in these fine fabrics was a consequence of innovations in loom design, the development of a skilled local workforce, and the

43 See Arthur Young, *Tour in Ireland (1776–1779)*, vol. 1 (1892), 229, 256.   **44** H. McCall, *Ireland and her staple manufactures* (1870), 304. See also C. Ó Gráda (1994), 282–3.   **45** *Linen trade of Ireland*, evidence of Peter Besnard, 27. His estimate of 60,000 weavers appears much too high. Julius Besnard, a Cork linen merchant, did an extensive trade through the port of Gibraltar, and also shipped to the West Indies and America (*Linen trade of Ireland*, evidence of Julius Besnard, 78).   **46** Sets of 9°° to 10°° were valued at about 12*d*. per yard, and higher sets earned more. See *Minutes of the Trustees of the Linen and Hempen Manufacturers ... 1816* (1817), Appendices from which 1816 data is extracted.   **47** This term is commonly used to refer to the area of intensive linen manufacture, whose boundaries, although sometimes disputed, were Lurgan, Lisburn and Dungannon.   **48** *Linen trade of Ireland*, evidence of John Stevenson Ferguson, 51.

gravitation of buyers to markets where they could procure large quantities of specific cloth.[49]

While market specialization in districts that fell within Ulster's historic Linen Triangle varied, other districts cohered around single branches of manufacture. In 1822, for instance, John Stevenson Ferguson noted that weavers in the swathe of territory encompassing southern and western Cos. Tyrone, Cavan, Monaghan, Longford, and parts of Londonderry, as well as regions of north Antrim, produced goods whose values were considerably lower than in Lisburn and Belfast.[50] The majority of webs sold in the Coleraine market in 1816 were 'seven-eighths' valued at 2*s*. per yard. They were used in home markets for shirts and other articles. 'Coleraines' also had a reputation for being the finest of their set in Ireland, and were so prized in the English market that some unscrupulous dealers had webs that had been woven in Cavan and Longford stamped as 'coleraines' for sale in London.[51] Maghera's market focused exclusively on these seven-eighth-wide webs, which varied in price from 1*s*. to 3*s*. 6*d*. per yard, and were used in the fine shirt trade for warmer climates. Co. Tyrone markets shared this specialization: Strabane's seven-eighth-wide linens commanded higher prices than those of Dungannon, but were of a similar description. Most of the seven-eighth cloth woven in these areas was bleached locally before being sent to England. The markets of Cookstown, Stewartstown, Newtownstewart, Fintona and Omagh also constituted parts of this specialist region in central and central-western Ulster.

Middle and northern Antrim formed another distinctive district of manufacture, producing three-quarter-yard-wide cloth. Remarking on Ballymena, John Greer declared it to be 'the greatest market of three-quarter wide Linens in the Province, from 5*d*. to 1*s*. 8*d*. per yard'.[52] James Corry also reported in 1816 that it maintained a specialization in such webs, which measured fifty-two yards in length and sold at £2 per piece, or 9*d*. per yard: some 1,200 brown webs of this variety were sold weekly. Weavers in Ballymoney, in north Antrim, also produced these webs, which were shipped to Dublin, England and America. The Ballymoney market also had a small trade in the seven-eighth webs that were the province of the small, nearby market of Ahoghill and others which bordered

---

49 Remarking on linen production in the district, J. Dubourdieu (1812) claimed that 'lawns' and 'cambrics' were distinguished by their cost, with sets priced over 5*s*. per yard described as cambrics (390). In some districts weavers were employed in workshops, but in most centres, rural domestic production, either independent or contracted, prevailed (392–3).   **50** *Linen trade of Ireland*, evidence of John Stevenson Ferguson, 35–6. Greer's 1784 accounts of markets, in which he speaks of few other classes of goods, testify to this concentrated production (*Report of John Greer, inspector general for Ulster, of the state of the linen markets in said province*, PRONI, Belfast, D/562/6225, 615–18). This region was known for weaving 'seven-eighth-wide' linen webs. On his tour through Ireland, Arthur Young was told that Ireland had no competitors in weaving such cloth (1892), 132. Young also noted its dominance in manufacture of three-quarter-yard-wide webs.   **51** *Linen trade of Ireland*, evidence of John Stevenson Ferguson, 51.   **52** *Report of John Greer*, 601.

the 'seven-eighth' region in Tyrone and Londonderry. Indeed, in these border areas, market differentiation between seven-eighth and three-quarter-wide web specialization was less pronounced: Coleraine's market had a trade in three-quarter wides, which at 5*d*. per yard, were cheaper than Ballymena linens, and were exported to England and then sent to the West Indies and other hot climates for linings and shirts. But, as the meeting point of two specialist districts, it also did a large trade in seven-eighths cloth.[53]

South Ulster was a more diverse manufacturing region. Cootehill specialized in linen sheetings and yard-wides. Seven-eighth cloth was the mainstay in Ballynagh, Killeshandra and Arvagh markets, averaging only 7½*d*. per yard. And Monaghan's cloth trade was in a range of sets, from 6°° to 12°° and valued between 8½*d*. and 14½*d*. per yard. The heterogeneity of this last 'linen region' of Ulster was pronounced, but its trade was generally in coarser and lower-priced webs.

There was some correlation between local yarn supply and cloth specialization in these regions; the 'peculiar' character of Ballymena-spun yarn, for instance, was credited for local weavers' specialization in light linen cloth.[54] But in most districts, weavers could obtain yarn beyond that supplied by local spinners. In western areas of Ulster, especially in Donegal and Fermanagh, and also in parts of Connacht, an extensive commercial hand-spinning industry supplied distant weaving markets with yarns.[55] This feature of the trade changed by the 1830s, when mill-spinning expanded the output of yarn, diminishing the scale of a traditional female form of domestic employment, removing them from direct market relations, and opening the weaving trade to greater female participation in many areas of the province.

MEN, WOMEN AND WEAVING WORK IN THE 1820S AND 1830S

Weaving remained predominantly male work through the 1820s, although female weavers had previously been engaged in the trade on a modest scale, as Edward Wakefield observed earlier in the century, when he claimed that changes in weaving technology — especially the adoption of the fly-shuttle in place of the hand-shuttle — enabled female weaving by reducing the physical exertions of such work.[56] Still, outside a small group of female weavers whose numbers grew and

---

53 Coleraine also had a distinctive system of web measurement. Speaking to the assistant hand-loom commissioners in the late 1830s, John Adams, a bleacher in the Coleraine district, stated that webs produced in that neighbourhood were measured by a local standard of a 37–inch reed, not the 40–inch reed used elsewhere in the calculation of sets, and therefore a 9°° Coleraine web was 'nearly equal in fineness' to a 10°° web manufactured in Cos. Down and Armagh (*Royal commission on handloom weavers*, Report of R.M. Muggeridge, 715).   54 H. McCall (1870), 208.   55 Further west, in Donegal, sail cloth was produced by the 1820s (*Linen trade of Ireland*, evidence of John Stevenson Ferguson, 36).   56 E. Wakefield, *An account of Ireland, statistical*

then contracted during the French Wars,[57] social relations of work, gender and authority continued to demarcate it as a male skill.

Technology is pre-eminently a social product.[58] It develops and is incorporated within economic systems, and also within powerful cultural and gender systems.[59] It can disrupt, strengthen and reshape existing ideologies of gender and work: hence contests over the proprietorship of new technology and technical skill in linen, as in other sectors, were often fraught. In weaving, despite ongoing technical improvements to loom design there was no significant technological breakthrough in the 1820s and 1830s. The handloom, however, long upheld as a tool for masculine work, began to be used by large numbers of women during those decades. Female weavers were received within the weaving workforce in ways that upheld their secondary role in domestic production, and also buttressed the social authority of the male weaver. These changes in the workforce were linked to the spinning sector, in which technological developments induced reassignments of weaving labour in domestic industry.

The chief technological developments in the linen industry during this time involved transformations in systems and technologies of yarn production. Yet the heralded technological 'revolution' in the 1820s obscured precedents that had, much less comprehensively, moved spinning from farms and cottages to larger, centralized settings.[60] Early experiments with dry mill-spinning, for instance, proved ill-suited to fine yarn production, and in 1825 James Kay developed a process by which the elasticity of linen fibres could be enhanced by water, offering new possibilities to harness the motive power of steam. From 1825, when some English mill-spun yarn began to undersell the hand-spun Irish variety, some manufacturers began to adopt British 'wet-spinning' techniques.[61] Mechanized spinning in Scotland attracted the attention of the Board of Trustees, who despatched William Marshall, the inspector of linen and flax for the port of Londonderry, to report on the state of the Scottish trade.[62] There, and in England, mill-spun yarn had been used from the late-eighteenth century.[63] In Ireland such

---

and political (1812), vol. 1, 697–8. See also W.H. Crawford (1993), 7. To contrast the productivity of a hand- and fly-shuttle, see the evidence of John Duff of Aughauleague, Laghore Parish, Co. Armagh in *Royal commission on handloom weavers*, Report of R.M. Muggeridge, 714. See also *Royal commission on handloom weavers*, Report of C.G. Otway, 596, for a discussion of the putative physical exertions of weaving work and their relationship to the sexual divisions of labour.   **57** A. McKernan (1994).   **58** See C. Cockburn (1985); A. Game & R. Pringle (1983). **59** B.D. Wright, et al. (1987); G. de Groot & M. Schrover (1995). For studies of gender and technology in the British industrial context, see C. Hall (1982); J. Schwarzkopf (1999).   **60** There were several early efforts to adopt centralized 'dry-spinning', beginning in Cork in 1805, where a mill was established to produce canvas yarn. See A. Takei (1994). When J. Dubourdieu toured Co. Antrim, he identified two such dry-spinning mills in the county, one in Crumlin and the other near Ballymena (1812), 399–400. Indeed, the Board of Trustees provided funds for dry-spinning machinery in the first decade of the nineteenth century, mainly to produce yarn for sail-cloth, canvas and duck (J. Horner [1920], 185).   **61** *Linen Trade Circular*, 7 May 1852.   **62** *Linen trade of Ireland*, evidence of William Marshall, 50–67.   **63** E.J. Boyle (1977), 1–2 and 12–4.

mechanization was delayed for a number of reasons. Until 1825, the Irish spinning industry was effectively protected from British and continental competition
by regulations which mandated that yarn sold in Irish markets was to be made up
in hanks containing twelve cuts of 300 yards — a standard of measurement not
used elsewhere.[64] Mechanization was also deterred by a plentiful supply of low-
cost female Irish hand-spinners; indeed it was estimated that early in the nineteenth century women could be employed at the wheel for as low as 2*d*. per day.
While daily factory wages averaged 8*d*., labour costs in even the more remunerative classes of domestic hand-spinning were cheaper by 25% to 50%.[65] The
abundant supply of cheap female labour challenged the logic of capital-intensive
mechanization in Ireland. But by the 1820s, the large output of cheap mill-spun
British yarn spurred Irish investment in mechanization.

Mechanization took place within a context of unstable prices and fluctuating
demand. In the late 1810s and early 1820s, American demand for linen, especially
for coarse Irish products, fell under heavy competition from cotton and continental linen suppliers.[66] Demand for finer classes of goods also slumped, even as markets for Irish linen expanded in British colonies and parts of Latin America.
Demand for linen was depressed in some markets by the rise of cotton cloth, which
was considerably cheaper.[67] Competition between the two was especially acute in
coarser qualities of linen.[68] The two Irish textile industries also vied for labour. Cotton provided more lucrative employment for Irish weavers and in the early decades
of the nineteenth century it attracted skilled weaving labour from the linen sector.[69]
But by the late 1820s, the Irish cotton sector entered into a period of contraction as
it faced British competition and a diminution of 'extra-British' trading links —
despite the success of some branches of the trade in Ireland's low wage environment.[70] Many male handloom weavers shifted from cotton to linen production,
which required similar skills.[71] By the 1830s, Belfast linen weavers were earning

---

64 E.J. Boyle (1977), 14.   65 C. Coote in E. Wakefield (1812), 684–5.   66 *Linen trade of Ireland*, evidence of Thomas Greer, 22.   67 Testifying in 1822 on the practice of illegally describing cotton as Irish linen, William Marshall suggested that an incentive lay in higher prices that
would be paid for linen: cotton shirtings that cost 1*s*. 4*d*. per yard in cotton calico would rise to
2*s*. 8*d*. to 2*s*. 10*d*. if the fabric were linen (*Linen trade of Ireland*, evidence of William Marshall,
71).   68 *Linen trade of Ireland*, evidence of Thomas Greer, 22. See also the Report from the
Select committee on handloom weavers' petitions, with minutes of evidence and index (341), HC
1835, vol. xiii [hereafter '*Handloom weavers' petitions*'], evidence of John Chadwick, q. 2721.
69 C. Ó Gráda (1994), 276. In 1812, during a period of prosperity in the Ulster trade, cotton
handloom weavers were said to earn 18*s*. to 1 guinea, while the weekly wages of a linen weaver
were 7*s*. to 8*s*. See J. Dubourdieu in B. Collins (1997), 234; L. Kennedy (1985), 3.   70 D. Dickson (1977). Still, as F. Geary has suggested, the Belfast cotton sector suffered less from the problems of competition, to which some branches had successfully adapted, than from the direction
of capital towards the linen industry, whose spinning sector was undergoing transformation (in
C. Ó Gráda [1994], 278)   71 Cotton weaving had been organized through putting-out and therefore weavers' historic experience of work organization and market status contrasted with that of
many handloom linen producers. See *Handloom weavers' petitions*, evidence of John Boyd, q.
1180.

8*s*. to 12*s*. weekly, and their counterparts in cotton only 5*s*. to 8*s*. Workers gravitated to linen as the cotton sector shrank, expanding the pool of skilled weavers.[72]

The first investments in the mechanization of yarn production by harnessing the power of steam also began in the late 1820s. Steam power displaced the rural spinning wheel within a decade and a half. By 1833, ten steam-powered flax mills operated in the Belfast region alone.[73] The impact of large-scale capital investment on yarn output was dramatic, with important consequences for the weaving end of the linen industry — and for gender relations in cottage industry. The ranks of former hand-spinners, almost exclusively female, grew, their skills now largely obsolete. *Ordnance Survey* writers in the 1830s and 1840s found many former spinners in want of employment.[74] The impact on hand-spinners' earnings was striking. In 1835 hand-spinners were estimated to be earning 1*s*. 6*d*. weekly in a district of Co. Down — in contrast with 4*s*. to 5*s*. in 1815; evidence from south Antrim suggests a decline from 5*s*. to 6*s*. weekly to 6*d*.,[75] and in the 1830s, a report to the handloom commissioners recorded that they had collapsed from 6*d*. per day to between 1*d*. and 2*d*.[76] With the exception of finest qualities of yarn, production was now based in mills, where female workers predominated.[77] This restructuring of yarn production also led to a revision of household labour allocation. Some fomer hand-spinners turned to work in mills — and many to domestic weaving.[78] But in Ireland's western counties, where the reduction of female spinners was exceptionally precipitous, opportunities for mill spinning and domestic weaving were limited. There was no transition to the mill system and no turning to the handloom, and in counties such as Donegal, which had supplied hand-spun yarn to other regions, the linen sector decayed. The result was a more concentrated region of linen manufacture in Cos. Antrim, Down and Armagh, where both weaving and mill-spinning were based, and what Frank Geary has shown to be a marked deindustrialization in Connacht, replicated to varying degrees in many western districts of Ulster that once supplied hand-spun yarn to linen weavers.[79]

---

72 *Royal commission on the condition of the poorer classes in Ireland*, Appendix C, Part I, State of the poor and charitable institutions in principal towns in Ireland [35], HC 1836, vol. xxx, Report on the town of Belfast, 5.   **73** W.E. Coe (1969), 61.   **74** See, for instance, A. Day & P. McWilliams (eds), *Ordnance survey memoirs of Ireland*, vol. 39, *parishes of County Donegal II, 1835–6: Mid- West and South Donegal* (1997), 168.   **75** *Royal commission on the condition of the poorer classes in Ireland*, Appendix E, Baronial examination relative to food, cottages and cabins, clothing and furniture, pawnbroking and savings banks, drinking; supplement [37], HC 1836, vol. xxxii [hereafter '*Poorer classes, appendix E*'], Supplement to appendix E, evidence of Revd H. E. Boyd, Drumara, 332 and evidence of Revd Robert Trail, Ballintoy, 264.   **76** In *Royal commission on handloom weavers*, Report of C.G. Otway, 596.   **77** E.J. Boyle (1977) has constructed a valuable analysis of occupations in the Irish linen industry in which she redistributes the unspecified category of weavers and spinners in census years according to the fabric on which they worked. This redistribution is based on a ratio devised through an analysis of the distribution of the labour force in ancillary industries (Appendix 4). By her estimate, the number of hand-spinners in Ireland declined from 202,419 in 1841 to just 56,258 by 1851 (49).   **78** E.J. Boyle (1977), 61.   **79** F. Geary (1996)

FEMALE WEAVERS AND FEMALE WEAVING

Mechanization and centralization of yarn production supported the handloom weaving trade by increasing yarn supplies and expanding the weaving labour-pool. Mill-spun yarn was hailed for allowing weavers to produce webs of a higher and more consistent quality.[80] In addition to improving yarn qualities, reductions in yarn prices enabled Irish piece goods to advance against competitors in markets such as South America.[81] Mechanization also had a major impact on systems of weaving production, increasing the scale of commerce in some markets, and enhancing the power of manufacturers, who purchased yarn directly from mills and supplied it to weavers. Beyond these economic and commercial impacts, there was a significant series of social developments as females entered the weaving trade in large numbers.

Many male weavers complained that an influx of female weavers diluted their earnings in the trade. But they also asserted that women's weaving was a 'secondary' activity concentrated in lower-skilled work.[82] These assertions reinforced an emerging sexual division of weaving work and reproduced status divisions in previous systems of domestic linen production. Women wove in specific branches of the trade without disrupting relations of gender and social authority in households. Classical labour supply perspectives on weaving income would see a diminution of weavers' earnings as a consequence of the expanded weaving labour pool — provided that male and female labour were applied to the same tasks. Indeed, some male weavers — mainly weaving coarse and cotton-linen 'union' cloth — experienced a marked decrease in earnings. But there were durable barriers to females' entry into many other branches, which sustained a gendered hierarchy of skill and sexual divisions of labour for many decades. Among these barriers were restrictive apprenticeship systems; prohibitive entry costs into such remunerative work as damask weaving; and exclusionary strategies developed to defend male 'craft' skill. Some of these branches remained male preserves through the end of the nineteenth century.

Although the entry of female weavers into the workforce led to claims that they were reducing the status and earnings of weavers generally, the impact of the emergence of a sexually-mixed labour force on weavers' earnings is difficult to measure. Most evidence suggests that wages fell in the 1830s and 1840s. But this was an acceleration of diminutions that began well before women entered the

---

80 One manufacturer in Banbridge claimed that weavers with the skills to weave a 10°° to 15°° web with hand-spun yarn could produce a 15°° to 22°° count with the mill-spun variety, although weavers of very fine goods still used hand-spun yarn, mostly from continental Europe. See *Royal commission on handloom weavers*, Report of C.G. Otway, 639; P. Solar (1988), 18.   81 F.W. Smith (1876), 76.   82 The entry of females into the trade was said in 1838 to have effected a reduction in male earnings. *Royal commission on handloom weavers*, Report of R.M. Muggeridge, 748.

weaving workforce, and was due to a variety of technical and commercial developments. Thomas Greer, for instance, described the industry in the early 1820s as being 'much depressed' on account of several factors, including the presence of foreign competition, especially in the coarser classes of the export cloth trade.[83] Weavers' wages had diminished alongside demand with the conclusion of the Napoleonic Wars: in 1833 the price of labour in Ireland was estimated by one contemporary to be one-half the level of 1813.[84] The impact on weavers' *real* wages during this period is more open to debate.[85] William Armstrong, a civil engineer, surveyor and land valuator who also held land in Co. Armagh, testified before the Select Committee on Agriculture that weavers had benefited from the downturn in agricultural prices during this period and had maintained or even increased their standard of living.[86] Developing measurements to test such claims is difficult, especially given the scarcity of sources for constructing reliable time series. This problem is compounded by the failure of real wage series to account for the subsistence pattern of agricultural labourers in the period. Many, as Joel Mokyr has noted, were 'self-employed workers in agriculture and rural industry'.[87] Rent dues for many weaving-labourers were often met through field labour.[88] This meant that there were many critical non-cash elements to household economies. But while such substitutes for price and wage series as Mokyr's 'subjective impoverishment' index suggest deteriorating material conditions for many people in Ireland, the general condition of many Irish rural industrial workers between 1815 and 1830 seems less miserable. Indeed, several people testifying before a commission investigating the poor in Ireland asserted that farmers were in a far worse position than weavers and other artisans who had benefited from declining food costs.[89] This

83 *Linen trade of Ireland*, evidence of Thomas Greer, 21–2. 84 *Select committee on the state of agriculture in the United Kingdom* (612), Minutes of evidence, HC 1833, vol. v [hererafter referred to as '*State of agriculture*'], evidence of William Armstrong, q. 9074–9077 and 9091. In Scotland, weavers of various fabrics saw their real income fluctuate, but generally decline, in the period after 1810 (N. Murray [1978], 46–7, 115). 85 See F. Geary & T. Stark (2004). 86 *State of agriculture*, evidence of William Armstrong, q. 9,193–6; *Poorer classes, appendix E*, see the evidence of Revd William Filgate, for instance, 332. By contrast, in some areas, such as Lambeg, a local clergyman, Revd John Bradshaw, testified that despite the depressed state of the linen trade, weavers continued to bring up children in the trade, though they were working fifteen to sixteen hours a day and not earning 5s. weekly (264). 87 J. Mokyr & C. Ó Gráda (1988). 88 It was valued in several linen districts of Cos. Antrim and Down in the mid-1830s at around £1 10s. to £1 5s. annually for a cabin let from a small farmer — and twice to three times that amount if it included a garden. *Poorer classes, appendix E*, evidence of Revd Henry Simspon, Saintfield, 329; evidence of Revd William Filgate, Dromore, 332; evidence of Revd A. Patterson, Kirkinriola and Ballyclug, 277. 89 Despite evidence suggesting that the weavers' position was stable, Henry McLaughlin, a Roman Catholic priest in Ballymoney, Co. Antrim, remarked that 'spinning is done, and weaving is little better than labouring work' before the commissioners inquiring into the condition of the poor in Ireland (*Poorer Classes, appendix E*, evidence of Revd Henry McGlaughlin, 269). Returns to the *Royal commission on the condition of the poorer classes in Ireland*, appendix C, Part I, State of the poor and charitable institutions in principal towns in Ireland [35], HC 1836, vol. xxx, Report on the town of Belfast. It suggested that oatmeal prices had declined from £ 1 2s. to 10s. (measurement not given), and pork from £3 10s. to £1 4s. between 1814 and 1834 (6). See also the *Royal com-*

evidence corroborates Liam Kennedy's claim that the supposed decline in the earnings and status of handloom weavers before 1840 has been exaggerated.[90] Even in difficult economic conditions, handloom weaving attracted and retained large numbers of workers, especially a growing number of female operatives. Yet the *status* of weaving was the subject of considerable anxiety. The poetry of several prominent male weavers, such as Peter Burns, emphasized immiseration in the 1820s:[91]

> Then worst of all, the weaving trade
> I had to leave and lift the spade,
> As only half my time I staid
> Where I was bound;
> The cause of which, work was ill-paid,
> The nation round.[92]

Undoubtedly, weavers experienced difficult adjustments to a lower wage environment after 1815, which encouraged households to revise their labour strategies and, in especially unremunerative branches of manufacture, to reassign females to weaving work. Women wove lower sets of cloth, long the least remunerative work and the easiest to take up with relatively little training. One man told the assistant handloom commissioner R.M. Muggeridge that some women had moved to the production of inferior mixed cloths and to seasonal harvest work as part of their induction into weaving.[93] Others remarked that female weaving labour had generally been confined to cottons, unions and 'light and less valuable fabrics'.[94] This development reflected a correspondence between lower-paid work and the secondary value assigned to most female paid labour — part of a wider ideology of gender and paid work which had long underpinned the organization of cottage production. The stability in masculine dominance of higher-paid work was maintained through the transition to a sexually-mixed labour force. Indeed, men tended to remain the proprietors of household looms, maintaining a form of social authority over production which remained remarkably durable for the next half-century.

Sexual occupational segregation has generated debate over the causes of earnings 'gaps' between males and females during industrialization. Some have argued that they were outgrowths of the cultural assignment of women's work to

mission on handloom weavers, Report of C.G. Otway, 635. The decreasing cost of living during this period has been shown in John O'Brien's research on Cork and by Peter Solar's subsistence indices, both of which suggest a decline of between one-quarter and one-third between the period of the Napoleonic Wars and the late 1820s (in C. Ó Gráda [1994], 82–3). **90** L. Kennedy (1985), 9. **91** See, in the Scottish case, N. Murray (1978), 171–2. **92** In J. Hewitt (1974), 24–5. **93** *Royal commission on handloom weavers*, Report of R.M. Muggeridge, 725–6. **94** Ibid., 747, 750.

a secondary status relative to men.[95] Others have suggested that the wage gaps expressed material differences in the quality of men's and women's work, which may reflect barriers to skills-development, rather than innate features of either sex.[96] Some have even argued that sexual segregation and work sex-typing were an integrated strategy that advanced the material well-being of households over-all by upholding the ideology of the male 'family wage'.[97] In the Irish handloom industry, there are indications that women's output was lower than that of men, but there were powerful cultural constraints on women's regular paid labour that had important influences over their earning power. Men and women were engaged in unpaid domestic tasks at different rates, and had markedly differen-tial access to skills training at the loom. Damask was one linen branch in which men enjoyed historic, exclusive access to lengthy apprenticeships.[98] Costs of entry into the trade were prohibitive for most weavers.[99] Requiring many years of training and access to expensive looms, often supplied by manufacturers, it remained predominantly a male preserve while females entered branches with fewer or weaker entry restrictions. Indeed, as late as 1907, it was said that damask weaving still 'appears to descend from father to son'.[1] That such gender divisions remained resilient over six decades suggests the power of cultural constructions of skill in relation to sexual stratification in the handloom trade. These influences were powerful enough to maintain rigid sexual segregation of workforces well after the 1830s, when the barriers to female weaving dissolved and new bound-aries between masculine and feminine weaving emerged.

As for the gendering of work in mills, now the principal sites of yarn produc-tion, men and women were received within exclusive sets of industrial occupa-tions.[2] In contrast with the mills of Leeds and Scotland, those in Belfast employed a considerably younger female labour force at lower wages,[3] which enhanced the competitive advantage of Irish mill-spinning and extended historic wage differ-entials that had once enabled Irish hand-spun yarn to compete with British mech-anized production. As early as 1835, parliamentary returns showed that the majority of flax mill employees in the north of Ireland were female, and a large majority was under the age of 21.[4] In mills, female workers were concentrated in

---

95 M. Berg (1993); D. Valenze (1995). **96** J. Burnette (1997). **97** See, for instance, S. Horrell & J. Humphries (1997) and (1995). **98** For a wider discussion of the gendering of skill, see J. Burnette (1997) **99** W. Charley (1862), 93. Indeed, it was reported by C.G. Otway that one Belfast employer had claimed that the damask weavers apprenticing at his concern had all been weavers before 'learning the damask mode of weaving' (in *Royal commission on handloom weavers*, Report of C.G. Otway, 633). **1** W.R. McMurray, 'Handloom linen, cambric and damask weaving, and linen embroidery', in W.T. Macartney-Filgate (ed.), *Irish rural life and industry, with suggestions for the future* (1907), 162–7. **2** By 1839, there were 40 mills in Ire-land, 35 of them in Ulster, and by 1856, some 11,000 mainly-female workers were employed on 237,000 spindles in Belfast. See A.G. Malcolm, 'The influence of factory life on the health of the operatives, as founded upon the medical statistics of this class at Belfast', *Journal of the Statis-tical Society of London*, 19 (1856), 170. **3** E.J. Boyle (1977), 40. **4** Return of persons employed

1.1 Selected occupations in Co. Antrim, by sex, 1841

Occupation	No.	Male (%)	Female (%)
Linen weavers	4,486	87.2	12.8
Unspecified weavers	12,526	83.4	16.6
Spinners of flax	5,958	0.4	99.6
Unspecified spinners	19,565	0.0	100.0[1]

Source: *Report of the commissioners on the census of Ireland, 1841* [504], HC 1843, vol. xxiv.[1] 19 males were recorded in this category.

1.2 Selected occupations in Co. Antrim, by sex, 1851

Occupation	No.	Male (%)	Female (%)
Damask & linen weavers	19,959	65.8	34.2
Unspecified weavers	4,322	59.8	40.2
Spinners of flax	1,622	1.1	98.9
Unspecified spinners	1,640	0.5	99.5

Source: *Census of Ireland, 1851*: pt. VI: General Report [2134], HC 1856, vol. xxxi.

a narrow range of tasks such as spinning. They were excluded from high-status supervisory roles involving technical control over machinery that were represented as demanding masculine skill. As in handloom work, the assignment of roles in the mill had an unmistakably gendered hue that reflected broader relations of social authority, and valorized male 'technical expertise'.[5]

GENDERED LABOUR AND STRUCTURAL CHANGE IN THE LINEN TRADE

As these social and technological developments changed the face of the linen industry, females gravitated to spinning mills and also took up weaving, and overall costs of production fell. During hostilities with France, the linen trade

in the cotton, worsted, flax and silk factories of the United Kingdom (138), HC 1836, vol. xlv.   **5** As mills grew, they continued to employ a disproportionate share of female labour, at more than two-thirds of workers in 1850, 1856 and 1862. See *Reports of the inspectors of factories to the secretary of state for the Home Department for the half-year ending 31 October 1862* [3076], HC 1863, vol.

had been buoyed by home demand and wages were boosted by competition for labour with Ulster's expansive cotton industry. But following 1815, it slumped into a protracted period of depressed prices and wages: between 1816 and 1821, for instance, sales in Ulster's linen markets declined from £2,232,962 to £2,073,122 16*s.* 4*d.*[6] The market for linen goods during this time was erratic, as the prices in figure 1.3 suggest.

1.3 Average prices of selected goods, per yard,
in selected markets, 1816 and 1820

Market	Description	1816	1820
Strabane	Seven-eighths (32" broad and 52 yards long)	14*d.* to 20*d.*	14*d.*
Belfast	Stout yard-wides (38" broad and 25 yards long)	3*s.*4*d.*	20*d.*
Armagh	7°°-8°° (51 to 54 yards long)	9*d.*	7½*d.* and 9*d.*
	9°°-10°° (51 to 54 yards long)	12*d.*	10½*d.* and 1*s.*
	11°°-12°° (51 to 54 yards long)	15*d.*	14*d.* and 16*d.*

Source: *Minutes of the trustees* (1817), Appendix, 31–2, 42–4, 77–9, and Horner (1920), 189–96.

It is important to emphasize the extent to which lower prices were not simply an outgrowth of spinning's mechanization, but rather an extension of longer-term developments discussed earlier in this chapter, that had seen both the cost of labour and prices of goods diminish significantly after 1815.[7] The gendering of weaving work was influential in maintaining this trend through the 1830s. But there were remarkable improvements in weaving productivity too.[8] By the end of the 1830s it was said that a weaver took half the time to produce a web, compared to twenty years earlier.[9] This trend continued in subsequent decades, as figures 1.4 and 1.5 illustrate. In his analysis of cambric weavers, for instance, Hugh McCall suggested that between 1828 and 1858, lengths of some webs doubled, while in some cases prices halved. But weaving a 72-yard piece by 1841 took the same amount of time as a 58-yard piece in 1831.[10] The *Linen Trade Circular* also noted on 6 August 1852 that the diminution in cloth prices had outstripped the decreases in raw material values (which had declined 20 to 30%). Increases in

xviii, Report of Robert Baker, 126–9.   **6** J. Horner (1920), 168, 198. This apparent decline must be approached with caution, as it may be partly attributable to the movement of trade outside the market. **7** See *Linen Trade Circular*, 6 August 1852 for an illustration of the decreases in cloth prices between 1805 and 1852.   **8** L. Kennedy (1985), 9.   **9** *Royal commission on handloom weavers*, Report of R.M. Muggeridge, 748–9.   **10** H. McCall (1870), 255.

1.4 Prices of classes of 'yard-wide family linens', per yard, 1805–52

Set	1805	1815	1820	1830	1835	1845	1850	1852
14°°	2s. 0d.	2s. 0d.	1s. 6d.	1s.5½d.	1s.4½d.	1s. 3d.	1s. 2d.	1s. 1½d.
18°°	3s. 4d.	3s. 1d.	2s.10d.	2s. 6d.	2s. 1d.	1s. 10d.	1s. 8d.	1s. 3½d.
20°°	4s. 4d.	3s. 9d.	3s. 6d.	3s. 2d.	2s. 10d.	2s. 5d.	2s. 1d.	1s. 7d.
22°°	5s.11d.	5s. 3d.	5d. 0d.	4s. 6d.	4s. 2d.	3s. 4d.	2s. 6d.	2s. 2d.
24°°	10s. 6d.	9s. 6d.	9s. 6d.	8s. 6d.	6s. 0d.	4s. 10d.	3s. 6d.	2s.10d.

Source: *Linen Trade Circular*, 6 August 1852.

1.5 Wages for yard-wide linens, before deductions,
52 yards long, 1831–38

Set	Days to produce a web	1831	1832	1833	1834	1835	1836	1837	1838
12°°	15	11s.	10s.	10s.	10s.	9s. 6d.	8s. 6d.	8s.	9s.
13°°	15	12s.	11s.	11s.	11s.	10s. 6d.	9s. 6d.	9s.	10s.
14°°	15	14s.	13s.	13s.	13s.	12s. 6d.	11s. 6d.	10s.	11s. 6d.
15°°	18	18s.	16s.	16s.	16s.	14s. 6d.	12s. 6d.	11s.	12s. 6d.
16°°	18	21s.	18s.	18s.	18s.	16s.	14s.	12s.	14s.
17°°	18	23s.	20s.	20s.	20s.	18s.	16s.	13s.	15s. 6d.
18°°	21	27s.	23s.	23s.	23s.	20s. 6d.	18s.	14s.	17s.
19°°	21	32s.	28s.	28s.	28s.	24s.	20s.	16s.	19s.
20°°	21	36s.	32s.	32s.	32s.	28s.	22s. 6d.	18s.	22s.
21°°	26	42s.	38s.	38s.	38s.	32s.	25s. 6d.	20s.	25s.
22°°	26	48s.	42s.	42s.	42s.	36s	28s.	24s.	30s.
23°°	28	56s.	48s.	48s.	48s.	42s.	33s.	30s.	35s.

Source: *Royal commission on handloom weavers*, Report of C.G. Otway 639–40.

1.6 Prices of various sets of Irish cambric handkerchiefs,
by the dozen, 1833, 1838, 1848

Set	Price of set in 1833	Price of set in 1838	Price of set in 1848
A	8s. 3d.	7s. 0d.	2s. 10d.
B	9s. 3d.	7s. 9d.	3s. 2d.
C	10s. 3d.	8s. 3d.	3s. 6d.
D	11s. 6d.	9s. 0d.	4s. 0d.
E	12s. 9d.	10s. 0d.	4s. 6d.
G	14s. 3d.	11s. 6d.	5s. 2d.
H	16s. 3d.	14s. 0d.	6s. 0d.
I	18s. 9d.	15s. 6d.	7s. 3d.
J	21s. 3d.	17s. 0d.	8s. 9d.
K	24s. 0d.	19s. 0d.	10s. 6d.
L	27s. 6d.	22s. 6d.	12s. 6d.
M	31s. 0d.	25s. 0d.	15s. 0d.
N	35s. 0d.	28s. 0d.	18s. 0d.

No details of the sets were given, although the prices suggest that set A may be treated as the coarsest set, with progressively higher sets through set N.
Source: G.R. Porter, 'Examination of the recent statistics of the cotton trade in Great Britain', *Journal of the Statistical Society of London* 13, 4 (1850), 305–12, especially 309.

1.7 Prices of sets of cambric goods, 1828–53

Year	Length	Set 1	Set 2	Set 3	Set 4
1828	58 yards	17s.	27s. 0d.	44s.	60s.
1838	72 yards	11s.	17s. 6d.	27s.	37s.
1850	100 yards	12s.	17s. 6d.	26s.	35s.
1858	104 yards	17s.	22s. 6d.	30s.	40s.
1853	120 yards	14s.	16s. 6d.	23s.	32s.

Source: Hugh McCall (1870), 255.

weaving productivity were partly due to technical improvements and intensified production, rather than to new technologies of production, and they were evident among both male and female weavers.

As prices fell through the 1830s, demand in home and export markets grew for goods that had once been far beyond the reach of most consumers, including finished goods such as linen handkerchiefs, whose manufacture was centred on the districts of Lurgan and Portadown. Irish cambric handkerchief-makers had long supplied London markets with luxury articles. Now, declining retail prices, illustrated in figures 1.6 and 1.7, spurred wider demand for cambric goods. These developments were remarkable given the increasing supply of cheaper French cambrics in home markets,[11] and the extensive smuggling of French goods into London. Lower labour costs in mechanized spinning and handloom weaving gave Ulster's cambric industry a structural advantage over its French competitors and its output expanded as new markets opened after the 1830s.[12]

In the 1830s and 40s, weavers partly limited the impact of the lower earnings environment through gains in labour productivity; females were also increasingly assigned less remunerative weaving work as sexual divisions developed in the trade. Despite changes in systems of yarn production, and in the sexual complexion of the weaving workforce, this exploration of technological, social and economic developments in the industry before weaving's mechanization shows that the sexual assignment of weaving labour tended to overlay existing forms of stratification in the trade. Mechanization inaugurated an era marked by the large-scale entry of females into weaving; it was accompanied by a gendering of weaving skill that assigned male and female workers to different branches of work. Females now wove in large numbers as part of a mixed labour force — but continuing male proprietorship of most household looms, pervasive barriers against skills acquisition by females in high-paid branches of work, and divisions between male and female branches of production point to boundaries between men's and women's weaving that influenced 'feminine' and 'masculine' experiences of work in the Irish linen trade.

---

11 *Linen trade of Ireland*, evidence of Leslie Alexander, 76.   **12** Improvements in 'mechanical appliances' for printing on Irish cloth contributed to a rise in the export trade, especially to the Caribbean, South America and the Mediterranean. See James MacAdam, 'On schools of design in Ireland', *Transactions of the Dublin Statistical Society* 1 (1849), 6. Ireland still lagged behind the Swiss and French in the development of intricate designs on cambric articles, but it was said to be producing cambric linens at lower costs in 1849 (6–11).

2

Linen, steam power and the handloom from the 1830s to the 1860s

Periods of coextensive hand and mechanized production are often presented as transition stages in the progress from domestic to factory modes of industrial production. This is especially true in studies of early-modern European textile trades. While European historians have noted pronounced contrasts in the periodization of these transitions, depending on national, regional and local contexts and available technology, prolonged periods of coextensive hand and mechanical production have not tended to be seen as representing a 'logical' production strategy. The theory of proto-industry once offered a rationale for the neglect of such periods; it regarded them as relatively brief transitions between phases of domestic and factory production. Incorporating agrarian, social and institutional factors as determinants of local industrial organization, it theorized the relationship between dispersed rural production and subsequent centralized mechanical manufacture.[1] Yet the explanatory value of this theory is now substantially deflated. In the Netherlands, in France and elsewhere, the putative linear movement from seasonal industrial and agricultural work to more intensive, centralized industrial production has been questioned by historians who have proved that mixed agricultural and rural industrial work were stable, long-term strategies in rural settings.[2] In Ulster's linen trade there is little evidence of a single path towards

1 F. Mendels (1982). The theory of proto-industrialization gained currency after its formulation in the early 1970s by Mendels (1972), who aimed to situate European industrialization within a wide chronology of development. Historians have subsequently expanded the variables that Mendels first proposed as factors in rural industrialization and have developed related demographic theories. By the 1980s, the range of enabling factors included local agrarian structures, social and institutional features (such as the local social hierarchy and land-holding patterns), business factors (such as costs of the organization of production and capital investment strategies) and cultural influences, including the intensity of local labour resistance to centralized production. The institutional context of the agrarian setting has also been identified as a key factory by P. Hudson (1986), who explores how contrasting agrarian bases and institutional factors engendered divergent systems of production in the wool and worsted sectors. There were important demographic developments in proto-industrial theory which historians have examined; see P. Kriedte, et al. (1993). Liberation from these constraints was accompanied by a revolution in a district's demographic regime (S.C. Ogilvie & M. Cerman [1996], 1–3; D. Levine, [1985]). For a comparative discussion of the Irish, Scottish and Flemish linen industries that tests elements of proto-industrial theory, see J. Gray (2003); for case studies of its application in Ireland see L.A. Clarkson (1989a), E.L. Almquist (1979). 2 G. Gullickson (1986), (1983), (1982) and (1981) has discovered differential patterns of marriage based on sex, which were in turn influenced by sexually-specific employment opportunities for men and women in nineteenth-century Auffay. She regards the sexual division of labour in regional industry and agriculture as critical to supporting domestic textile production there. F. Hendrickx, in his study

factory industrialization or of a cursory period of coextensive production systems.[3] In exploring the diverse character of the linen sector between the 1830s
and the 1860s, this chapter outlines the structural complexity of an industry
whose development over the course of the nineteenth century defies generaliza-
tion. It also explores links between the market status of linen weavers and the
structure of agrarian economies, illustrating several paths which the linen sector
followed into an industrial age.

MANY PATHS: THE TERRAIN OF LINEN PRODUCTION IN THE 1830S

In the late 1830s and in 1840, assistant handloom commissioners (part of a wider
team which had fanned out throughout the United Kingdom to investigate various
branches of the country's textile sector) tabled reports that vividly described conditions in Ulster's linen industry. They offer a window onto diverse systems of production and exchange in the Irish linen industry, and illuminate contemporary
views of the sector's development. At their core was a belief that the industry was
on a linear march towards the factory system. A putative transition phase sustain-
ing both mechanized and hand production was seen as the awkward precursor to
a moment at which capital penetrated the industry and, allied with new technology, effected a comprehensive transformation in commerce and production, to the
irrefutable benefit of manufacturer and operative alike. This belief was underpinned by assumptions that the linen trade was progressing from atomized independent domestic production to rationalized, homogenized systems. Certainly the
experience of the British cotton sector — whose weavers' work we now recognize
as more varied than was once appreciated — were influential in shaping ideas
about the Irish linen industry, and about the potential for capital and technology to
bring about economic and social transformations. Yet, on the ground, diverse
workforces continued to operate in a structurally varied trade, and experiences of
mechanization were varied and complex.

   Ballymena was among many markets visited by the assistant handloom commissioners in their inquiry into the linen trade, and it attracted curiosity as a specimen of resilient open-market activity. Situated on a bank of the Braid Water a
few miles beyond its confluence with the Kells Water and the River Main, the
town of Ballymena was at the centre of a basalt plateau. In the Glens of Antrim

of the nineteenth-century Netherlands (1997) and (1993), also presents a regional demographic system
at variance with that of the proto-industrial model, especially challenging the transitional character of
mixed agricultural and domestic industrial work. For similar comments on the durable pattern of
labour in commercial agriculture and rural industry, see B. Collins (1997) and J. Chartres (2000), 1105.
J.H. Quataert (1995), (1988) and (1985), in her investigation of rural industry in Germany, argues that
the failure to account for the industrial activity of the rural small-holding class constitutes a major
weakness in proto-industrial theory.   3 P. Gibbon (1975).

on the east coast of the county, the black basalt sheets ended in dramatic cliffs.[4] Lowland Scots settled the region in the seventeenth century: relative political stability, population expansion and Scottish economic growth during this period spurred migration and capital investment in Ireland.[5] The human links between Scotland and this region of Ulster were reinforced by land proprietorship: part of the lands which later formed the Ballymena Estate had passed from Sir Faithful Fortescue to William Adair, Laird of Kinhilt, Wigtonshire in the seventeenth century.[6] From the mid-seventeenth century, the town became the commercial and administrative centre of a predominantly rural Presbyterian district. In a series of leases, the Adairs and other landlords parcelled out land for mixed arable and pastoral farming. Ballymena was the regional market centre for these farms, and its economy featured some urban production and processing, in corn, textile and paper mills. By the early years of the nineteenth century, it was the district's major inland market centre, organizing the commerce of an expansive agricultural hinterland.

The boundaries of the 'mid-Antrim' district in this study are not rigid. Its rural components were defined more by their relationship to Ballymena as a regional centre of exchange than by the borders of any single jurisdiction, although those which demarcated such units as the poor law union and petty sessions district often overlapped, encompassing the town and its rural environs. The coherence of the mid-Antrim district was primarily expressed through the integration of surrounding rural areas within commercial, administrative and productive regimes organized through the town. Such functions brought professionals, market officers and ancillary businesses, from public houses to inns, to Ballymena. The local market and the market-house, built by subscription and with funds from the Adair family, were key urban institutions, and the height of the market-house's 1754 tower announced its importance to the surrounding district. The town's market serviced an area of extensive agricultural cultivation whose topography was described in 1832 as 'generally undulating', the principal tillage crops being oats, potatoes and flax.[7] Linen was the main rural manufacture and was credited with the vibrancy of Ballymena's textile market. Textile finishing was also an important rural industry and was organized on a large scale on bleachgreens employing scores of workers.

4 F. H. A. Aalen, et al. (1997), 11, 15.   **5** R. Gillespie (1985) provides a detailed account of this settlement in chapter 2, 'The human background', 28–46. See also V. Morgan & W.A. Macafee (1981). For a comprehensive treatment of earlier Jacobean settlement, see M. Perceval-Maxwell (1973).   **6** The remaining portion was acquired through the marriage of Adair's son Robert to a daughter of the neighbouring landlord, and the estate was confirmed to him by patent of Charles I. See [Ballymena] *Observer*, 18 February 1865.   **7** A. Day et al. (eds), *Ordnance Survey memoirs of Ireland,* vol. 23, *parishes of County Antrim VII, 1831–5, 1837–8: Ballymena and West Antrim* (1993), 88. Early in the nineteenth century, an urban butter market was established, with others in the nearby town of Ballymoney and village of Broughshane (J. Dubourdieu, *Statistical Survey of the County of Antrim* [1812], 425). In 1824, market days fell on Saturday for linen, Tuesday for pork and Wednesday for grain (*Pigot and Company's City of Dublin and Hibernian provincial directory* [1824], 339).

The Ballymena linen market suffered through the vicissitudes of the 1820s, when the average value of its webs, principally three-quarter-yard-wide, 52-yard-long brown linens, declined in value, following a trend which was evident in many other branches of the trade.[8] Estimates of the size of Ballymena's linen market relative to other centres in Ulster also suggest volatility during this decade — a period in which open-market trading declined in some centres. Figures compiled for the Board of Trustees indicate that weekly sales in Ballymena's brown linen market in 1784 were exceeded in Ulster only by Armagh, Dungannon, Lisburn and Lurgan. But in 1824, as figure 2.1 illustrates, Ballymena's brown linen market was recorded as the eleventh-largest in Ulster — almost certainly a reflection of some trade shifting to venues outside the market, and the lower value of its local, specialized webs, rather than a contraction of the trade *per se*.

2.1 Value of brown linen sold in Ulster markets, 1824

Town	Value of brown linen
Armagh	£ 335,260 8s. 4d.
Lurgan	121,455 16s. 8d.
Tandagree	112,083 6s. 8d.
Lisburn	96,018 0s. 0d.
Belfast	90,000 0s. 0d.
Strabane	86,284 0s. 0d.
Dungannon	85,702 16s. 6d.
Londonderry	78,156 0s. 0d.
Banbridge	77,550 0s. 0d.
Coleraine	74,138 2s. 8d.
Ballymena	73,610 18s. 10d.

Source: *Select committee on the laws regulating the linen trade of Ireland*, Report, minutes of evidence, appendices (463), HC 1825, vol. v, 185–6.

The market was a central urban institution that channelled and distributed resources in the district. Rural farms benefited from an extensive transportation infrastructure that integrated Ballymena into a wider network of urban centres and created a system for distributing farm produce and goods. The town was situated on an inland route connecting Londonderry and Belfast. The Davison family of Raceview, owners of a local woollen mill, advocated a rail line between the two

---

8 See the *Minutes of the Trustees of the Linen and Hempen Manufactures of Ireland ... 1816* (1817), Appendices, 83–4; *Irish Textile Journal*, 15 September 1888, 104.

places in 1836. It was realized a decade later under the patronage of leading land-
ed and industrial figures, including the Mulhollands of Belfast and the tenth Vis-
count Masserene.[9] Representations accompanying railway proposals to the House
of Commons stated that £23,000 was issued on a weekly basis by Ballymena
banks at the local market and that thirty linen beetling and bleaching concerns
operated in the district: nine on the Braid Water, ten on the Kells Water and eleven
on the River Main.[10] In 1848 the railway was completed. In its new Railway Age,
the imperative of preserving and developing Ballymena's market became acute
as Belfast's regional commercial hegemony grew. In 1850 the poet John Gallagher vividly described the throngs of traders who assembled in town on mar-
ket-day:

> On Saturday morning all is bustle and din,
> With jaunting-cars, phaetons and carts driving in.
> And great preparations are made for the day;
> All are eager and willing their goods to display!
> And the train's long, loud whistle is heard through the town
> At ten, when the brave Belfast merchants come down;
> And country drapers, good luck to them all,
> That keep up the trade in our great linen hall.
> And the yarn-stores are all prepared for the weavers,
> My brave country-fellows, that do their endeavours;...[11]

Although the market that Gallagher extolled served as a centre of exchange for
local agriculture, linen played a pre-eminent role within it. Indeed, the assistant
handloom commissioners praised its vibrancy as they examined a number of districts and found varied systems of textile manufacture and exchange operating
within them.

REGIONAL MARKETS AND REGIONAL WORKFORCES

In Ballymena and elsewhere, the assistant handloom commissioners' reports illustrate the remarkable structural heterogeneity of the trade in the 1830s, rather than
suggesting that it was on a trajectory towards centralized production — a development which many contemporaries anticipated and which the assistant commissioners also desired. The years in which they undertook their inquiry brought
protracted dullness to many textile branches, including linen: in 1835, for

---

9 W.A. McCutcheon (1984), 120 and J.R.L. Currie (1973).   **10** Quoted in 'Elevation and plans,
Hotel, Ballymenagh C. Antrim [*sic*]', PRONI, Belfast, D/929/HA12/F4/11/4.   **11** Excerpted from
John Gallagher's 'Old Ballymena' (1995).

instance, weavers in the Belfast area were said to be in a very 'depressed state', earning less than 5s. weekly for a long workday of fifteen to sixteen hours.[12] In these poor conditions, assistant handloom commissioners C.G. Otway and R.M. Muggeridge embarked upon an extensive tour of the province. The Irish commentators were particularly interested in assessing the position of handloom weavers in light of industrial changes associated with the mechanization of spinning — and with technological advances in cotton weaving, which they believed might soon be applied to the linen trade. Indeed their perspectives on the linen sector were informed by assumptions about commercial and industrial development that expressed a teleology of organizational rationalization influenced by their observations of the British cotton sector.[13]

Surveying the Irish textile sector, Otway suggested that British operatives' wages out-stripped those in Ireland.[14] Yet, in his view, the position of the Irish handloom weaver compared favourably with that of the agricultural labourer. The weaver had an industrial skill that elevated him above the common labourer, and contributed to a marginally higher status in the rural social order — one that was undermined by labourers' entry into the trade.

> The advantage which the handloom weavers in the rural districts enjoy over the great mass of the labouring population, in having a resource open for their labour when a demand for agricultural labour has ceased, reacts with most injurious effects on the former; for the agricultural labourer, finding that his harvest is participated in by the weaver, while he is debarred from any participation in their periods of employment, a temptation is held out to him to learn weaving, and to bring up his children to it, and so adds to the number of persons not capable of being employed profitably as handloom weavers, either to themselves or their employers, as compared with the demand for handloom labour.[15]

Otway also argued that such occasional producers were susceptible to 'serve two masters' and that they failed to place their households on sounder footings through

---

12 *Royal commission on the condition of the poorer classes in Ireland* [37], HC 1836, vol. xxxii, Supplement to appendix E, remarks of Revd John Bradshaw, Lambeg, 264. Observers in centres of the British linen trade, such as Leeds, remarked on an influx of Irish weavers, which, they claimed, exacerbated low earnings (*Royal commission on handloom weavers*, Assistant commissioners' reports (43–II), HC 1840, vol. xxiii, West Riding of Yorkshire, Macclesfield, &c., Report from Solomon Keyser, 475–6).   **13** If these expectations were partly nourished by the experience of Britain's cotton industry, historians have now shown that the development of an exclusive factory labour force in that sector was also unrealized for many decades. See G. Timmins (1993); J.S. Lyons (1989).   **14** *Royal commission on handloom weavers*, Assistant commissioners' reports, pt. III (Yorkshire, West Riding; Ireland) (43–II), HC 1840, vol. xxiii (hereafter '*Royal commission on handloom weavers*'], Report of C.G. Otway, 594.   **15** Ibid., Report of C.G. Otway, 594.

the acquisition of appropriate skills.[16] This comment echoed those of other observers in 1833[17] — and Arthur Young fifty years before. Seasonal weaving, so long a dominant characteristic of domestic linen production, became a feature of fewer branches. Otway and Muggeridge expressed general satisfaction with the 'progress' of Ulster's linen sector. According to them, a new era for the linen trade, founded upon rational principles of commercial and industrial organization, was dawning. It offered lucrative new opportunities for full-time weaving, decoupling textile and agricultural labour and ending the seasonal character of linen production. With increasing demand for cloth in home and foreign markets, and an expanded supply of yarn, labour in the linen sector would, in their view, move inexorably to more advanced forms of organization. But only some markets displayed features that they could laud as harbingers of a new golden age for linen. In many others, they saw few, or very modest, indicators of the sector's 'modernization'.

A VARIED LOT: HANDLOOM WEAVERS IN THE 1830S

Surveying weavers 'as a body', Otway concluded that at least half were young males and females, aged 12 to 20,[18] with those above fourteen and below seventy earning from 9*d.* to 1*s.* per day in 'the least profitable of all trades in Ireland'.[19] Households sought to mitigate low earnings in times of distress by deploying women and children to household weaving or mill work.[20] Indeed, he commented that the expansion of mill-spun yarn, and the 'greater ease with which it is woven' had facilitated the entry of women and young workers into the trade. But he also noted that they were received into a workforce in ways that promoted male dominance in remunerative ends of the trade. While Otway lauded the expansion of the labour force, he cautioned that the participation of juvenile and female labour, enabled by the use of mill-spun yarn, 'must still be taken into account in forming a proper estimate of the nature of the remuneration obtainable for all handloom labour'.[21] He also observed that the growth of putting-out had transformed weaving households that had once been autonomous producers:

> Forty years ago, almost the entire weaving of the country was done by, or on account of the weavers. Each man bought, or raised and prepared his own materials, from which he made his linen web, and sold it in the pub-

16 Ibid., Report of C.G. Otway, 594–5. **17** Minutes of evidence of the *Select committee on the state of agriculture in the United Kingdom* (612), Report, minutes of evidence, appendix, HC 1833, vol. v, evidence of William Armstrong, q. 9108. Arthur Young, *Tour in Ireland (1776–1779)*, vol. 1. (1892). **18** *Royal commission on handloom weavers*, Report of C.G. Otway, 596. **19** Ibid., 600. **20** Ibid., 622. **21** Ibid., 596.

lic market, or by private contract, to agents or travellers who went round
the country to make purchases ...

At this period, many weavers, who were small farmers also, had from
three to six or eight looms in their houses. The spinning and various
preparatory processes which the flax underwent, were chiefly performed by
the female branches of the family. The owner, his apprentices and journey-
men, worked either at the loom, or in the field, as interest prompted, or the
seasons dictated; and as, at this time, the demand almost invariably exceeded the supply of linen, high remunerative prices were obtained. This may
perhaps be regarded as 'the golden age' of the linen weavers of Ireland.[22]

In contrast to the 'golden age' of domestic industry, the assistant handloom
commissioners observed a patch-work quilt of production throughout Ulster,
reflecting different levels of capital penetration and diverse ways of organizing
production. In some centres, the volume of transactions outside open markets
appeared to grow as manufacturers took control of the trade. The degree to which
this occurred was linked to local agrarian systems and the extent of structural
changes within them. Districts in which weaving cottiers occupied very small
plots of land were generally places where the movement towards putting-out and
workshop production was most pronounced. In Rathfriland, Co. Down, for
instance, C.G. Otway found few small farmers in the open market. There, for the
most part, manufacturers dominated the trade, selling cloth directly to bleachers
and Belfast-based agents.[23] In Banbridge, Co. Down, Otway met an employer of
950 weavers who described new systems of production and exchange. Previously he, or agents acting on his commission, had purchased webs from weavers,
small manufacturers and jobbers in open markets, and then had them bleached.
Now he was putting out yarn, and profitably circumventing open markets by
avoiding both commissions and time-consuming negotiations.[24] In describing
Banbridge and other centres, the assistant commissioners distilled the markets of
Ulster down to three types:

1 Those in which weavers worked on their own account 'or, as it is technically
   expressed, for the market, and occupying, besides, small holdings of land';

2 those in which weavers worked for manufacturers, including workforces of cottier-weavers who did not possess land, and weavers who held small plots; and

3 those in which weavers worked for manufacturers in weaving-shops or factories.[25]

22 *Royal commission on handloom weavers*, Report of R.M. Muggeridge, 703–4.   23 *Royal commission on handloom weavers*, Report of C.G. Otway, 635–6.   24 Ibid., 638–9.   25 *Royal commission on handloom weavers*, Report of R.M. Muggeridge, 709.

Open markets were vibrant in Ballymena, Ballymoney and Coleraine (which were described as being 'noted for the sale of the finest qualities of linen').[26] Weavers here were direct participants in the market. Unlike C.G. Otway, his fellow assistant commissioner R.M. Muggeridge wrote with approval of this system, emphasizing the extent to which small producers retained control over production, while having the option of entering the temporary employment of manufacturers if they calculated it to be more remunerative.[27] But Muggeridge also saw risks for weavers in the open market, in which households were governed by precarious systems of credit and fluctuating prices.[28] One Coleraine weaver working on his own account described the ardour of independent production and claimed that colleagues had immigrated to America due to diminishing prospects at the loom.[29] Indeed, the open market in Rathfriland was operating on a smaller scale than in previous decades. For a 54–yard cloth of a set of 20°°, woven in a fortnight working fourteen to sixteen hours daily, weavers could receive 22s., but from this sum they deducted 5d. to 6d. for dressing the web, and 1s. for warping the chain and winding the weft if outside help was required.[30] The district's weavers were working under several different systems of production; as elsewhere, their status as industrial producers was linked to their status as either farmers or paid labourers in local agriculture. Otway observed that the former class of farmer-weavers, occupying 10 to 20 acres, had fallen off. As in Ballymena, where they predominated to a greater degree, small farmers on land from 4 to 10 acres remained independent participants in the linen market, shifting between seasonal textile production and work on their smallholdings. The weavers employed by manufacturers, by contrast, were former day-labourers for farmers who engaged in fieldwork or in weaving.[31] In Dromore, Co. Down, where weaving families had on average two looms each, this class of landless labourers was the mainstay of the putting-out workforce: they held cottages under terms which still obliged them to perform agricultural service during the busiest times of the year.[32] There, the scarcity of such labourers sometimes led to agricultural wages of 9s. to 11s. 8d. per week, outstripping the earnings of most weavers, and encouraging textile workers to shift activities.

By contrast, in the district around Lurgan, Co. Armagh, as in mid-Antrim, Otway found a relatively large independent weaving class occupying 5 to 15 acres of land and working it themselves. The town's parallel workforce of

---

26 Ibid.   27 Ibid., 710.   28 Ibid.   29 Ibid., 715.   30 *Royal commission on handloom weavers*, Report of C.G. Otway, 636. In Barnsley, linen weavers deducted a total of 2s. 6½d. weekly for such expenses as winding, dressing and brushes, loom rent (6d. weekly), candles and the wear and tear of implements. See the *Royal commission on handloom weavers*, Reports of the assistant handloom commissioners (43–II), HC 1840, vol. xxiii, West Riding of Yorkshire, Macclesfield, & c., Report of Solomon Keyser, 479. *Net* earnings stood at 5s. 6d. per week.   31 *Royal commission on handloom weavers*, Report of C.G. Otway, 636.   32 Ibid., 641.

weavers working for manufacturers, like its counterpart in Rathfriland, comprised cottiers.[33] In the view of Otway and other contemporary observers, the seasonal producer was less likely to develop skills for highly-paid weaving work. In many such branches where casual labour predominated, female weavers were becoming numerous by the late 1830s. But male small farmers also wove as independent producers in many markets, including Lurgan. There, Otway found many weavers selling goods on their own account. Some grew or bought their own flax, wove cloth and sold it in the local market, 'which is one of the principal brown linen markets of the north of Ireland, next to Ballymena, which is the most extensive'.[34] Just as he looked favourably on districts in which manufacturers dominated the trade, Otway decried the condition of Lurgan's independent weavers, many of whom were weaving for the specialist lawn branch. He argued that their counterparts who had withdrawn from the open market enjoyed greater stability in their earnings, and also improved their skills.[35] And although he admitted that it was impossible to gauge their incomes, Otway contended that 'all the evidence on this head goes to prove that they make less than those employed by manufacturers also, and that their profits are most injuriously fluctuating'.[36] Open markets such as Ballymena and Lurgan were described as being in a state of gradual displacement as underlying agrarian structures transformed. In the 1840s the Belgian observer Auguste Moxhet described the number of weavers in Ulster working on their own account as 'insignificant' and contrasted their decline favourably with the continuing independence of Belgian weavers.[37] Indeed, by 1852, the *Belfast Linen Trade Circular*, the organ of the Belfast Linen Trade Committee and a clarion of the triumphalist narrative of factory industrialization, declared that 'Linens are no longer sold, in any quantity, in the open market by individual weavers.'[38] Instead, activity in such places centred on exchanges between merchants and manufacturers, with only a handful of markets now serving as important sites of exchange between weavers and merchants.[39]

Ballymena, like Lurgan, was a centre in which the open-market system prevailed after the 1830s, principally as a site for negotiations between manufacturers and merchants. Indeed, it was described as possessing 'an important feature that, while all the other brown markets of the kingdom have been rapidly declining, it has been increasing'.[40] One correspondent with the assistant commissioners, the bleacher Thomas M. Birnie of Dunminning, wrote that the town's linen

---

33 Ibid., 643.   34 Ibid., 642.   35 Ibid.   36 Ibid., 645. Even in this redoubt of independent production and open-market exchange, commercial practices such as redemption expressed the blurred lines between commercial systems. Under redemption, weavers hired yarn from manufacturers, wove webs and then sold them independently, paying the manufacturer 1*s.* for yarn hire, in addition to the actual price of the yarn. See ibid., 643.   37 P. Solar (1988), especially 20–1.   38 *Linen Trade Circular*, 4 June 1852.   39 J. Sproule (ed.), *The resources and manufacturing industry of Ireland, as illustrated by the exhibition of 1853* (n.d.), 288.   40 *Royal commission on handloom weavers*, Report of C.G. Otway, 642.

trade had grown just as neighbouring markets disappeared altogether. He attributed its resilience 'to the fact that, in all other parts of Ulster, the trade is much more in the hands of manufacturers'. Since manufacturers sold large quantities of linen to bleachers on credit, they could often circumvent the market. In Ballymena, however, Birnie claimed that 'the trade, though to a great extent in the hands of manufacturers also, is carried on principally for cash bargains'.[41] Local manufacturers sometimes employed hundreds of weavers, and they continued to use the market to negotiate with buyers: Sir William Crawford remarked in 1910 that forty years earlier 20,000 webs were sometimes on sale in the weekly market.[42] Observers were divided about the extent to which women had entered the trade in Ballymena, and in other branches and regions. In districts surrounding the city of Londonderry, where the handloom was declining, few women had taken up weaving. In other centres, women wove in large numbers, though commentators were quick to point out that their work was 'lesser-skilled' and concentrated in lower-paying branches. Indeed, as part of the repertoire of strategies to defend skill in the trade, several observers argued for a more clearly-defined and rigorous apprenticeship system — explicitly expressing their hope that handloom weaving would thereby become more remunerative.[43] Damask weaving was identified as the exemplar of skilled work — and also as an exclusively male trade. The French Jacquard loom was adopted by Irish damask weavers in first decades of the nineteenth century to produce figured work. The loom was an elaborate and expensive device, the operation of which required many years of specialized training.[44] The preparation of perforated cards in the damask loom, which were used to inweave patterns in the cloth, was judged to require 'considerable skill' by the author William Charley, 'and is almost a special business of itself'.[45] The weaving of broadcloths by handloom often required a number of hands: one damask tablecloth, for instance, required the labour of four weavers and twelve boys assisting at the loom.[46] The restrictive character of damask weaving apprenticeships, through which boys were trained from a young age, contrasted with the relative ease of entry characterizing female-dominated branches of manufacture as the decades passed, and served as a demarcator of masculine craft.

The systems of production for which the assistant handloom commissioners reserved most generous commendations were those which removed weavers from the market altogether, ending mixed agricultural and textile labour. Between putting-out and workshop systems, the workshops won higher plaudits, but the

---

41 *Royal commission on handloom weavers,* Report of R.M. Muggeridge, correspondence of Thomas M. Birnie, 756–8. **42** Sir W. Crawford, *Irish linen and some features of its production* (1910), 12. **43** *Royal commission on handloom weavers,* Report of R.M. Muggeridge, 715. **44** A. Ure, *The philosophy of manufactures* (1861), 595. **45** William Charley, *Flax and its products in Ireland* (1862), 93. **46** W.A. McCutcheon (1984), 307–10.

assistant commissioners also welcomed the growth of the putting-out system as a precursor to comprehensive modernization in the sector. 'Already the advantages of concentrated capital and ingenuity and enterprise, over the isolated efforts of the lowly and industrious rural weaver are rapidly developing themselves in Ireland,' they reported, 'and day by day are transplanting the loom from the cabin of the cottier to the factory or weaving-shop of the manufacturer.'[47] In Lisburn, Co. Antrim, in the late 1820s, the damask manufacturer Messrs Colston was among few local firms operating under the putting-out system, but it grew in many branches of the trade, especially in parts of the Linen Triangle, where the cost of yarns used to weave high sets of goods proved prohibitive to independent weavers, and where transaction costs fell under putting-out and workshop systems.[48] In some districts, production became centred on workshops, while in others dual systems of dispersed and centralized weaving prevailed.

Centres of industrial centralization won generous praise from the assistant commissioners. Considerable commercial reorganization had occurred in Banbridge by the 1830s: there, C.G. Otway wrote, 'some of the first manufacturers who invested large capital in the linen trade, established themselves, and here the great experiment of placing the linen trade of Ireland on a new foundation was tried'.[49] By one account, no more than one weaver in one hundred now wove on his or her own account.[50] In this market, famous for fine linen, Otway remarked that the dissolution of the Board of Trustees, the repeal of protective duties, and Scotland and England's early adoption of mill-spun yarn had spurred local manufacturers to reorganize production. This enhanced the role of merchant-manufacturers who controlled spinning and putting-out, and who also bleached cloth and exported it, or sold it to merchants through factors.[51] Banbridge's weavers were the same class of landless cottiers who predominated in several other districts. In domestic weaving, women continued to perform ancillary tasks such as winding their own weft, and also winding warps for manufacturers.[52] Weavers lived in small cottages held by their employers near workshops where they wove.[53] And although the organizational framework under which they worked was different from that of other districts, household labour remained the basis of domestic and workshop weaving, with wives and young children attending weavers' looms.[54] Otway encountered several Banbridge manufacturers, one of whom employed 2,000 handloom weavers and another 1,700 looms. They spoke of their success in displacing French competitors in lucrative American markets, and described bright prospects that attended their trade.[55] The status of workers under the putting-out system won

---

47 *Royal commission on handloom weavers*, Report of R.M. Muggeridge, 710.   **48** Ibid., 713.   **49** *Royal commission on handloom weavers*, Report of C.G. Otway, 637.   **50** Ibid., 639.   **51** Ibid., 637.   **52** Ibid., 638.   **53** Ibid.   **54** Parents who were not skilled in the trade would often send their child to apprentice with a weaver, (Ibid., Report of C.G. Otway, 641).   **55** Ibid., 638.

praise from the assistant handloom commissioners, but they looked most favourably on centralized systems of production.

Weavers employed in workshops worked for manufacturers who owned the premises and the looms. This system was described as widespread in Co. Down, and also present in parts of Cos. Antrim, Londonderry and Armagh in the 1830s. Workshops were especially prevalent in urbanized districts where the textile work-force had become disconnected from the seasonal demand for labour in agriculture. This was the case in Belfast, where the urban workforce comprised landless renters, many of whom were migrants to the town. In Belfast, some 700 of the town's 900 linen weavers were workshop employees. Belfast's linen industry was still small compared to its cotton sector, and its weavers were mainly employed in canvass, sacking, single and double damask and coarse linens.[56] While weavers expressed some reluctance to enter workshops, C.G. Otway reckoned that they were the most secure of all handloom operatives, as they were sheltered from the market and their work mostly subsumed under the wage system.[57]

Workshop employment involved a change in the status of weavers from inde-pendent producers (in the open-market system) or contracted workers (under putting-out) to employees. It entailed routinized work, close monitoring of pro-duction, and a relationship of exclusive employment.[58] In other important dimen-sions, however, workshop production reproduced dynamics of social authority and maintained systems of labour that were prevalent in domestic weaving – especially when family members aided the workshop weavers. The manufactur-er Daniel Currell reported to an inquiry in 1841 that he had 35 boys (almost two-thirds of whom were aged 13 or under) and 28 girls (just under half of whom were aged 13 or under) working in his Belfast weaving-shop, the youngest wind-ing bobbins for the loom. But most of the young children in his factory were hired directly by the weavers whom they assisted — the weavers being described as 'very often' their parents. Since they were recruited by weavers rather than by workshop owners, and were unwaged, units of production in workshop weaving resembled domestic weaving, in which the collective work of the household was rewarded by a single wage.[59] The engagement of young workers directly by workshop weavers was also common in William Orr and Co.'s Belfast concern, where it was said that 'parents, or other workmen … bring the children in to wind

56 Those manufacturing sailcloth could earn 10*s.* weekly (*Royal commission on handloom weavers,* Report of R.M. Muggeridge, 718).   57 *Royal commission on handloom weavers,* Report of C.G. Otway, 634.   58 To many manufacturers, this system deterred embezzlement — which was seen as a serious problem associated with putting-out in the 1830s. Muggeridge heard from the secretary of the County Londonderry Committee, for example, that yarn theft was widespread and he was urged by manufactures to obtain strengthened legal instruments to punish embezzlement severely, even with hard labour. *Royal commission on handloom weavers,* Report of R.M. Muggeridge, 705 and of C.G. Otway, 651–2.   59 Evidence collected by T. Martin, *Royal commission on children's employ-ment in mines and manufactories,* 2nd Report (manufactures) II [432], HC 1843, vol. xv (hereafter 'T. Martin — *children's commission*'), n. 6.

for them, and have the entire management of them'.[60] While the employers provided meat and clothes to the children 'at discretion', they offered no separate wages to them — 'this is the same as if they were in the parents' house'. Only young persons who were employed as weavers in their own right drew wages: in the drill-weaving factory of Abraham Walker, for instance, the earnings of young weavers engaged in plain work were estimated to be 5s. to 6s. weekly, with 'fancy weavers' earning 7s. to 7s. 6d.[61] Therefore, despite transformations in relationships between producers, manufacturers and the market, workshop weaving reproduced household systems of labour governed by divisions of sex and age. Just as the entry of female labour into the weaving trade had been negotiated with reference to historic gendered relations of labour status and authority, so the development of workshop labour tended to endorse, rather than challenge, the social relations that governed cottage production.

The practice of drawing on household labour remained intact in the workshop, but the dominant site of linen production in Ulster remained the rural farm or cottage in the 1830s, when in many cases seasonal production continued. Most markets incorporated a diversity of workforces and commercial and organizational systems. Between the experience of Banbridge, where putting-out predominated and drew a large workforce of cottiers into weaving, and Lurgan and Ballymena's more resilient open markets, where smallholders predominated, there were places such as Tandagree, Co. Armagh, which retained, more tenuously, elements of independent production. The class of farmer-weavers owning larger plots of land — upwards of 20 acres — and those engaged in seasonal weaving were declining.[62] Here, C.G. Otway found evidence of the vaunted new system of putting-out. One weaver, Joseph Pedlow, claimed that in competition with manufacturers, he began to weave using expensive hand-spun yarn to meet demand in the open market. In consequence of higher raw-material costs, Pedlow said he could earn only 10d. daily, whereas weavers working for manufacturers (making cloth of a set from 13°° to 14°°) could earn far more, without relying on their own credit to purchase yarn.[63] Until the previous May, Pedlow reported that his *net* earnings were 6s. weekly, lower than the 9s. that, he claimed, could be earned by weavers working for manufacturers. His reflections on independent production mixed regret and stiff resistance: 'I had a sort of pride in me, and, having a little farm, I did not wish to be subject to fines, if I had not my web in by a certain time.'[64] In these markets, some with parallel systems of independent production, putting-out and workshop weaving, the decline of the small farmer-weaver was a primary factor behind the relative decay of open-market work.

---

60 T. Martin — *children's commission, n.* 13.   **61** Ibid., *n.* 16.   **62** *Royal commission on handloom weavers,* Report of C.G. Otway, 646.   **63** Ibid., 645.   **64** Ibid.

Weaving under workshop and putting-out systems and the relative decline in independent production were broad trends in textile production and commerce that the assistant commissioners welcomed. But general decay had also set in through many districts of linen manufacture in Ireland, undermining prospects for the industry. In Drogheda, Co. Louth, for instance, which specialized in the same coarse ranges of cloth produced in British centres such as Barnsley and Dundee, C.G. Otway found an immiserated class of urban weavers, earning wages of around 3*s.* 4*d.* to 5*s.* weekly and 'reduced to the level of common labourers'.[65] The town had once been a vibrant cotton and linen centre, specializing in sheetings, dowlas and 'market linens' using home-spun yarn.[66] In 1820, 53,697 pieces had been stamped in the open market, but by 1834 that volume had slumped to 19,524 pieces.[67] In the 1830s cotton had declined as well. Local manufacturers blamed a number of factors for the local trade's distress: the former Linen Board regulations on yarn measurement, which precluded them from using continental yarns; the introduction of cheap substitutes, such as union cloth, which contained cotton weft; disputes between weavers and manufacturers; and an English poor law regime which extended parish allowances to weavers and enabled them to work at lower rates.[68] Under heavy competition from firms in Britain that adopted mill-spun yarn earlier than in Ireland, Drogheda experienced acute distress.[69] Indeed, it was reported in the 1830s that weavers' wages did not surpass 4*s.* weekly for plain goods, and 8*s.* for fancier cloth, including the work of a winder and involving sixteen hours of work daily.[70] Drogheda cloth was described as easily woven, and the ease of entry into the trade was identified as a cause of industrial decay as 'secondary' workers flooded the market, depressing wages further.[71] These claims served as clear expressions of the threats that many male weavers attached to the expanding pool of female labour. But conditions in Drogheda also reflected deeper structural changes that were transforming the geography of linen production in Ireland. Other historic linen centres experienced outright contraction. In Co. Donegal, for instance, independent weavers now wove primarily for home-use, and those weaving for the market earned comparatively low wages. In Co. Sligo, the trade was declared virtually extinct, the old system having 'died a natural death', leaving a small class of weavers in poverty and weaving mainly for their

---

65 Ibid., 629. 66 *Royal commission on the condition of the poorer classes in Ireland*, Appendix C, Part I, State of the poor and charitable institutions in principal towns in Ireland [35], HC 1836, vol. xxx, Report on the town of Drogheda, 45. 67 *Select committee on handloom weavers' petitions* (492), HC 1835, vol. xiii, Analysis of the evidence taken before the *Select committee on handloom weavers' petitions* (1834–35), Part I: Distress and its results, 4–5. 68 Ibid., 45. Indeed, in the face of these problems, many weavers were reported to have emigrated to British centres of the trade (46–7). 69 *Royal commission on handloom weavers*, Report of C.G. Otway, 629–31. 70 Report on the town of Drogheda, 47. 71 *Royal commission on handloom weavers*, Report of C.G. Otway, 631.

own purposes.[72] Dungannon, Co. Tyrone was another specimen of decline, this time in a formerly vibrant 'seven-eighths' weaving district in Ulster: its market had diminished, and manufacturers had not sought weavers there as production shifted eastward to areas in the historic Linen Triangle.[73] Cos. Antrim, Down and Armagh were now centres of a condensed region of intensive linen manufacture.

In markets that had developed along regional lines since the eighteenth century, rates of organizational change in the 1830s varied markedly. From the desperate plight of landless, urban Drogheda coarse cloth weavers to the diminishing numbers of small farmers in the Rathfriland linen market, to cottiers weaving in the workshops of Banbridge and small farmers seasonally active in Ballymena, labour forces and production systems remained remarkably diverse as the structural features of the Irish linen trade changed. These divergent experiences were extensions of the intrinsic regionalization of linen manufacture in Ireland, strengthened by diverse forms of industrialization and uneven rates of agrarian change. Clearly, some observers such as Otway and Muggeridge hailed the decoupling of agricultural and weaving work as a foundation for prosperity and improved weaving skills. They also warmly welcomed the development of centralized production as a sound underpinning for the sector's 'modernization', heralded by the diffusion of new technologies.

THE FITFUL BIRTH OF A FACTORY AGE

If the industry's heterogeneity was one of its historic features, and was sustained through the transformations of the 1830s and 1840s, the 1850s offered new promise for those who believed that steam technology would be the agent of the sector's transformation — and perhaps of its homogenization. Now technology, and not commercial change, nourished hopes of industrial transformation. Yet commercial conditions and technical limitations privileged the handloom in many linen branches, defying predictions of its eclipse. While the rapid transformation of linen yarn-spinning in the 1820s and 1830s has been highlighted in many accounts of the industry, weaving has been less comprehensively analyzed — partly because it presents a much more ambiguous case of sectoral 'modernization'.[74] The contrasts between the two ends of the sector are significant. The displacement of hand-spinning in Ulster was relatively swift and complete; even the small demand for super-fine yarn that survived after mechanization drew on con-

---

72 Ibid., 650.   **73** The market specialized in coarse 9°° sets, but had seen a considerable falling off as buyers sought larger supplies of cloth and longer credit terms through manufacturers who supplied them with webs manufactured elsewhere in the province (Ibid., 648).   **74** L.M. Cullen (1972), 106–9, 124–5; C. Ó Gráda (1994), 282–92; E.J. Boyle (1977), 33–53.

tinental suppliers. In weaving, mechanization was much more uneven. Related social experiences of work also contrasted with spinning, where technology contributed to a much more thorough and decisive 'eclipse' of rural hand production with the emergence of mill workforces.[75] In contrast with spinning, the study of technical processes in weaving after the 1840s has been limited, though several historians have argued that the uneven timing of steam mechanization requires greater attention.[76] The prospects for mechanization certainly proved seductive to contemporary observers, who anticipated far more revolutionary industrial transformations than those that occurred in the 1850s and 1860s. In 1852, for instance, the *Belfast and province of Ulster directory* quoted J. MacAdam's comments in the *Journal of Design* in which he predicted the demise of the handloom:

> There are many reasons for believing that the future progress of the Irish linen trade will at least keep pace with its past development. One cause of linen fabrics being dearer than cotton is, that the great mass of the latter are woven by power, while all the former, except some of the coarsest kinds, are woven by hand. Although many attempts have been made to adapt the powerloom to linens, they have hitherto not been successful, chiefly owing to the fact, that flax-fibre is not so elastic a substance as cotton-wool. Nevertheless, late experiments have given more satisfactory results, although not yet sufficiently matured to warrant the belief that the powerloom can be soon made generally available...It is scarcely possible that the difficulties which have heretofore prevented powerloom weaving from being adopted in the linen manufacture, should prove insuperable. Mechanical science has achieved many triumphs, where much greater obstacles lay in the way. We may, therefore, conclude that, sooner or later, the system will be fully carried out, and its results will have a powerful effect on the advancement of the manufacture.[77]

There is little doubt that MacAdam and others believed that they stood on the threshold of a new era in weaving. Remarking in 1851 on two transformations which nourished visions of dramatic change — mechanization of British cotton weaving and Irish flax spinning — James Haughton predicted that prosperity would soon attend steam-loom weaving and expressed enthusiasm in 'anticipa-

---

75 G. O'Brien (1921), in his critique of the economic implications of Union, saw the experience of the linen industry as less severe than others. Potentially drastic social consequences were mitigated by the absence of technological changes in the weaving end before the Famine (315–35) **76** E.J. Boyle (1997) does not study the social history of the handloom weaving labour force, but underscores the extent to which they remained an important part of the workforce, 59–78. Similarly, Ó Gráda (1994) underlines the extent to which handloom weaving remained important in several sectors of the trade during mechanization, 289. See also E.R.R. Green (1949), 121–3. **77** *Belfast and province of Ulster directory for 1852* (1852), vol. 1 , 47.

tion of the happy prospects which await Ireland, when the further triumph of mechanic power shall enable the manufacturers of these lands, to overcome the difficulties now in the way of spinning and weaving linen yarn'.[78] These remarks were allied to a commentary on manufacture in urban centres, where, in contrast to rural districts, Haughton believed that a 'much higher standard of intelligence, and a much stronger appreciation of the blessings of freedom' were to be found.[79] But the changes which such commentators anticipated were belied by the size of the handloom labour force for many decades — a fact which led C.F. Bastable to write in 1884 that the linen trade 'commenced with a system of *domestic* manufacture, which is not, even now, entirely swept away by the competition of the powerloom'.[80] Capital investment in mechanization proceeded unevenly in the trade, effecting different levels of commercial reorganization and defying the hopes of some observers in the 1830s. Similarly, changes in production systems were halting and incomplete, as the limits of new technology became apparent. By the end of the 1860s, thousands of weavers remained at the handloom and continued to work in the trade for decades.

FAMINE AND LABOUR IN THE LINEN TRADE

The coincidence of technological developments and population decline in Ireland was hailed by many observers of the trade as a foundation for its modernization. The late 1840s witnessed considerable anxiety over the size of handloom weaving's labour pool as Famine emigration diminished Ireland's population. But far from heralding its eclipse, the 1840s and early-1850s witnessed a spatial redistribution of Ulster's linen weavers, with an increasing concentration in north-eastern counties of the province. In Connacht, depopulation induced contractions in cottage industry, while in Ulster the geography of production shifted eastwards towards Cos. Antrim, Down and Armagh — especially towards Belfast — and away from regions which traditionally supplied yarn to weaving districts.[81] This continued a pattern of geographic contraction that, since the 1820s, had seen the linen sector in western parts of Ireland, and the markets of Co. Louth and other places, diminish in scale. Even within this smaller area of manufacture, production remained highly regionalized, with one commentator noting:

78 James Haughton, 'The application of machinery to manufactures, beneficial to the working classes', *Transactions of the Dublin Statistical Society* 2 (1851), 11.   **79** Ibid., 7.   **80** C.F. Bastable, 'Economic conditions of industrial development, with special reference to the case of Ireland', *Journal of the Statistical and Social Inquiry Society of Ireland* 8 (1884), 461–73; this quotation appears on page 466. See also the excellent study by O. Greeves (1969).   **81** In F.W. Smith, *Irish linen trade hand-book* (1876), 82. For a discussion of the state of the trade, see P. Ollerenshaw (1985), 73–4.

As is always the case in kindred manufactures, the different sorts of linen fabrics are confined to certain localities. Thus, in Ireland, coarse linens for blouses, &c., and for the common kinds of export goods are chiefly made in the county of Armagh; medium and fine kinds of export cloth about Ballymena and Coleraine; damasks and diapers at Lurgan, Lisburn, and Belfast; lawns at Lurgan and Dromore; cambrics at Lurgan, Waringstown, and Dromore; heavy linens and sheetings for the home market at Banbridge; hollands in the counties of Antrim and Armagh; shirt fronts, woven in plaits, at Dromore; and the coarsest fabrics, such as bed-ticks, coarse drills, &c., at Drogheda.[82]

The continued use of the handloom in many of these areas defied predictions from the newly-established trade journal of the Belfast Linen Trade Committee, the *Linen Trade Circular*, that population decline and technological developments would result in its displacement. To some contemporary observers, these two trends appeared to be converging in the 1850s, leading them to believe that population loss would choke off labour supply and that technical improvements to powerloom design would facilitate wider mechanization. In short, they believed that the powerloom offered an avenue through which a crisis in labour supply could be averted.[83]

The *Linen Trade Circular*, surveying the industry in 1852, claimed that emigration had substantially reduced the number of weaving smallholders and hailed the development of new weaving technology as a means by which emigrating handloom weavers could be replaced. The pessimism expressed in predictions of an impending labour scarcity was mitigated by a firm belief that steam-weaving would soon prevail:

Up to the period of the famine of 1847, hand-labour was so cheap and plentiful that this question remained in abeyance. The wide social changes brought about by the failure of the potato crop have, since then, materially affected this important department of manufacture. The weaving of linens, in the North of Ireland, was chiefly carried on by small farmers, cottiers and labourers, seldom as a separate employment, but as an adjunct to the work of the farm. Consequently, at the more pressing periods of field-labour, such as seed-time and harvest, the production of linen cloth was greatly curtailed, by the transference of the weavers to out-door work, on the conclusion of which they again returned to their looms, and the production at once increased. Some inconveniences resulted from these fluctuations, but they were practically of little influence on trade. Since the

82 A. Ure (1861), 599.   **83** J. Sproule (n.d.), 288.

loss of the potato, however, a great change has occurred, which already seriously affects the entire question. The class of small farmers is gradually becoming extinct, because they have found it difficult to live on the produce of their farms, and the labour of their looms, after deducting rent and other permanent charges.[84]

Weavers' earnings rose markedly from the mid-1840s, when the trade was shaken by the Famine — a event which nonetheless inspired optimism that the sector would find surer footings after the upheaval. Contemporary perspectives on the workforce in the early-1850s were corollaries to those of the pre-Famine period, when observers such as the Belgian consul in New York believed that the abundant supply of weaving labour had served as a strong disincentive to mechanization.[85] By the early-1850s, as the *Linen Trade Circular* claimed that handloom weavers had been disappearing since the mid-1840s, its concerns centred on the limited *extent* of handloom weaving labour. A related concern revolved around the *productivity* of weavers, especially with earnings rising significantly.[86] Observers worried that such high earnings would promote irregular labour.[87] Indeed, after decades of falling earnings, returns to poor law commissioners for a district comprising Cos. Antrim, Armagh, Down, Londonderry and Tyrone show them rising sharply after 1851. They began in fact to far surpass those of agricultural labourers, as figure 2.2 illustrates, providing an incentive for seasonal rural labourers to focus a higher proportion of their energies on textile production.

2.2 Average wages of agricultural labourers and weavers in Lt-Col. Clarke's district, comprised in the counties of Antrim, Armagh, Down, Londonderry, and Tyrone, 1846–53

Occupation	1846	1847	1848	1849	1850	1851	1852	1853
Agricultural labourers	5s. 0d.	5s. 0d.	5s. 0d.	5s. 0d.	5s. 3d.	5s. 3d.	5s. 3d.	5s. 3d.
Weavers	5s. 6d.	5s. 3d.	3s. 9d.	4s. 3d.	5s. 3d.	6s. 0d.	7s. 6d.	7s. 6d.

Source: *Sixth annual report of the commissioners administering the laws for relief of the poor in Ireland* [1645], HC 1852–53, vol. i, Appendix, 153.

It must be noted that no specific reference was made to linen weavers in the above return, and that there were still cotton weavers who remained at the handloom in areas of Ulster. These weavers were said to be among the lowest-paid in the textile workforce. See an account of the weavers in Ballymacarrett, *Banner of Ulster*, 19 February 1847.

84 *Linen Trade Circular*, 29 October 1852.   **85** P. Solar (1988), 20–1.   **86** *Linen Trade Circular*, 29 October 1852.   **87** *Linen Trade Circular*, 6 August 1852.

The belief that these conditions imperiled the supply of labour remained wide-spread throughout the decade. In a half-yearly factory report, T.J. Howell remarked that linen manufacture was slowed by emigration. He also believed that in a climate of higher earnings, weavers reduced their time at the loom to maximize leisure, adding to widespread anxiety about the regularity of their work and the stability of labour supply.[88] At several points in the decade, bottlenecks created by increased spinning output and restricted weaving capacity were credited with leading to higher yarn exports. Manufacturers' anxieties about handloom weavers found repeated expression in the *Linen Trade Circular*. Fluctuating commercial conditions also deepened concerns about stability in the trade,[89] though they also partly account for the fact that, despite concerns about the extent and productivity of handloom labour, manufacturers resisted adopting the powerloom even in branches for which it was available.

Despite concerns about the decline of the weaving labour pool, there is evidence of growth, not contraction, in the number of weavers employed in the trade. While the census suggests that the number of weavers in Co. Antrim grew between 1841 and 1851, there was a significant shift in the sexual composition of the weaving labour force, as females continued to enter linen branches.[90] The extent of feminization by 1851 can be exaggerated: the printed census, for instance, suggests that a large number of males worked at the loom in this period. Certainly, specific branches became feminized as households re-gendered weaving and skilled work became coterminous with remunerative branches of weaving and masculine labour. Many men remained at the loom — especially as the gendering of work and skill reduced direct competition with female workers.

PROMISE DELAYED? THE LINEN TRADE IN THE 1850S

New weaving technology was received within these complex contexts, and in a commercial environment that initially discouraged its adoption. Despite manufacturers' concerns about the reliability of handloom labour, the 1850s did not witness a large-scale reorganization of linen textile production. As in spinning, weaving's mechanization had several precedents in previous decades.[91] Yet it was

88 In *Linen Trade Circular*, 18 February 1853.   **89** Conditions in the trade after 1850 have received considerable attention. See E.J. Boyle (1977); O. Greeves (1969); P. Ollerenshaw (1997); P. Solar (2005).   **90** Edward Wakefield's account of the linen industry included records that showed that the introduction of new shuttles had reduced the exertions of weaving to such an extent that by 1808 the Linen Board was offering looms and shuttles to several classes of female workers, including women who had woven over 200 yards in the year ending 1806. See E. Wakefield, *An account of Ireland, statistical and political* (1812), vol. 1, 697. A. McKernan (1994) has also shown the extent to which female weavers were employed in the industry during the Napoleonic Wars.   **91** H.D. Gribbon (1969), 98–102.

not until the 1840s that steam power was adopted, when a few manufacturers such as the Ballymena bleacher Daniel Currell erected steam-powered machinery in Belfast. During the 1840s and early-1850s, the diffusion of steam-weaving was limited in the Irish trade. While it was prevalent in the British linen sector where, with only a few exceptions such as the fine trade of Dunfermline, coarser branches predominated, powerlooms were ill-suited to finer Irish linen manufacture, and the substitution of hand-power by steam was far from comprehensive. If the technical requirements for mechanization were at hand in some branches, conditions that would render it a profitable business strategy were not yet in prospect. During the 1850s, despite high American tariffs, Ireland's linen trade continued to grow overall, especially with Australia. Holland, Belgium, Spain, Portugal, Sardinia, Austria, Russia and Norway reduced import duties on linen goods.[92] As figure 2.3 illustrates, although the early part of the decade saw an upturn in exports, it was also punctuated by periods of protracted dullness — and cotton continued to be a competitor. In 1854, manufacturers reduced the number of handloom operatives in their employment as demand slackened. A two-year period of low demand retarded the erection of powerlooms,[93] and, combined with high costs for flax, also depressed the spinning trade. In November 1854, prices in the trade were especially depressed, owing to an expansion of spindle capacity in 1852 and 1853 (amounting to a 20 percent increase in output), which had 'glutted foreign markets'.[94] The Russian War also reduced the supply of foreign flax, resulting in a downturn that ended in 1856, when improved conditions led to a revival of interest in mechanization.[95] In such an unstable commercial climate, manufacturers approached powerlooms cautiously. In the mid-1850s, some manufacturers experimented with them, and it was reported in 1855 that a number of manufacturers were adopting steam technology.[96] It was also reported that the production of ordinary light export linens by powerloom had progressed in 1856, and that a large proportion of the 25 firms and 2,200 powerlooms in operation that year were manufacturing heavy linens for the home trade, as well as coarse drills and some light sets of goods.[97]

Throughout the vagaries of the 1850s, the *Linen Trade Circular* continued to declare that 'handloom weavers have become so scarce, and their wages so high, that, were it not for the likelihood of powerlooms coming more and more into use, the cost of production might be such as seriously to interfere with the prospects of the export trade, while there would be considerable difficulty in securing a sufficient make of goods'.[98] Pressure to lower prices led some manufacturers to con-

---

92 F.W. Smith (1876), 94.   **93** Ibid.   **94** 'Address delivered at the opening of the eighth session of the society, by Jonathan Pim, esquire, one of the vice-presidents', *Journal of the Dublin Statistical Society* 1, Pt1, (1855), 23.   **95** *Linen Trade Circular*, 19 January 1857.   **96** F.W. Smith (1876), 97. **97** *Linen Trade Circular*, 19 January 1857.   **98** Ibid.

sider reducing relatively high labour costs through mechanization. But unstable market conditions discouraged the levels of capital investment that mechanization required, and even after the spurt of powerloom production in 1856, new problems delayed their further adoption. The end of the Crimean War, which some observers believed would herald prosperity, was followed by a commercial panic in the United States in October 1857. The resulting deep downturn in America reduced demand for Irish linen goods. The number of packages of linen imported into the key entrepôt of New York stood at 13,238 during the first nine months of 1857, in contrast to 22,564 in the corresponding period one year earlier.[99]

2.3 Linen exports from the United Kingdom, quantity and value, 1840–70

Year	Quantity Exported (yards)	Value Exported (£)	Year	Quantity Exported (yards)	Value Exported (£)
1840	88,741,000	3,306,088	1856	143,709,586	4,887,780
1841	↑	3,347,555	1857	131,654,381	4,516,880
1842		2,346,749	1858	119,613,996	4,124,356
1843	Average of 84,682,490	2,803,223	1859	135,482,564	4,604,587
			1860	139,216,826	4,804,803
1844		3,024,800	1861	116,322,469	3,852,341
1845	↓	3,036,370			
1846	84,610,898	2,830,808	1862	156,894,813	5,133,936
1847	89,108,057	2,958,851	1863	181,637,300	6,508,973
1848	88,901,519	2,802,789	1864	210,675,054	8,172,813
1849	110,343,274	3,493,829	1865	247,186,459	9,156,990
1850	120,140,713	3,947,682	1866	255,632,385	9,576,245
1851	127,345,027	4,107,396	1867	211,363,068	7,438,382
1852	131,052,649	4,231,786	1868	210,114,382	7,113,873
1853	131,653,601	4,758,432	1869	214,792,554	6,800,141
1854	109,560,031	4,108,457	1870	226,470,696	7,248,345
1855	115,707,436	4,118,013			

Source: *Flax Supply Association annual report 1895* (1896), 33.

---

99 Ibid., 23 November 1857.

2.4 Declared value of linen exports from the United Kingdom
to the United States of America, 1856–61

Year	Value of exports
1856	£2,154,490
1857	£1,425,156
1858	£1,344,634
1859	£1,989,823
1860	£1,893,427
1861	£642,696

The above figures are for cloths of all kinds
and cambrics.
Source: *Linen Trade Circular*, 28 February
1859, 20 February 1860, 24 February 1862.

In the month of November alone, the comparison was even starker: a little
more than one-eighth of the volume of trade in linen fabrics was transacted in
1857, compared with the previous year. The *Linen Trade Circular* lamented that
these events had dimmed bright prospects for the steam-loom.[1] Indeed, in 1858,
it was reported by Messrs D. Dewar and Co. that the powerloom was making
only halting progress in Ulster, though there were some 3,000 such looms in operation, mostly in the regions of Bessbrook, Co. Armagh, Lurgan and Belfast.[2] The
trade recovered in 1859, but, as figure 2.5 shows, the number of powerlooms[3] in
Ireland stood at only 3,633.[4] That year, the small number of powerloom manufacturers were said to be well-supplied with orders for forward delivery, and the
Linen Trade Circular remained a champion of the new technology, declaring that
the powerloom remained a superior mode of production.[5]

THE PERSISTENCE OF HAND PRODUCTION:
A TECHNICAL PERSPECTIVE

Before the 1850s, the adoption of the powerloom in most Irish linen branches was
impeded by the limits of weaving technology to spin flax, which did not have the
elasticity of cotton. Improvements to powerlooms, and better dressing of linen
warps to increase their elasticity, resulted in the extension of the powerloom to a

---

1 Ibid., 4 January 1858.   **2** A. Ure (1861), 584.   **3** This is the total number 'employed and unemployed'.   **4** F.W. Smith (1876), 99.   **5** *Linen Trade Circular*, 2 January 1860.

2.5 Linen powerlooms in Ireland, at various years, 1850–1904

Year	Total	Year	Total
1850	88	1881	21,779
1856	1,871	1882	22,279
1859	3,633	1883	23,677
1861	4,933	1885	24,300
1864	8,187	1889	26,360
1866	10,804	1890	26,592
1868	12,969	1892	28,233
1871	14,834	1894	28,764
1872	18,169	1897	31,484
1873	19,155	1899	32,245
1874	19,331	1900	32,245
1875	20,152	1902	30,927
1877	20,958	1903	31,114
1879	21,153	1904	31,174

Source: *Flax Supply Association annual report 1904* (1905), 17.

wider range of yarns in the 1850s.[6] In some British centres of linen textile production, the powerloom was used to weave canvasses, bagging and drills at the beginning of the decade.[7] In Ireland, where finer goods were generally produced, both this specialization and the abundant supply of cheap labour discouraged powerlooms, even as British firms began to adopt them. One Castlewellan manufacturer, for instance, who employed 700 handloom weavers, reported to the assistant handloom commissioners in the 1830s that he had set up powerlooms for coarse sets and unions, but he had abandoned them when he mechanized the spinning end of his business, judging that 'powerlooms would never be able so to compete with handloom labour as to drive it out of the market'.[8]

Powerloom production was first directed to coarser cloth, and in some branches it came into direct competition with hand producers as it was adopted.[9] By the

---

6 Sir R.L. Patterson, 'The British flax and linen industry' (1903), 141.   **7** A. Ure, *Dictionary of arts* (1875), vol. 3, J–Z, 122.   **8** *Royal commission on handloom weavers*, Report of C.G. Otway, 635. **9** In A. Ure (1861), 590.

late 1850s, the earnings of handloom weavers working on such webs fell, as figure 2.6 shows. By 1875, for instance, a factory operative working ten hours a day
was said to earn more than handloom weavers who had once worked fourteen-
hour days on comparable coarse cloth.[10]

2.6 Average daily wages of linen hand- and steam-loom weavers:
Belfast and neighbourhood, 1855, 1856, 1857, 1860

Weavers	*Cloth*	*1855*	*1856*	*1857*	*1860*
Linen, by hand	Coarse	9*d*. to 1*s*.	9*d*. to 1*s*.	6*d*. to 9*d*.	6*d*. to 9*d*.
	Medium	1*s*. to 1*s*. 6*d*.	9*d*. to 1*s*. 2*d*.	9*d*. to 1*s*. 2*d*.	10*d*. to 1*s*. 4*d*.
	Fine[1]	1*s*. 6*d*. to 2*s*. 6*d*.	1*s*. 3*d*. to 2*s*.	1*s*. 3*d*. to 2*s*.	1*s*. 6*d*. to 2*s*.
Linen damask,	Coarse	1*s*. 8*d*.	1*s*. 8*d*.	1*s*. 8*d*.	1*s*. 8*d*.
by hand	Medium	3*s*. 4*d*.	3*s*. 4*d*.	3*s*. 4*d*.	3*s*. 4*d*.
	Fine	5*s*.	5*s*.	5*s*.	5*s*.
Linen,	Coarse	1*s*. to 1*s*. 2*d*.	1*s*. to 1*s*. 1*d*.	1*s*. to 1*s*. 2*d*.	10*d*. to 2*s*.
by power	Medium	—	—	—	—
	Fine/	—	—	—	—
	Superfine				

¹ 'Fine and superfine' are the descriptors in 1855 and 1857.
Source: *Return of wages published between 1830 and 1886 (Industrial Workers in the United Kingdom)* [C.5172], HC 1887, vol. lxxxix.

The machinery involved in making powerlooms was similar to that used in
cotton. Consequently, British engineering firms were able to build linen looms
with some ease.[11] Powerloom suppliers to the linen trade were mainly based in
northern Britain, and although some innovations in damask-loom production
were made by firms in Ulster, local businesses were not generally involved in the
large-scale production of steam-looms or in the diffusion of new technology in
the weaving end of the trade. The cost of erecting looms was estimated in 1862
to be around £14 each, which amounted, when calculated alongside the costs of
motive power and related factory infrastructure, to £42 per loom.[12] These were
fixed costs, whether or not the looms were engaged in production, and such high
levels of investment required a promise of stable demand and profitable returns.
By contrast, the cost of a handloom at the same time amounted to around 30*s*.,
with an equal amount for heddles and reed.[13] This cost was often borne by the

10 A. Ure (1875), 122. 11 W.E. Coe (1969), 69. W.A. McCutcheon (1984) names in particular the
English firms of Aherton, Hall and Northrup (307–9). C. Gill (1925) also refers to a machine-maker
from Leeds establishing a branch in Belfast in 1852 (328). 12 W. Charley (1862), 92. 13 Ibid., 96.

weaver, who also paid for materials and, if required, additional labour to prepare and attend the loom.

The reluctance of manufacturers to adopt the powerloom, despite the encouragement of the *Linen Trade Circular*, partially centred on these high costs of mechanization, especially at a time when returns were unpredictable and handloom labour remained available. Another critical disincentive to mechanization in this period related to the technical limits of weaving technology itself. They limited powerlooms to low sets of cloth through the 1850s and 1860s, and provided many exclusive preserves for hand production.[14] Writing in 1862, William Charley endorsed the view of the *Linen Trade Circular* that supplies of handloom cloth were diminishing 'and there are many circumstances which would seem to indicate, that while the days of progress in powerlooms have unquestionably set in, those of decadence in handloom weaving give warning of approach'. Still, Charley noted that the powerloom was suitable only for coarse and medium-quality sets, with finer cloths from 18°° to 26°° remaining preserves of the handloom.[15] This range narrowed as the province of powerlooms expanded: they could by 1875, for instance, weave cloth up to a count of 16°°. Indeed, in one factory, an 18°° set had been made up by power, but not profitably. The varying suitability of linen's many branches to powerloom manufacture was a critical factor promoting coextensive hand- and powerloom production in the second half of the nineteenth century, when the forward march of mechanization was not as unyielding as many had expected. Handlooms, instead of being an organizational mode which was 'backward and transaction-cost heavy',[16] remained the only viable mode of production for many webs.[17] In many branches the threat of mechanical displacement was not acute, since the powerloom was not in direct competition with the handloom, and the status and earnings of handloom weavers remained high. Indeed, even when the sector experienced unparalleled prosperity in the 1860s, and powerlooms were widely adopted, many branches of handloom manufacture were resilient and remained so for half a century.

CIVIL WAR, PROSPERITY AND MECHANIZATION

From the late 1840s to 1853, Irish linen exports grew in quantity and value, but the downturns of 1854–5 and 1857–8 militated against capital investment in

---

14 In A. Ure (1861), 590. **15** W. Charley (1862), 89. **16** A. Raaschou-Nielsen (1993). For a more dated argument, see P.J. Coleman (1964), 68; he identifies a lack of entrepreneurial 'nerve' as a cause of retarded mechanization. **17** There were also cases of labour resistance to mechanization, although they were limited to branches in which the threat of displacement seemed acute. In Lurgan in 1857, the manufacturer James Malcolm introduced powerloom production to the town, and faced a large assemblage of weavers who gathered to protest mechanization. Many details of events in this period remain obscure. There is a report from the *Irish Textile Journal*, 15 October 1907, which provides some details.

powerlooms at a time when weaving technology was developing.[18] It took a much greater increase in demand in foreign markets to provide the impetus to adopt powerlooms. These conditions arrived with the outbreak of hostilities in America. The Civil War spurred mechanization in weaving, although its initial impact on the linen industry in Ireland was severe and negative. The United States supplied the large majority of raw material to the British cotton industry, but in 1861 the blockade of southern ports by the Union navy had a devastating impact on the supply of raw cotton to Britain, and affected linen exports from the UK too.[19] The Flax Supply Association reported in 1861 that shipments to America had declined from 41% to 18% of U.K. linen exports. Ballymena linens had fallen 25%, with Lurgan damasks falling even further.[20] The resulting distress among Ulster's weavers was acute: the *Ballymena Observer* noted on 20 December 1862 that a weaver 'toiling to midnight, was unable to earn more than 4*s*. a week, and in many cases not more than 3*s*. 6*d*.'[21] But the newspaper suggested optimistically that good weavers were earning closer to 5*s*. 6*d*. As the year ended, conditions improved.

Indeed, by the turn of 1862, the Irish linen trade became the beneficiary of a cotton famine precipitated by the American Civil War. There are few extant records from manufacturers, but two weavers' books show wages paid during the 1850s and 1860s for various sets of hand-woven linen cloth — and illustrate the impact of the outbreak of the American conflict. The putting-out books of Edward Gribbon (who was active in north Antrim and north Londonderry) and John Keightley, a merchant in the Magherafelt and Ballyronan districts, list handloom goods produced between 1855 and 1862. Gribbon's weavers' book lists work that ranged from very low sets of cloth to webs as high as 22°°. In 1859, one of his weavers, Daniel McNaul, was paid advances and wages of 11*s*. for a thirty-inch-wide web of a set of 17°°, the length being a standard 52 yards: for higher sets or 21°° and 22°°, £1 and £1 2*s*. 6*d*. was paid, respectively.[22] In 1860 these rates remained stable, but they declined by 1861, with the 21°° cloth realizing earnings of 17*s*. Although earnings varied according to each weaver's skill, a decline in prices, especially in higher classes of cloth, from 1855 to 1862, was a feature common to most classes of goods.[23]

---

18 E.J. Boyle (1977) argues in Appendix 7 that the comparative cost advantage of powerloom labour over handloom labour was very modest — less than one penny per bundle of yarn (295–6).   **19** E.J. Boyle (1977), 80–1.   **20** F.W. Smith (1876), 103.   **21** It continued: 'We understand that, at present, a good weaver may ear. ʔbout 5*s*. 6*d*. per week; but, when, out of that pittance, he pays the absolutely necessary expenses oɪ house rent, candles, and fuel, what remains for the provision of his own food, and the maintenance of a helpless family?—Ed.'   **22** Putting-Out Book of Edward Gribbon, PRONI, Belfast, D/1191/29; see pages 46, 283, 379.   **23** Earnings declined further to 16*s*. 6*d*. in 1862.

2.7 Prices of 'light' linen sets, 1860–4

Set	1860	1862	1864
10°°	8*d.*	9*d.*	10*d.*
15°°	11*d.*	12*d.*	13*d.*
20°°	19*d.*	19*d.*	18*d.*
25°°	31*d.*	22*d.*	29*d.*

Source: McCall, *Ireland and her staple manufactures,*
(1870), 310.
The cloth description appears as given by McCall.

After two years of a deep downturn associated with the disruptions of war, the linen industry rebounded, as the severe disruption of cotton markets provided a lucrative entrée for linen manufactures. Demand for linen grew rapidly in the United States, where it was used for military uniforms and other purposes.[24] Markets in continental Europe also opened after the completion of a supplemental treaty between Great Britain and France in 1860, reducing tariffs on Irish yarns and linens.[25] With surging demand, prices rose. Exports to the United States reached new heights in 1862,[26] reversing price trends that had generally shown marked diminations since the end of the Napoleonic Wars, as figures 2.7 and 2.8 illustrate.

2.8 Prices of 'heavy' linen sets, 1860–4

Set	1860	1862	1864
10°°	12*d.*	13*d.*	16*d.*
15°°	17*d.*	18*d.*	19*d.*
20°°	24*d.*	24*d.*	27*d.*
24°°	39*d.*	40*d.*	42*d.*

Source: See previous table.

Exports of linen goods rose from 116,322,469 in 1861 to 255,632,385 in 1866. This demand provided a strong incentive for the expansion of spinning capac-

---

24 E.J. Boyle (1977), 85.   **25** *Linen Trade Circular*, 7 January 1861.   **26** Ibid., 12 January 1863.

ity, which saw the number of spindles rise to 894,272 by 1868.[27] Power-spinners saw a great increase in their profit margins, and on their rates of return on fixed and current assets: Emily Boyle has estimated that the rate of return for one company, Richardson Sons and Owden of Bessbrook, grew from 6.4% in 1862 to 27.1% in 1864.[28]

2.9 Linen mills and factories in Ireland in 1850, 1856 and 1862

Year	Spinning mills	Spindles	Weaving factories	Power looms	Spinning & weaving mills
1850	67	396,338	1	58	1
1856	85	567,980	13	1,691	9
1862	60	592,981	15	4,666	19

Source: *Reports of the inspectors of factories ... for the half-year ending 31 October 1862* [3076], HC 1863, vol. xviii, Report of Robert Baker, 110.

During this boom, the traditionally conservative banking sector in Ireland readily supplied credit for industrial expansion — often with disastrous results when conditions changed in the 1870s.[29] As construction of new facilities continued, demand for factory and mill labour grew and wages rose: mill-spinners' wages increased from 4s. and 4s. 6d. per week in 1850 and 1851 to 8s. and 9s. per week by the mid-1860s.[30] The infusion of capital in the weaving end of the trade was remarkable, with the number of powerlooms rising to over 10,000 by 1866.[31] Powerloom manufacturers were said to be supplied with ample forward orders, buoyed by incentives to expand capacity. Weaving factories opened new commercial warehouses and stores in Belfast.[32] Political instability in America impacted on the commercial foundations of the trade, shifting it to highly-capitalized, large firms as credit terms became more restrictive. The small number of agents acting on behalf of Ulster concerns increased, as the system of settlement by notes at six and eight months was replaced by cash payments in ten days, with a 6% trade discount, or in one month with a 5% discount.[33]

At this point, hesitant experimentations with the powerloom gave way to widespread investment in the technology, at least where it could be effectively applied, especially in coarser branches of manufacture. Yet the Irish linen sector and its

27 R.L. Patterson (1903), 130.   **28** E.J. Boyle (1977), 90.   **29** Ibid., 185; P. Ollerenshaw (1987), 105–14.   **30** *Reports of the inspectors of factories to the secretary of state for the Home Department for the half-year ending 31 October 1865* [3622], HC 1866, vol. xxiv, Report of Robert Baker, 73. **31** *Annual report of the Flax Supply Association for 1905* (1906), 17.   **32** *Linen Trade Circular*, 11 January 1864.   **33** *Irish Textile Journal*, 15 May 1887.

workforces encountered this new climate in a variety of ways. The fortunes of the coarser end of the trade were especially buoyed in the first years of the war, spurred by demand for military clothes and canvasses used for military purposes in the American market.[34] This demand boosted the trade in Dundee (which specialized in such coarse sets) as well as similar branches in the Irish industry. By contrast, the fine trade, in which handloom weavers increasingly specialized, was relatively less buoyant. This was an important feature of the trade, since it interacted with technological developments that supported mechanization in coarser branches. Technical advancements made the production of coarse cloth by powerloom even more feasible in the early 1860s, which winnowed handloom preserves. Indeed, by 1865 the *Linen Trade Circular* reported that powerlooms were producing heavy sheetings and 'all descriptions of serviceable Linens in general use'. They had also been used to weave coarse damasks and cambrics, and it reported that 'Already the handloom is being rapidly superseded, save in the production of very fine fabrics.'[35] As the steam-loom factory workforce developed, females became pre-eminently associated with the operation of the new weaving technology: many contemporaries emphasized the extent to which the physical exertions associated with handloom work, especially in coarse ranges, were now lessened by the powerloom.[36] While it could relieve the physical demands of weaving, many handloom weavers insisted that the powerloom could not displace skills of dexterity and intellect demanded in their work. The adoption of powerloom-weaving technology created a context for the reconstruction, and regendering, of weaving skill. As a factory weaving workforce developed, the sexual segregation of women and men by sets of cloth and branches of manufacture characteristic of the handloom trade dissolved into more conventional forms of occupational segregation associated with mass industry. Women attended the looms, retaining some elements of craft status through the adoption of a piece rate structure of remuneration. Yet in contrast with the intricate stratification of handloom piece earnings by make and 'count' of cloth, differentials in earnings collapsed throughout branches of powerloom production. While formal systems of factory authority can obscure the rich and complex hierarchies that emerged within occupational categories,[37] male skill and authority was affirmed by their domination of supervisory and machinery-minding tasks.[38] Proprietorship of technical expertise and 'command of the machine' became the paramount features of masculine claims to authority in the powerloom factory.[39] Weaving technology, therefore, involved a major regendering of work,

---

34 O. Greeves (1969), 95–100. **35** *Linen Trade Circular*, 9 January 1865. **36** H. McCall (1870), 296–7. **37** See M. Cohen (1997) for a detailed account of female factory labour in the weaving industry. **38** The payment system in mechanized weaving, which was based on piece-work, preserved elements of the 'craft' tradition in the factory milieu. For women's participation in mechanized weaving, see C. Gill (1925), 333 and M. Cohen (1997a), 182–4. **39** For a discussion of similar processes in the English hosiery trade, see H. Bradley (1995).

but less a radical reorganization of status distinctions as male workers assumed authority over both technology and workforces. The adoption of powerloom technology also impacted on gender relations within the handloom trade, supporting masculine claims of craft control in remaining, highly-remunerative handloom preserves which were more immune from mechanization.

Clearly, the factory labour force created by high levels of capital investment in powerlooms was encouraged by the favourable climate of the early-to-mid-1860s, in which demand and prices for coarse goods were high. These branches were also especially amenable to mechanization, but others were not. Handloom wages in 1862 stood at between 15*s*. to 20*s*. weekly for first-class handloom weavers, while second-rate weavers earned half as much and apprentices 4*s*. or 5*s*.[40] There was generally a correspondence between these rates of pay and the gendered divisions of handloom work that assigned females to lower sets of goods. 'Female branches' faced especially acute threats of mechanical displacement, but anxiety over this possibility was more widespread. Indeed, the threat of the steam-loom led the famous autodidact of mid-Antrim, David Herbison, the 'Bard of Dunclug', whose work was widely published in the local press, to lament the diminished autonomy of some weavers. Indeed, Herbison portrayed mechanization as a final blow to independence, following the decisive subordination of small hand-producers to the commercial dictates of manufacturers.

> We then had nae drapers the poor to oppress;
> We wove our ain wab and we drank our ain glass,
> And aye had a shilling to spend or to spare,
> The heart to mak' glad that seemed weary wi' care;
> Contented we were when we had in our bag
> A very fine score, or a six hundred rag;
> Our sweethearts aye met us wi' joy in their face,
> Mirth reigned in their pride, and made happy ilk place;
> Our coats were hame spun, and our sarks were the same,
> And warmly we welcomed a frien' whan he came;
> Our rent was aye paid whan the rent day came roun'
> When I was a boy in my ain native toun.
> [...]
> Oh had I the power the past to restore,
> The reel wad still crack, and the spinning-wheel snore,
> Mill-yarn wad sink doun as it never had been,
> Trade flourish as fair as it ever was seen;
> Distress and oppression flee far frae our view,

---

40 W. Charley (1862), 96.

> Our hamlets rejoice and their beauties renew;
> The profligate band that brought want to our door
> Should labour or starve on a far foreign shore;
> A wab in a steamloom should never appear,
> Our country to steep in affliction and fear;
> Peace, pleasure and plenty, and happy hearts roun',
> And times wad revive in my ain native toun.[41]

This poetry expressed anxiety over the diminished status of the handloom craft as an outgrowth of commercial reorganization, rather than technological encroachment or the sexual reassignment of weaving work. It reflected nostalgia for a skill status which had been partially eclipsed by power, and for an independent market status which had been in decline since the rise of manufacturers. It also expressed a desire for a restoration of social relations of production in which women's work was confined to spinning. Herbison's 'The Auld Wife's Lament' echoed these sentiments:

> For, ah! I'm sure I'll never see
> Such joys as charm'd my youthfu' e'e –
> The days are past when folk like me
>   Could earn their bread,
> My auld wheel now sits silently
>   Aboon the bed.
>
> And well may Erin weep and wail
> The day the wheels began to fail,
> Our tradesmen now can scarce get kail
>   Betimes to eat,
> In shipfuls they are doomed to sail
>   In quest of meat.
>
> For that machine that spins the yarn
> Left us unfit our bread to earn.
> O Erin! will you ne'er turn stern
>   Against your foe,
> When every auld wife can discern
>   Your overthrow![42]

Here the threat of mechanical deskilling was portrayed as a disruption to gender relations and as an agent of status diminution. But weavers devised strategies

---

41 D. Herbison in J. Hewitt (1974), 122–4.   **42** In J. Hewitt (1974), 120–2.

through which they resisted threats to the stability of their craft. The first set of responses have been detailed already — the evolution of a sexual segregation of handloom work, sustained by gender ideologies of labour value, which upheld male authority, valorized the primacy of masculine weaving and maintained the stability of male dominance in 'craft' ends of the trade. In many branches that were largely ill-suited to powerlooms, even as technology improved through the 1860s and 1870s, handloom weaving remained the dominant form of production — and the sexual segregation and stratification of weaving work prevailed. Damasks, diaper and cambric handkerchiefs, and finer shirtings remained specialist provinces of the handloom. Districts such as Lurgan and Portadown in Co. Armagh, where these industries were historically centred, were capitals of Ulster's handloom trade in the second half of the century — and arenas in which relations between sex and skill were reconstructed.

LOCAL PERSPECTIVES: REGIONAL HANDLOOM LABOUR FORCES

The Lurgan district was an area in which specialist cambric handloom manufacture was based through the 1860s and beyond.[43] Here, handlooms were much more prevalent than powerlooms in the mid-1860s: indeed, a correspondent to the Children's Employment Commission estimated that they outnumbered powerlooms by fifty-to-one, with only 450 hands employed in powerloom manufacture.[44] Weaving-shops had proven unsuccessful, owing to 'the trouble of inspection', and so had been largely abandoned.[45] During the Civil War boom, weavers could earn from 5s. to 12s. weekly — but as low as 3s. in 'down times'. In such depressed conditions, workers were compelled to weave twenty-four hours a day, through 'relays' of household members.[46] Long after the 1860s, the handloom was the mainstay of the district's cambric trade and as late as 1888 the number of handloom weavers 'directed by' manufacturers and merchants in the Lurgan district was said to as high as 18,000.[47]

Portadown, specializing in fine classes of goods as the seat of damask cloth production, was another centre of hand production during linen weaving's 'Factory Age'. There were three steam-powered weaving factories in the town by 1864, but handloom weaving of fine webs, especially damask cloth, retained its

43 McCall (1870), 255. *Royal commission on the employment of children in trades and manufactories not regulated by law,* Second Report, with minutes of evidence (3414), HC 1864 vol. xxiv, Evidence upon the handloom weaving and hosiery manufactures in Ireland and Scotland, collected by Mr. J.E. White, statement by manufacturers of Lurgan, q. 13.   **44** Evidence upon the handloom weaving and hosiery manufactures, extract from a letter from J. Henning relating to the preceding statement, q. 14.   **45** Evidence upon the handloom weaving and hosiery manufactures, statement by manufacturers of Lurgan, q. 13.   **46** Ibid., q. 13.   **47** G.H. Bassett, *Book of County Armagh* (1888b), 359.

primacy in the local textile economy.[48] Henry Cinnamon, a Portadown linen manufacturer, claimed that the handloom produced a finer finish on webs, and that on fine work, stoppages of powerlooms due to thread breakage obviated their utility. Overall, he reckoned that in the production of fine goods 'there is not much difference in the profit in the two ways, except that as a powerloom will do two webs where a handloom can do one, money is turned twice instead of only once in the same time'.[49] While Cinnamon and others still largely relied on handlooms, weavers were ambivalent about their prospects in their trade. The Portadown weaver Thomas Foy testified in 1864 that his entire family worked on the four looms in his house. His daughters, aged 9, 8 and 7, wound yarn, as his children did not begin weaving until the age of 12 or 13, with girls beginning weaving at an earlier age. Foy enjoyed paramount social authority as the organizer of production and the proprietor of looms. His house and loom-shop cost 14*d*. weekly, and he had paid £3 for each loom (instead of renting them for 2*d*. a week or 8*s*. annually), but he was required to pay for shuttles and gear to equip the looms, and his income could be lower after deductions for the late return of webs. In comparing his position with that of factory weavers, Foy declared:

> I believe that we should do much better in factories, and wish that I had gone and got my family in. It would have been worth £200 to us by now, my brother says. There is no loss of time there such as we have. There is a day lost in going to get the stuff out from the manufacturer and nearly another in putting it into the loom and starting.[50]

In Portadown, there were likely other weavers such as Foy who regretted remaining at the handloom. There were probably many households that had members engaged in both handloom and factory work, and others who had calculated that fine domestic weaving could be remunerative. Yet the handloom remained the primary instrument of fine damask production into the twentieth century, with Portadown as the seat of the trade.

While handloom workshops were expanding, especially in the damask trade, a good deal of weaving in the 1860s was still based in domestic settings and organized using family and household labour. In Lurgan, Portadown and other regions, the Children's Employment Commission heard of weavers' dependence on children — first as young winders and then, as they progressed through informal household apprenticeships, as weavers. This was also the case in the handkerchief district around Portadown and in the Loughgall district of Co. Armagh, where

---

48 Evidence upon the handloom weaving and hosiery manufactures, evidence of Alexander Brandon, M.D., q. 5. **49** Ibid., evidence of Henry Cinnamon, q. 3. When they graduated to weaving, children earned 2*s*. 6*d*. to 3*s*. weekly, with adults earning 6*s*. to 7*s*. a week — and 10*s*. for the finest class of work. **50** Ibid., evidence of Thomas Foy, q. 2.

coarse linen was produced in farms and cottages. There, W. Hallagan, the bailiff of a large estate, testified that one manufacturer in the district employed 300 looms in a relatively low-paid branch, and that girls were employed at weaving 'because boys are of more use out of doors', where the value of their labour was greater.[51] The young, the elderly and the infirm engaged in winding, and households without labour to undertake this task turned to the workhouse to supply children to undertake paid work. Winders brought in from the workhouse (who were generally older than household winders) were housed and boarded in weavers' homes, and earned 8s. to 10s. per quarter, reducing the *net* income of weaving households.[52] Still, even with these additional expenses, during the linen boom weavers' earnings were high, leading Hallagan to declare that:

> All the linen weaving districts are very prosperous now, and people can live much more comfortably by weaving than by small farming. It was usual for weavers to go out to work in summer, but now even those who formerly were begging for labour cannot be flattered out…A good weaver can make 1s. 6d. a day and a woman or girl as much as a man. Three or four years ago, not more than half that amount could be earned. I know of no distress; people are not leaving, and he must be a very lazy person who is in want.[53]

This portrait of linen manufacture in two districts of Co. Armagh suggests that the handloom was especially resilient in several branches in the 1860s. Indeed, as late as 1903 it was noted that a small Irish handloom weaving labour force continued to specialize in a narrowing range of fine webs — mainly in these two districts of Ulster.[54] Handloom production remained resilient, profitable to manufacturers and remunerative to weavers who remained in the trade at the turn of the twentieth century; it also remained organized around poles of sex and age.

THE HANDLOOM AT WAR'S END

If the outbreak of the American Civil War heralded distress and then general prosperity in the Irish linen trade, its resolution was bracing for an industry that had so rapidly and extensively expanded its capacity. Improved conditions in the fine end — which prospered, but did not experience the dramatic price and demand increases of the coarser trade — actually sustained remunerative production for a longer

---

51 Ibid., evidence of W. Hallagan, q. 11.   52 Ibid., evidence of William Graham, q. 10.   53 Ibid., evidence of W. Hallagan, q. 11.   54 R.L. Patterson (1903), 142.

period, as a continuing substitution effect privileged linen for shirtings and other purposes even as cotton prices fell. By 1867, powerloom goods and coarser descriptions of handloom cloth declined in value. By contrast, finer sets had seen relatively less falling off, 'as the production of these had not been stimulated to any degree corresponding with medium and coarse fabrics'.[55] The *Linen Trade Circular* warned that falling cotton prices would induce manufacturers to diminish mill and factory production, and in 1867 over-capacity resulted in serious problems for the industry, to which manufacturers responded by reducing their output.[56] These new problems associated with mechanization drew the attention of the Flax Supply Association:

> Owing to the immense expansion which the export trade with America received during the war, the productive power which was developed at that period, it was found impossible to contract in the same ratio, now that a reaction in the demand for that market had set in. In times gone by, when such a state of things arose, although it would have doubtless pressed hard upon the weavers thruoghout the country, the curtailment of production would have been much more rapidly effected than its expansion, and whilst the loss would have been shared more equally by all, trade would have recovered its lost ground much sooner; but the unyielding nature of the factory system, thus put to its first practical test, soon became apparent; and the centralised power was slow to accommodate itself to the altered circumstances of the times. Whatever advantages powerloom weaving had in comparison with the more ancient one of hand-labour — and those advantages are admittedly great — its concentrated powers were evidently unfavourable to capitalists, when brought face to face with suddenly reduced demand.[57]

While the number of powerlooms continued to grow, now much more slowly than before, the greatest period of prosperity in the Ulster linen trade had drawn to a close with an incomplete displacement of hand power. Alexander Knox, medical poor law inspector, noted in 1870 that post-Civil War conditions had depressed manufacturing in parts of Ulster, but still remarked that handloom weaving was 'pretty general, in different parts, but especially in the districts adjoining Belfast, Newtownards, Lisburn, Banbridge and Ballymena'.[58]

---

55 F.W. Smith (1876), 128.   **56** *Linen Trade Circular*, 3 February 1868. The quantification of handloom cloth's overall contribution to Irish cloth output is impeded by imprecise employment numbers in the handloom trade and by the frequent adoption of short-time and idle looms throughout the trade in much of the 1870, 80s and 90s.   **57** F.W. Smith (1876), 132.   **58** *Reports from poor law inspectors on wages of agricultural labour in Ireland* [C.35] HC 1870, vol. xiv, Dr Knox's Report, 144.

The post-Civil War era witnessed worsening conditions and capped a decade of significant reorganization within the linen trade, during which the triumph of the steam-loom was remarkably incomplete. Varied levels of agrarian change and industrial reorganization characterized districts in which the trade was carried on. After the 1830s and 1840s, the main influences in the resilience of the handloom were technological impediments and restricted capital investment in expensive machinery while the sector's fortunes remained unstable. This provided employment for a weaving workforce in the linen handloom trade for many decades — with some workers competing directly with machines (and often succumbing after a brief period of co-existence) and others remaining relatively immune to displacement. Men predominated in these latter branches, especially in damask, as skills access remained restricted and male weavers fashioned a robust defence of their trade premised on the family wage and on a gendered craft identity. In marked contrast to it, most branches of handloom weaving survived precariously, and as they faced mechanical encroachment and their status and earnings diminished, the profile of handloom labour changed.

3

The textile workforce in mid-Antrim, 1851–1901

Sexual divisions in the linen handloom workforce require analysis alongside agrarian, social and economic structures in charting and explaining rural industry's resilience in late-nineteenth-century Ireland. Research into diverse systems of European textile production in this and earlier periods has explored the influence of economic and social structures in promoting parallel hand and mechanized manufacture.[1] The organization of industrial labour around overlapping poles of sex and skill also shaped diverse work experiences. This chapter focuses on the profile of handloom labour in Ulster, and outlines how features of the workforce, especially its sexual profile, changed. A case study of mid-Antrim's shirting weavers in the last half of the nineteenth century provides a prism for examining relationships between gender, work and the demarcation of skilled labour in the contracting handloom trade.

While historians of factory production have examined sexual divisions of labour and contests over the social construction of skill in mills and factories, these themes have received less attention in rural industry. In Ireland, rural industrial workers have been over-shadowed by a focus on other segments of agrarian society.[2] Although Ulster's shipyards and linen factories were among the largest in the world, rural districts were also important sites of industrial production — especially in textile and garment manufacture. Alongside these industries, smaller-scale 'home industries' such as tweed weaving operated in the countryside, some as adjuncts to mass manufacture and others as craft trades. In the early-twentieth century there was a widespread belief that some branches of handloom production were exemplars of indigenous peasant craft skill and part of an Irish handicraft tradition. In explaining why handloom weaving remained more resilient in mid-Antrim than in other districts, the industry's pioneering historian, Conrad Gill, claimed that peculiarities of geography enabled mid-Antrim to 'survive' as an oasis of putting-out and hand production into the factory age.[3] D.A. Farnie later asserted that handloom weaving after 1900 'survived only as a curiosity in districts isolated by mountain, forest, or sea (as in the remote "Celtic fringe" of the United Kingdom)'.[4] But in the last half of the nineteenth century the handloom was more

---

1 Many of the key works are cited in Chapter 2, n. 1. **2** By contrast, in British historiography, urban industrial hand production has received greater attention. See D. Bythell (1978); J.A. Schmiechen (1984); J. Lown (1990); J. Rendall (1990); J. Morris (1986); and N. Osterud (1986). The Leeds garment industry, which was structured though urban sub-contractors, is documented in K. Honeyman (2000a). See also D. Bythell (1993). For Glasgow, see A.J. Albert (1990). **3** C. Gill (1925). **4** D.A. Farnie (1958), 580. See also J.H. Clapham (1963) in which he identifies Wales, the Highlands

than a curious instrument of small-scale craft production. Mid-Antrim's weavers were integrated within an extensive regional commercial network, signaled by steam trains which moved yarn, webs and commercial agents between Ballymena and other urban centres — and then onward to domestic and foreign markets. Large spinning concerns such as Belfast's York Street Spinning Co. gave out work directly through agents in the town's Linen Hall.[5] And linen handloom weaving generally was centred on districts that could hardly be regarded as remote — Lurgan, Portadown, and Lisburn. Like these other centres, however, Ballymena's trade was highly-specialized. Fine shirting linens dominated its market, and several broad trends were evident in the local workforce from the 1850s. One was *social differentiation*, as the population from which weavers were recruited changed. This change was accompanied by the marked *casualization* of handloom labour and the *feminization* of the workforce. Relationships between these three processes, which developed as the principal article of local manufacture changed, require close attention.

SPECIALIZATION

This study has emphasized the regionalized geography of linen production in Ireland. It remained pronounced as the sector industrialized and the scale of the handloom weaving trade contracted after the 1860s. In spite of the encroachment of the powerloom into some preserves of handloom manufacture, contemporary observers predicted that it would survive for years in regions where weavers produced cloth to which steam technology had not been applied.[6] Handloom weavers specialized in branches for which such technology was ill-suited throughout the UK's textile trades.[7] Weavers found lucrative niches in cotton, silk and linen production, even as mechanization brought the majority of manufacture into the factory. This strategy was pursued by weavers in mid-Antrim, too. Their later-nine-

and the Hebrides as vestigial areas of handloom production in his discussion of the woollen sector (83).   **5** Varieties of yarn from which light ordinary Ballymenas were produced — described repeatedly in the late 1880s and 1890s by the *Linen Market* as ranging from 30 to 120 leas — were spun at the Braidwater Mill, which produced line yarns from 10 leas to 150 leas (*Irish Textile Journal*, 15 September 1888, 106). Yarn measurements describe the lightness of the yarn — the number of 300–yard measurements of yarn to the pound.   **6** W. Charley, *Flax and its products in Ireland* (1862), 97.   **7** Specialization was an important strategy for handloom weavers in many regions of Britain and Ireland. Of the several handloom weaving populations which have been studied during the era of mechanization, the cotton weavers of Lancashire and Paisley, and the silk weavers of Coventry feature most prominently. Coventry's ribbon trade focused on the fancier end of production, in contrast to neighbouring centres. Some historians have argued that local strategies of social administration and trade organization — especially poor relief policy and the so-called 'list of prices' which set uniform rates of pay — also played a role in extending hand production. See J. Prest (1960); P. Searby (1977); P. Mathias (2001), 242–3. Paisley's weavers also found a niche in specialized fine shawl production, for which the powerloom could not be adopted. See T.C. Smout (1979); T. Clarke & T. Dickson (1982).

teenth-century specialization in shirting cloth contrasted markedly with the principal manufacture of earlier decades, as they moved from weaving three-quarter-
yard-wide webs to yard-wide cloth. In 1784 John Greer described Ballymena as
'the greatest market for three-quarter wides' in the province. During James Corry's
1816 tour through Ulster, most of the town's trade was in such webs — 50 to 52
yards long and 28 inches broad.[8] But by the 1850s, three-quarter-yard-wide cloth
had been superseded as a staple of the local trade by webs that became so closely
identified with the district that they bore the name of its principal market.[9] 'Ballymenas' were light, yard-wide linens used for shirtings, collars and cuffs. Weavers
shifted to this cloth partly in response to powerloom cotton's competition with, and
displacement of, linen shirtings by the 1830s and 40s.[10] As the substitution of cotton for linen increased, demand for handloom articles produced in the Ballymena
district was restricted to high counts of yard-wide cloth, which was the preferred
measurement in home and export markets. In 1898 Clara Collet, a collaborator
with Charles Booth on *The life and labour of the people of London* and a leading
civil servant, author and social commentator, noted in a report to the Board of Trade
that Ballymena weavers had moved to finer production as powerlooms erected in
the district after 1870 were employed to weave cloth. 'There was no actual displacement of labour,' she wrote, 'but rates of payment for handloom work fell, and,
the weavers had to move up to the finer goods.'[11] Evidence of extensive handloom
manufacture from the accounts of an East Londonderry manufacturer, John Keightley, also suggest that weavers still worked on 'seven-eighths' in that district, but
that they too were focused on high counts for which mechanization was not suitable in the late-1850s and early-1860s (cloth from 18°° to 26°° remained the product of handloom manufacture at this time).[12] Weavers in contiguous mid-Antrim
were producing webs of a wider measurement, but of a similar high count. In the
fine, yard-wide light cloth branch, supplying the high-end shirting trade in home
and export markets, they found a niche that resisted substitution by cotton and, for
several decades, direct competition with powerlooms.[13]

---

8 It was the custom to cut the web in two and sell it in two 25–yard pieces (*Irish Textile Journal*, 15
September 1888). Corry estimated that some 1,200 of these webs were traded during the Saturday
market, averaging £2 per piece. This cloth, which also dominated trade in neighbouring markets, was
principally made up in a brown state, then sent to Dublin or exported to England and America. By
contrast, trade in other goods was relatively small: fewer yard-wide webs (25 yards long and 38 inches broad) were exchanged, at an average value of £2 10s. per piece. See *Minutes of the Trustees of the
Linen and Hempen Manufactures ... 1816* (1817), Appendices, 83   **9** See also *Irish Textile Journal*,
15 September 1888.   **10** See *Report from the select committee on handloom weavers' petitions*, with
minutes of evidence and index (556), HC 1834, vol. x, Minutes of evidence, evidence of Hugh
Mackenzie, q. 1021–23.   **11** *Board of Trade report by Miss Collet on changes in the employment of
women and girls in industrial centres*, Part I, *Flax and Jute Centres* [C.8794], HC 1898, vol. lxxxviii , p. 52. The shift can be detected early in the era of halting mechanization: yard-wides predominated in weekly market reports published in *The Belfast News-Letter* in the 1850s.   **12** See Weaver's
Book of John Keightley, PRONI, Belfast, MIC/26/1, 239). A. Ure, *The philosophy of manufactures*
(1861), 591.   **13** Hugh McCall claimed that £20,000 changed hands annually in the local market

Despite this strategy, shirting weavers faced mounting challenges in the last quarter of the nineteenth century that undermined their branch's immunity to steam and contributed to its decline. Ballymena cloth was used in the American shirt-, collar- and cuff-making trade, centred on Troy, New York. Previously serviced primarily by agents of Ulster concerns,[14] the number of agents involved in the lucrative trade increased during the American Civil War.[15] Ballymena sets from 18°° to 20°° were used by Troy shirt-makers for collars and cuffs, and Ballymena and Co. Down handloom linens were also mainstays of the high end of the shirt trade, the *Irish Textile Journal* reporting on 15 July 1886 that 'Troy does not take kindly to powerlooms in the finer sets'. But in cheaper, ready-to-wear lines, American firms purchased 15°° to 17°° sets, and sometimes web counts as low as 14°°.[16] To meet this demand, Ballymena weavers produced a range of their eponymous cloth — with counts ranging from 14°° to 21°°. The latter, finer article commanded a price of 14s. in 1888;[17] it took sixteen days to weave a web 63 to 64 yards long. This work was meticulous and time-consuming, in contrast with the powerloom's rapid production of cloth of lower counts.[18] Yet unlike looms employed by weavers in other handloom branches, those used for Ballymena shirtings could be adapted to produce different sets of cloth. Indeed, the change in local handloom specialization required few adaptations to handlooms that produced the district's traditional staple.[19] This also enhanced the labour force's flexibility, allowing it to meet the range of demand for shirtings of varying qualities.[20] By contrast, looms used in the Lurgan fine cambric trade could not be so easily adapted to lower sets, precluding weavers from producing other qualities of cloth.[21] Yet, however flexible the response of weavers to changing conditions in the trade, their work attracted lower earnings through most of the last quarter-century. Local households' adaptations to this deteriorating earnings environment were most clearly expressed by transformations in the workforce.

---

during the prosperous 1860s (*Ireland and her staple manufactures*, [1870], 207).   **14** These firms were W. Wetherald and Young (representing Belfast's York Street Spinning Co.), William Redmond (representing James and Robert Young) and George Burgess (representing the Barklies of Larne). **15** *Irish Textile Journal*, 15 July 1886.   **16** Ibid.   **17** It was said to have once claimed a price of 30s. (*Irish Textile Journal*, 15 September 1888).   **18** In 1888, when handloom weavers won the backing of Colonel Edward Saunderson for legislative protection in the trade, one merchant opined that they were attempting to be paid on a weekly basis, as powerloom workers were, but that a 24°° web could not be finished in the same time as a 12°° web (*News-Letter*, 5 May 1888).   **19** *Irish Textile Journal*, 15 September 1888.   **20** *Irish Textile Journal*, 15 February 1887.   **21** In 1886, for instance, when demand for coarser cambric goods was high, many Lurgan handlooms remained idle because 'they do not suit the looms formerly employed at fine sets' (*Irish Textile Journal*, 15 November 1886).

THE WEAVING WORKFORCE IN ULSTER: CONTEXTS OF RESILIENCE
AND DECLINE

By the late-nineteenth century, shirting weaving was relatively unremunerative, as the trade faced protracted problems. Earnings varied within branches of handloom manufacture. Durable sexual divisions of labour upheld the diminishing amount of remunerative work as a masculine preserve. In Lurgan's damask trade, most weavers earned between 6s. and 8s. a week in 1864, but a 'first-class weaver' could earn 15s. to 20s., a 'second-class' weaver half that amount, and apprentices 4s. or 5s; this stratification continued through subsequent decades.[22] Earnings in the handloom handkerchief trade in Cos. Down, Antrim and Armagh, for instance, ranged from 7s. to 9s. per week in 1890, averaging 7s. 8d. for the relatively small number of skilled women in this branch, and 7s. 10d. for the male weavers who dominated the trade.[23] There was a correlation between the stratification of labour by sex and by earnings.[24] Differentiation was even starker *between* handloom branches: in 1897, in mid-Antrim, the earnings of the shirting weavers were estimated to average only 7s. per week — considerably lower than in other branches of handloom manufacture.[25] From these earnings, weavers deducted costs for weft winding, as well as for paste and tallow to finish their yarn. Indeed, one 1888 estimate placed the *net* earnings of mid-Antrim weavers as low as 5s.[26] In the mid-1890s, when a severe downturn in the linen market had an especially negative impact on the local shirting trade, prices and wages tumbled.[27] By then, while fine damask and cambric weaving remained handloom preserves, weaving of many shirting counts had been mechanized and most handloom production was undertaken by female weavers and aged men.

The diminution of the handloom workforce was not confined to the shirting trade. From the early-1870s to the twentieth century, the number of workers in most of the province's handloom branches diminished, though the extent of this

---

22 A. Ure (1861), 597; W. Charley (1862), 96; *Royal commission on the employment of children in trades and manufactories not regulated by law,* Second Report, with minutes of evidence (3414), HC 1864 vol. xxiv, Evidence upon the handloom weaving and hosiery manufactures in Ireland and Scotland, collected by Mr. J.E. White (hereafter 'Evidence upon the handloom weaving and hosiery manufactures in Ireland and Scotland'), statement by manufacturers of Lurgan, q. 13.   23 Return of the rates of wages in the minor textile trades of the United Kingdom with report thereon [C-6161], HC 1890, vol. lxviii, 69. Even this small weaving labour force was stratified between those earning 16s. to 20s. on a 60–66 yard cloth (no extra pay was realized on cloth over 60 yards), or about 5s. to 6s. per week, and those earning as much as £2 6s. for a fine 24⁰⁰ cloth of 60 yards, or above 10s. per week. Report on 'The agricultural labourer. Ireland', Ballymena, *Royal commission on labour*, Third Report (Agricultural Labour) (vol. IV, Ireland, part I), Reports from the assistant agricultural commissioners, HC 1893–94, [C.6894–XVIII], xxxvii, pt1 (hereafter 'R. McCrea report'), 87.   24 A. Ure (1861), 597; W. Charley (1862), 96; Evidence upon the handloom weaving and hosiery manufactures in Ireland and Scotland, statement by manufacturers of Lurgan, q. 13. 25 *Board of Trade report*, 53.   26 G.H. Bassett, *Book of Antrim* (1888a), 281.   27 See *Textile Manufacturer*, 15 February 1895: 'In handloom brown goods Ballymena linens experienced a sharp fall in values' (41).

change is hard to measure. In addition to the continuous revision of the ways in which occupational data was aggregated in the printed census,[28] the seasonal character of weaving often militated against its enumeration.[29] Fluctuating conditions encouraged both male and female weavers to withdraw from textile work periodically. In 1853, for instance, while trading conditions were poor, many male handloom weavers emigrated and joined the army.[30] In 1862 William Charley also noted that weavers enlisted in the militia during dull periods in the trade, and 'consequently, when the reaction comes, they are often in great demand, and obtain higher wages for a time'. He estimated that nearly half of militia recruits in northeast Ireland were drawn from its weaving population, 'many not being able to get regular work owing to the frequent panics in trade during the past three or four years'.[31] For many weavers, seasonal work in weaving and agriculture was more common — and an extension of the historic integration of agricultural and textile work in the region.[32] All of these features of handloom labour cloud estimates of the workforce's size. Some sources estimate that 40,000 weavers were working in Cos. Antrim, Down and Armagh in 1831.[33] Clara Collet wrote that the assistant handloom commissioners identified a Belfast workforce of 700–900 linen handloom weavers and 12,000–15,000 cotton weavers, but she also noted that this number differed from that in the 1841 census a few years later.[34] Because of its failure to comprehensively enumerate weaving work, census occupational data is more useful for identifying the geography of handloom production and the broad contours of growth and contraction in the workforce than for measuring the size of active workforces. For instance, while it indicates relative stability in the size of the handloom workforce between 1841 and 1851, it also suggests a diminution by 1861. Yet the 1861 enumeration occurred before the Civil War-era boom, when

28 In the 1821 and 1831 censuses, the employed population was classified according to criteria that assigned social 'heads' of families under one of a tri-partite designation, none of which was a clear indictor of production status.   **29** P. Solar (1988), 21. Weaving households often turned exclusively to fieldwork at several points in the year — especially in autumn and in spring. This is relevant to this analysis, since the census was taken in late-March in both 1851 and 1901.   **30** *Linen Trade Circular*, 13 January 1855.   **31** W. Charley (1862), 96.   **32** *Select committee of the House of Lords on land law (Ireland)*, First Report (249), HL 1882, vol. xi (hereafter '*Select committee of the House of Lords on land law*'), evidence of John Young, q. 3098, 3100; *Royal commission of inquiry into the working of Landlord and Tenant Act (Ireland), 1870 and the acts amending the same*, Minutes of evidence [C.2779–II], HC 1881, vol. xviii [hereafter '*Working of Landlord and Tenant Act (Ireland)*'], evidence of John Young, q. 5961, 5967, 5971. By some accounts this pattern was less prevalent by 1888 (*Irish Textile Journal*, 15 September 1888).   **33** In B. Collins (1997), 237.   **34** *Board of Trade report*, 49–51. In 1841 and 1851, it may be assumed that those workers enumerated under the occupational categories of 'Weavers of Linen' and 'Weavers (Unspecified)' and of 'Weavers of Damask and Linen' and 'Weavers (Unspecified)' were handloom weavers, but there were additional categories such as 'Manufacturers of Cloth' under which they may also have been placed. By 1861, a new caveat emerges: by then, powerloom weavers were operating in some branches of the trade. The occupational data for Ulster under the category of 'Linen and Damask Weavers' may be expected to encompass the large majority of weavers who still worked at the handloom, especially as the increased number of workers enumerated as 'Factory Workers (unspecified)' may have included powerloom weavers.

many weavers returned to the trade as it enjoyed a resurgence. From 1871, aggregate occupational categories in the printed census provide no divisions that clearly distinguish linen weavers from weavers of other goods, or separate handloom and powerloom weavers.[35] Contemporary qualitative evidence, much of which is broadly impressionistic, offers little to redress the limitations of the census. The former President of the Belfast Chamber of Commerce, R.H. Reade, responded to persistent entreaties to estimate the size of the workforce in the 1880s by remarking only that it was decreasing.[36] There is, however, evidence of a large handloom workforce after the 1860s: Clara Collet estimated that 30,000 handlooms were at work in Ireland in 1874. Even when this number was revised to 25,000, she surmised that it was greater than the powerloom workforce.[37] An 1888 directory estimated that 15,000 to 20,000 handloom weavers were employed in Co. Antrim alone,[38] and thousands more in Cos. Down and Armagh. In fact, the number of handloom weavers in Ulster 'directed by' manufacturers and merchants in the Lurgan district alone was said to be as high as 18,000.[39] But there is also evidence that the number soon declined significantly. In 1893 it was estimated that £220,000 were paid out to handloom weavers in Ireland.[40] Wages declined to £55,000 by 1910. By 1898 Clara Collet estimated that only 2,500 handloom weavers remained in Ulster. Fourteen years later, representatives of the Handloom Weavers' Society also claimed that their membership of 800 weavers represented the majority of 'heads' of linen weaving households, with another 300 heads not included on the association's rolls. They estimated that the cambric and damask handloom weaving labour force in Ireland numbered only 3,000.[41] A survey of this evidence suggests that while thousands of weavers worked in the trade after the 1850s, far fewer remained at the loom in the last decade of the nineteenth century.

Linen branches which remained exclusive handloom preserves diminished considerably during this period, pushing the decreasing workforce into a narrowed

35 The general term of 'Factory Labourers in Textiles' used in 1871 comprises a wide range of possible occupational claims, and the category of 'Flax, Linen – Manufacture' and 'Weaver-Undefined' are similarly imprecise: Charles Booth remarked on the imprecision of taxonomy in the Irish textile sector when commenting on the nineteenth-century census. In approaching the census data, for instance, he cautioned that the increase in people in Ireland enumerated under 'Flax, linen and damask manufacture' between 1871 and 1881 may be partly attributed to decreasing numbers in the 'weavers, spinners and factory hands (undefined)' categories. See Charles Booth, 'Occupations of the people of the United Kingdom, 1801–81', *Journal of the Statistical Society* 49, 2 (1886), 314–444, especially 346. **36** Minutes of evidence of the *Select committee on industries (Ireland)* (288) HC 1885–85, vol. ix (hereafter '*Select committee on industries (Ireland)*'), evidence of R.H. Reade, q. 11,623. **37** Board of Trade report, 52. **38** G.H. Bassett (1888a), 23. **39** G.H. Bassett (1888b), 359. **40** Sir W. Crawford, *Irish linen and some features of its production* (1910), 13; Alfred S. Moore, *Linen from the raw material to the finished product* (1914), 82. **41** *Report of the departmental committee with regard to the application of the National Insurance Act to outworkers in Ireland*, vol. II, Evidence and appendices [Cd. 7686], HC 1914–16, vol. xxxi [hereafter '*Outworkers in Ireland*'], evidence of representatives of the Handloom Weavers' Association, 404–9.

range of work.[42] The Ballymena handloom shirting trade fell off earlier than hand-loom cambric and damask production as (relatively cheaper) shirting powerlooms were introduced into the trade. While dispersed rural production was predominant, there were several urban handloom workshops in Ballymena in the 1860s, when Robert Chesney's Melbourne House opened a linen manufacturing, bleaching and finishing department 'specially made to take the place of the present exorbitant price of cotton'.[43] Chesney was also a partner in the Ballymena Linen Co.; which began operations in February 1863, employing 80 to 100 hands.[44] Urban female weavers operated looms that they rented from factory proprietors and were paid on a piece-rate basis. In one Ballymena workshop, 120 looms were at work in 1864.[45] As we have seen, workshops also drew on members of the weavers' fam-ilies: one widow weaving at a local workshop appeared before petty sessions in February 1866 to beg JPs not to incarcerate her son, aged 12 or 13, in order that he could continue to attend her at the loom.[46] The firms were relatively small enter-prises, requiring a limited capital investment in land, buildings and looms, but not demanding the much greater fixed capital investments of a steam-loom factory. From the mid-1860s, the town was also the site of a large spinning mill, the Braid-water Mill,[47] and of steam-weaving factories which arrived in Ballymena in the late 1860s and early 1870s.[48] Even so, the large majority of mid -Antrim's weavers in the 1860s were working in rural districts.

In the 1880s, the handloom trade in mid-Antrim was still associated with the eponymous light handloom pieces,[49] and its market remained a meeting place for merchants and manufacturers.[50] In 1880, for instance, a poor year for the trade, the York Street Flax Spinning Co. reported that Ballymena manufacturers had 40,000 webs on hand.[51] Yet in 1898 Clara Collet remarked that while 'the handloom industry still survives in the counties of Antrim, Down and Armagh', considerable emigration had drained Ballymena's handloom workforce.[52] By 1912 it had shrunk

42 *Irish Textile Journal*, 15 May 1888. See also *Irish Textile Journal*, 15 January 1889.   **43** *Observ-er*, 10 January 1863.   **44** *Observer*, 28 February 1863.   **45** *Observer*, 12 November 1864   **46** *Observer*, 24 February 1866. The widow claimed that she was 'unable to weave without the boy's assistance'.   **47** For wages in 1874 and 1878, see Braidwater Spinning Company machine book, PRONI, Belfast, D/1492/8.   **48** *Observer*, 9 June 1866. The newspaper reported that the steam-weav-ing factory was to employ a pair of 'horizontal expansive and condensing steam-engines of 120 horse-power to be supplied by Messrs Hicks and Hargreave, and Co., of Bolton. It was expected that the weaving workforce, 'chiefly females', would earn 12*s*. to 14*s*. per week.   **49** A small handloom labour force engaged in the production of woollen and worsted goods was centred on Newtownards and Letterkenny, with a small presence in the Ballymena district as well (*Irish Textile Journal*, 14 Feb-ruary 1886). In Newtownards, the staples of the handloom were 'plain and fancy fabrics such as Leno Curtains, Persian Shawls and Woollen Shirting' and production was organized by Glasgow manu-facturers (*Irish Textile Journal*, 15 March 1886, 30). Indeed, it was said that handloom work in 1886 was still the principal employment of men in Newtownards (*Irish Textile Journal*, 15 November 1886). In 1912 Grey Abbey, Co. Down was said to be the only centre of silk handloom weaving in Ulster, with a small handloom tapestry industry centred on Newtownards (*Outworkers in Ireland*, evi-dence of W.T. Macartney-Filgate, q. 192–5).   **50** *Irish Textile Journal*, 15 March 1886.   **51** W. Crawford (1910), 12.   **52** *Board of Trade report*, 52.

to such an extent that a representative of the Department of Agriculture and Technical Instruction in Ireland declared that the handloom trade in fine Ballymena shirtings was 'a dying trade. There are only a few hands left, and there are only two men, I think, who are giving out yarn or "chains".'[53] The pace and extent of the shirting trade's decline contrasted with the experiences of other specialist branches of handloom linen manufacture, such as the cambric and damask trades. In Lurgan it was estimated that £10,000 in wages were paid out weekly to the district's (mainly cambric) handloom weavers in 1877.[54] In 1888 the Tandagree-area manufacturer William John Turtle employed about 1,000 handloom weavers 'belonging to various places' and William Kilpatrick employed 500 at the handloom.[55] Despite the apparent vibrancy of handloom weaving there, in some branches weavers' fortunes declined. The manufacturer Thomas Shillington claimed in 1880 that most weavers' prospects were diminishing,[56] and Thomas Swann, a resident of the Lisburn area, shared his pessimistic outlook:

> In former times cotton and linen were manufactured by handloom in the cottages, but that trade has very much decreased of late. The cotton has almost deserted the country owing to the fact that it has been put into powerlooms in Glasgow and Paisley; linen is still affording a pursuit to cottagers in the country. The children that are not acting as weavers are always ready to come and act as farm servants, and labour is always plentiful.[57]

Through most of the late-nineteenth century, damask continued to be insulated from mechanization, and employed handloom weavers into the twentieth century.[58] But in other branches, weavers' earnings followed a long trajectory downward.

The fluctuating fortunes of Ballymena's weavers, and of the handloom trade generally, were part of a wider experience of instability throughout the linen sector.[59] Linen was susceptible to changing fashions, such as the popularity of coloured shirts, and to displacement by other fabrics, especially as flannel, percale and other fabrics gained widespread popularity.[60] In shirts, summer trouserings, handkerchiefs and other garments, cotton gradually but decisively superseded

---

53 *Outworkers in Ireland*, evidence of W.T. Macartney-Filgate, q. 262–3. **54** In C. Gill (1925), 2.
55 G.H. Bassett (1888b), 227. **56** *Working of Landlord and Tenant Act*, evidence of Thomas Shillington, q. 5,157. **57** Ibid., evidence of Thomas Swann, q. 6,160. **58** M. Cohen (1997a), 216–17. **59** P. Solar (2005) and (2003), provides an excellent overview of conditions in the post-Famine Irish linen industry, and in the wider European industry. **60** *Irish Textile Journal*, 15 September 1888. The 15 November 1887 issue illustrated the diminishing demand for linen drills, which had been superseded by cottons and had slumped from $2.5 million to a trade of $150,000 over fifteen to twenty years, a decrease not in value, but 'of consumption'. On 15 September 1888, the Troy correspondent noted that 'the fancy flannel craze has worked temporary injury to yard-wide cloth', as 'has the very large business done in French and German embroidered and many-plaited bosoms, not to mention piqués, Madras shirtings, and other fancy fads'.

linen fabric.[61] Its price advantage proved attractive to garment manufacturers and consumers alike: in its *General list for 1887*, for instance, the large London-based shirt firm of Welch, Margetson, offered fine yard-wide linen webs from 1*s*. 7*d*. to 2*s*. 3*d*. per yard, and yard-wide light frontings from 1*s*. 8½*d*. to 5*s*. 1*d*. per yard, but popular flannels generally were cheaper, and India Gauze cotton shirtings cost only 10½*d*. per yard.[62] By 1898, leading American collar- and cuff-makers advertised articles made of cotton materials and claimed that they matched linen in all features except cost.[63] As cheaper fabrics were substituted for linen shirtings, there was pressure to lower prices of lower grades of yard-wide linen cloth most vulnerable to displacement.[64] In the 1870s and 1880s, moments of bright prosperity were punctuated by deep downturns that reflected the unstable commercial environment. In 1880 a Ballymena web was valued at around £3, of which £1 represented the earnings of the weaver.[65] As prices diminished in their principal markets, weavers' earnings declined.

Ulster's linen trade also faced acute protectionist pressures in export markets, with varied impacts on different branches, especially as the United States sought to foster a domestic industry. Before 1890, the United States applied a tariff of 35% *ad valorem* on imported linens; most continental countries also adopted high duties.[66] That year, the McKinley Tariff Bill proposed to increase duties on imported piece linens and linen products — especially on sets that were thought to be potential specializations for a nascent American linen industry. Domestic shirt-, collar- and cuff-makers, who purchased Ballymena cloth, lobbied Congress for an exemption for yard-wide linen cloth and secured a delay in duties of 50% on piece goods over a count of between 9°° or 10°°.[67] Subsequent amendments also shielded Ireland's linen shirting trade (not only by exempting it from increased duties but also by effectively shutting out German and other competitors in the American collar market), yet demand for Ballymena handloom linens continued to decline. Despite winning a reprieve from the McKinley tariff in 1891, for instance, prices of 20°° Ballymenas remained low, some selling at between 33.5 and 34 cents per yard.[68] American shirt- and collar-manufacturers began to gravitate to powerloom cloth, which was easier to make up and provided 'greater satisfaction in wear'.[69] In 1889 the *Linen Market* reported that manufacturers in the Paris and Berlin shirt and collar trade also preferred powerloom shirtings to handloom Ballymenas,

61 Sir R.L. Patterson, 'The British flax and linen industry' (1903), 135.   **62** Cluett, Coon and Company Collection, Rensselaer Co. Historical Society, Troy, New York, box 1010A, 24–34.   **63** See, for instance, *Cluett, Coon and Co. Descriptive Catalogue of Fashions for 1898*, Cluett, Coon and Company Collection, Box 95, 21.   **64** *Irish Textile Journal*, 15 Jan 1890.   **65** Crawford (1910), 12.   **66** *Select committee on industries (Ireland)*, evidence of R.H. Reade, q. 11722.   **67** *Irish Textile Journal*, 15 April 1890; 15 June 1890; 15 July 1890; 15 October 1890.   **68** *Irish Textile Journal*, 15 January 1891. The journal advised readers to divide these figures by three to calculate approximate values in sterling.   **69** *Irish Textile Journal*, 15 October 1891.

'which are gradually falling into disrepute'.[70] A comparison between 1875 and 1895 is instructive. The value of a Ballymena 20°° web declined from 1*s.* 2 ½ *d.* per yard in 1875 to 9 ½*d.* in 1895 — a drop of 36%.[71] In the women's clothing trade, ruffings replaced linen collars in 1888, just as linen shirtings also slumped,[72] a Troy correspondent with the *Irish Textile Journal* noting that the declining price of Ballymenas 'is the old, old story with which we have opened each new season for a long, long time'.[73] In such conditions, some agents sold goods at a loss to maintain a presence in the market, hoping that they could profit from their toehold when conditions improved.[74] But depressed demand and competition from both powerloom cloth and other fabrics decisively undermined the handloom shirting trade by the century's end.

As wider problems in the trade became more severe, Ulster's struggling handloom weavers attracted the attention of one of the district inspector of factories and workshops.[75] He noted that earnings for weaving were very small, and in 1887 wrote that the powerloom was encroaching even upon the cambric handkerchief trade — long a remunerative handloom preserve. From March 1885 to the end of 1886, he surveyed 785 Irish weavers who were 'members of a family working in their own homes'.[76] In handkerchief districts of Cos. Down and Armagh, he observed systems of manufacture that continued to revolve around household labour. Young children were employed in winding and preparing yarn. When their labour was not available, weavers' earnings fell as they employed waged assistants (and, as was long the custom, also paid costs associated with paste-dressing and oil to light the room in which they worked).[77] But his comments on these weavers' conditions were suggestive of the twilight of domestic systems of labour. An 1888 article on mid-Antrim's handloom weavers affirmed his observations of an ageing weaving workforce, noting that weavers were 'mostly old men and girls, as the wages now earned do not tempt young men to the work'.[78] 'In many instances,' it continued, 'the old wife does the winding of the weft, but when there is no female in the family to do this, the weaver must get it done outside, at a cost of from 1*s.* 6*d.* to 2*s.* 6*d.* for each web, according to the set.'[79] With the exception of a small number of well-paid male weavers engaged in specialized production, most weavers drawn from these populations — rural women and aged men — served to observers as a barometer of the shirting trade's decline.

70 *Linen Market*, 7 December 1889. See also *Linen Market*, 11 January 1890.   **71** *Flax Supply Association annual report for 1895* (1896).   **72** *Irish Textile Journal*, 15 June 1888.   **73** *Irish Textile Journal*, 15 July 1888.   **74** In 1889, it was said that some were selling sets of 18°° at 29 cents a yard, 19°° at 31.5 cents, and 20°° at 33.5 cents — when the cost of landing a 19°° in New York was 34 cents per yard. See *Irish Textile Journal*, 15 November 1889.   **75** In 1878, the Domestic Workshops Act extended his remit to the workplaces of most handloom operatives.   **76** *Report of the chief inspector of factories and workshops to Her Majesty's principal secretary of state for the Home Department for the year ending 31st October 1886*, HC 1887 [C.5002], vol. xvii, 10.   **77** Ibid.   **78** *Irish Textile Journal*, 15 September 1888.   **79** *Irish Textile Journal*, 15 September 1888. For a 21°°

SOCIAL DIFFERENTIATION

As earnings in the Ballymena shirting trade fluctuated in the face of unstable demand, protectionism and competition after the 1860s, manufacturers began to tap different pools of labour in the district. The region had a long history of rural domestic production, and linen weavers occupied a distinctive place in rural society. The storied male 'farmer-weaver' of the late-eighteenth and early-nineteenth centuries had famously engaged in seasonal textile production. But by the 1850s a critical transformation in the workforce had occurred: the district's weavers tended to be landless waged labourers whose households straddled industry and agriculture. Seasonal weaving ceased to denote the commercial independence and rugged masculinity of the farmer-weaver and instead became a strategy adopted by cottiers as weaving's prospects declined. Most sources do not attest to the extent of this change. Many people recorded as 'labourers', for instance, wove on a seasonal basis; their weaving work went unenumerated in the census survey of occupations. Seldom did it record dual occupational claims. The most detailed occupational data in the census was associated with the adult male population, often leaving women's and children's extensive paid and unpaid work in textile production unrecorded. The profile of the rural workforce, and systems of labour that underpinned rural handloom weaving, are therefore only partially illuminated by the census. Church records, too, have significant limitations, and heavily bias the enumeration of male occupations. The recording of baptisms and marriages did not involve the systematic collection of occupational data, and the frequent attribution of age as 'major' or 'minor' militates against the precise comparison of marriage ages between cohorts over periods of time.[80] The quality and extent of the records also varied greatly between local churches: here I examine Presbyterian and Episcopalian church records in Ballymena in the 1850s and 60s. Male weavers are compared with co-religionist labourers and farmers, the two other occupations that predominate in the records of male work. In most cases they corroborate evidence of social differentiation in parliamentary papers that suggests that weaving-labourers predominated in rural mid-Antrim's textile economy by the second half of the century. In 1880, for instance, John Young of Galgorm, a local linen merchant and landlord, told the Irish Land Commission that few small farmers were left at the loom. Weaving was principally undertaken by cottier-weavers who were also employed seasonally in waged agricultural

---

web, for which 14*s.* was paid, and 4 yards produced daily, this additional cost of paid winding, combined with the cost of items for preparing the cloth, reduced the household's small earnings even further (*Irish Textile Journal*, 15 September 1888).   **80** There were few uniform principles or taxonomies in the recording of occupations. Often occupational designations varied from church to church and minister to minister. The degree to which occupational titles were claimed or attributed is also unclear.

labour.[81] If we employ literacy as an indicator of socio-economic status, the records from Ballymena's First Presbyterian Church support his observation of social differentiation. Labourers were much less likely than farmers to sign their names on marriage registers in this church, which had a large number of rural members. Instead they marked them with an 'x'. One in six farmers, and just under half the male labourers, signed with an 'x'. Just over 40% of the weavers marked an 'x'. This confirms weavers' social distance from farmers (with whom they had been associated in linen's 'golden age') and their relative proximity to rural labourers.

Episcopal church records in the district suggest more marked differences between these occupational groups, though they appear in a small number of records. In Craigs parish, between May 1845 and 1865, one-third of farmers did not sign the registers, compared to two-thirds of weavers and almost five out of six labourers.[82] Episcopalians and Presbyterians were not evenly distributed through the socio-economic strata of rural mid-Antrim, where Presbyterians tended to be over-represented among rural farming households. This indicator is based on a specific measurement of literacy — the ability to sign one's name — and does not offer information, as the census does, on the ability to read only.

Evidence from the 1851 census for the townland of Craigs, however, also suggests that males enumerated as farmers had markedly different levels of literacy from male weavers and labourers. While almost four-fifths of farmers could both read and write, approximately half the weavers and labourers could only read, the rest being able to both read and write.

Marriage records can also be used to measure endogamy within occupational groups, indicating the extent of fluidity between social boundaries demarcated by various occupations. Relative to weavers, male farmers were more likely to marry within their occupational group: indeed, well over two-thirds of farmer-grooms married farmers' daughters. Weavers displayed a lesser propensity towards endogamy, while labourers showed a very limited tendency. Like farming, weaving drew on systems of family labour and the household served as the primary site of skills transmission. Household production was maintained by recruiting spouses from weaving families, many of whom were trained at family looms from a young age. The imperative of preserving — and even expanding — farm holdings also guided farmers' marriage decisions and reinforced endogamy. In the cottier population engaged in paid labour, the maintenance of domestic sys-

---

81 *Working of Landlord and Tenant Act*, evidence of John Young, q. 5917, q. 5918, q. 5961, q. 5962. In other districts, people stated that opportunities for seasonal weaving were diminishing and weavers were shifting to agricultural work on a full-time basis (*Working of Landlord and Tenant Act*), evidence of Thomas Shillington, 5397–5413). **82** The total numbers of enumerated weavers in Craigs parish between May 1845 and December 1865 was 69, with 36 labourers and 9 farmers (Craigs parish register of marriages, Books 1 and 2, Deputy-Registrar's Office, Ballymena).

tems of labour was not an imperative guiding marriage decisions to the same extent as in farming and weaving households.

3.1 Occupations of grooms and brides' fathers, First
Presbyterian Church, Ballymena, marriage registers, 1857–67

			Bride's father's occupation	
Groom	*No.*	*Farmer (%)*	*Labourer (%)*	*Weaver (%)*
Farmer	89	71.9	1.1	12.4
Labourer	49	32.7	26.5	32.7
Weaver	86	25.6	15.1	50.0

Source: Marriage register of the First Presbyterian Church, Ballymena, PRONI, Belfast, MIC/1P/114/1.

Another indicator of rural social differentiation is intergenerational mobility. If we compare the occupations of grooms and fathers, we see a strong occupational correlation between farming fathers and sons: almost two-thirds of farmer's sons were recorded as farmers. Of the remaining number, the largest single occupational title, at a little over 11% of the total, was 'weaver'. This suggests that some farmers' sons entered other work, either permanently or temporarily, if they did not expect to inherit farmholdings (especially if they were younger sons). By supplying their sons to the weaving trade, farming households served as an important source of weaving labour in the 1860s. More than two-thirds of weavers' sons claimed their fathers' occupation during this period; about one in seven was recorded as a labourer, the next highest group, and under one in twenty as a farmer. Very few weavers' sons were likely to achieve the relatively higher status of farmer. Male weavers continued to work the loom as their children progressed from assisting them to full-time weaving through a system of skills transmission based in the household. Several decades later, the declining state of the shirting weaving trade discouraged the intergenerational reproduction of the weaving household: indeed commentators noted that in response to bleak conditions and even poorer prospects throughout the trade, children were no longer brought up to weave.[83]

83 G.H. Bassett (1888b), 277.

These records offer insight into the structure of the male weaving workforce in a decade that encompassed an unprecedented linen boom. It is likely that a cottier-weaving population in proximate, if somewhat higher, social position to regular rural labourers developed in the district since the 1820s and 1830s, when farmers ceased adjunct textile production and weaving cottiers emerged as the backbone of the labour force. However, a profile of female weavers is harder to construct, especially as women's work was unrecorded or underreported in many sources, often because it was one element in a repertoire of activities aimed at livelihood maintenance. In the 1870s, many cottier-weavers, male and female, remained at the handloom; indeed their numbers were estimated to be greater than those working at the powerloom in Ulster.[84] After the boom of the 1860s, weavers now found themselves in frequent conflict with manufacturers during a period of unstable demand for Irish linen and uncertainty over the future of the trade. Putting-out continued to be the dominant form of industrial organization in the mid-Antrim shirting trade, but as conditions worsened, frictions between weavers and manufacturers endorsed John Young's observation of accentuating social divisions within the trade. The most vociferous debate in mid-Antrim pitted weavers again manufacturers over the issue of web lengths.

In 1873 the local handloom industry around Ballymena was suffering from a downturn,[85] with a male weaver's weekly earnings at the loom, when assisted by a 'boy or woman', no more than 8s. per week.[86] By contrast, twenty years earlier, in 1853, the district's weavers earned 1s. to 2s. per day.[87] Relations between producers and manufacturers frayed as an increasingly large number of workers suspected that manufacturers exploited them as a cheap and flexible source of 'reserve labour'.[88] Local weavers objected to an increase in web lengths from 52 yards to between 60 and 65 yards, and claimed that there had been no corresponding increase in payments. In December 1872, weavers meeting near Kells resolved to limit handloom cloth production to lengths of 52 yards, and in January 1873 a thousand weavers assembled in Ballymena to hear the populist John Rea launch a scathing attack on linen manufacturers accompanied by a rambling discourse taking in many wider themes in Irish history.[89] Commenting on these protests, the *Observer* suggested that an open-market system could be re-established in the town, circumventing manufacturers to whom, the newspaper intoned sympathetically, 'the present race of operative weavers, formerly independent, have now, almost universally, become the hirelings'.[90] A correspondent to the

---

84 *Select committee on industries (Ireland)*, evidence of R.H. Reade, q. 11623. **85** Ibid., 137–8.
86 *Observer*, 18 January 1873. **87** *Select committee of the House of Lords on land law*, evidence of John Young, q. 3098–100; *Observer*, 25 January, 1873; *Royal commission to inquire into the state of fairs and markets in Ireland*, Part II, Minutes of evidence [1910], 1854–55, vol. xix, evidence of John Dickie [*sic*], q. 9885. **88** C. Nardinelli (1986). **89** *Observer*, 18 January 1873. Another example of the maverick Rea's populism can be found in S.A. Royle (1987). **90** The open market appears to have remained a point of contact between manufacturers and merchants. See *Slater's*

newspaper endorsed this view.[91] By the end of March 1873 workers had formed a local Weavers' Defence Association.[92] It was a harbinger of trade bodies established first at the local and then at the national level as weavers developed an infrastructure for wider mobilization, especially after 1884.

Manufacturers responded to these protests by circulating a statement in which they insisted that they could not accept any web lengths under 60 yards because the Belfast exporters who purchased their webs demanded longer cloth. On 1 March 1873, a deputation of weavers met with representatives of local manufacturing interests to discuss the matter at the Adair Arms Hotel in Ballymena. John Young, a leading member of the local linen gentry, Conservative Party organizer in the county, and insightful commentator on the local trade, chaired the meeting. After weavers and manufacturers failed to reach agreement, weavers announced plans for a meeting on the following Saturday at the Linen Hall. In expectation of a large protest, a reinforcement of the local constabulary arrived in Ballymena ahead of the meeting. When a thousand weavers marched to the Linen Hall to demand entry, they were refused admission.[93] Leading local linen merchants and the local estate agent, S.W. Perry, accompanied the weavers to the town's 'People's Park' and heard their grievances. As a meeting between representatives of weavers and manufacturers began, the weavers' ranks swelled to 3,000. At the end of negotiations, Young announced that a standard length of 56 yards had been agreed, to triumphant cheers from the weavers.[94]

It appeared rural bleaching merchants led by Young had successfully brokered an accord between manufacturers and weavers that satisfied weavers' claims to customary market rights. But Samuel Curry, a local linen manufacturer, warned that the manufacturers' delegation could not accept the agreement before consulting colleagues. On 11 March 1873, Young reported to the Office of the Lord Lieutenant that weavers were agitating throughout a district that stretched from mid-Antrim into Co. Londonderry. As Young had anticipated, the promise of harmony in the local trade was dealt a blow when manufacturers declared their 'regret that, with every disposition to carry out this compromise, the Manufacturers are rendered powerless in the matter by the resolution of their principal customers — the Belfast Linen Merchants — that Webs of less than 60 Yards they cannot buy'.[95] The district's weavers reacted to the manufacturers' announcement by accusing them of reneging on the agreement, and they circulated the following announcement:

late *Pigot's Royal national commercial directory of Ireland* (1870), 33.   **91** *Observer*, 18 January 1873.   **92** *Observer*, 25 January 1873.   **93** *Observer*, 8 March 1873.   **94** *Observer*, 15 March 1873.   **95** *News-Letter*, 21 March 1873.

NOTICE TO WEAVERS OF THE COUNTIES OF ANTRIM AND LONDONDERRY —
We beg to announce to Weavers in general that on account of the Manufacturers breaking through the Amicable Settlement that was agreed to by
the Manufacturers, Weavers, and Magistrates, we call a monster meeting of
all Weavers, to attend at Ballymena, on Saturday, 22nd March, 1873, *to
claim the rights of the settlement.*[96]

Although we know that females became a higher proportion of this workforce
between 1851 and 1901, it is not possible to reconstruct the profile of protestors
in the 1870s with much precision. The local workforce in the early 1870s comprised both male and female shirting weavers, and continued to be organized
around sexual divisions of labour which corresponded to poles of status and skill
in shirting weaving. Among the 60 weavers who were admitted to the Ballymena
Workhouse in 1875, for instance, 40% were female; over a third of the male
weavers, whose average age was over 52 (as opposed to 31 for female weavers),
were widowers.[97] These were the most destitute sections of the local weaving
population: most women were admitted with young children and without spouses, and like the aged widowers, could not offset their low weaving income with
other earnings from within the household. They were part of a heterogeneous,
sexually-mixed workforce in mid-Antrim that was experiencing distress in the
1870s. This weaving population was clearly drawn from local cottiers whose
earnings in the trade were diminishing after the Civil War boom and whose frus-
trations culminated in the 1873 agitations.

After weavers' leaders issued their call for a protest meeting in Ballymena,
unrest continued: two dwelling houses of weavers who were violating the strategy of collective resistance by manufacturing 60-yard webs were attacked the following Monday.[98] Authorities prepared for the Saturday protest meeting by
bringing 30 members of the Royal Dragoons to town, along with 50 men from
the 78th Regiment and one hundred extra police officers from across Ulster. Worried communications were exchanged between the resident magistrate, A.C.
Montgomery, and Dublin Castle.[99] Under heavy pressure, weavers and manufacturers agreed that workers would be paid a full rate for all webs over 60 yards
long. In exchange for a dilution of their demands over web lengths, weavers succeeded in re-establishing a small open market in the town. There, they could cir-

96 *Observer*, 22 March 1873.   **97** Admittance rolls from the Ballymena Union Workhouse, PRONI,
Belfast, MIC 15F/31 and 32. The year 1875 is chosen because it is among the earliest containing
details of 'employment or calling'. W. Nelson Hancock argued that differences in the operation of
poor relief regime in England and Ireland, especially rules governing out-relief, placed Irish weavers
at a disadvantage during period of distress in the early 1860s. See 'The differences between the English and Irish Poor Laws, as to the treatment of women and unemployed workers', *Journal of the
Statistical and Social Inquiry Society of Ireland* 3 (1862), 217–35   **98** *Observer*, 29 March 1873.
99 Correspondence of A.C. Montgomery, 11 March 1873, NAI, Dublin, CSO RP 1873 3433 and of
M. Alcock, CSO RP 1873 3939.

cumvent local manufacturers, and sell single webs directly to merchants and drapers. A.C. Montgomery, in correspondence with the under-secretary, declared that
the proposed revival of the open market was 'reasonable and desirable'.[1]
Weavers, for their part, represented it as a dilution of the manufacturers' monopoly over the market and as a restoration of customary relations in the trade. The
open market that the revived Co. Antrim Linen Committee superintended after
1873 operated on a very small scale through the last quarter of the nineteenth century, as the local trade declined and unremunerative weaving was reassigned to
rural women. This market conflict illustrated the growing tensions in a trade
which was increasingly polarized between a cottier class whose earnings were
declining and manufacturers who sought to develop greater control over dispersed rural labour. Changes in the sexual composition of the local workforce
after 1851 offer further evidence of worsening conditions in the shirting trade.

FEMINIZATION

In addition to the process of social differentiation to which many records attest,
there are indications of the feminization of mid-Antrim's weaving population. The
census's limited utility in documenting women's labour, paid and unpaid, bears
reiteration.[2] The omission of women's unpaid work from population surveys was
an expression of gender ideologies which privileged men's regular paid labour as
a focus of enumeration.[3] Another factor operating against the documentation of
women's paid work in textiles, especially in the rural setting, was its seasonality.[4]
Acknowledging these limitations, records show the rural shirting trade engaged a
much higher proportion of females by the end of the nineteenth century.

While their work was often undocumented, rural women gradually became the
foundation of the handloom shirting trade. The later-nineteenth-century enumerated handloom workforce drew mainly on widowed women and adult daughters
— both practicing skills that they had acquired in childhood and to which they

---

1 A.C. Montgomery to the under-secretary, NAI, Dublin, 24 April 1873, CSO RP 1873 5799.   **2** See
Introduction, footnote 37.   **3** The enumeration of the weaving workforce itself was also often imprecise: despite instructions in 1851 to ensure that the particular branch of textile manufacture, whether
woollen, silk or linen, be recorded, a variety of occupational taxonomies prevailed, including the
general designation of 'weaver' in manuscript returns. *Census of Ireland, 1851*: pt. VI: General
Report, appendix to the General Report [2134], HC 1856, vol. xxxi, cx. In 1901, similar instructions
were given to provide such details, 'so as to express distinctly the material which he [the weaver]
weaves' (*Census of Ireland for the year 1901*, HC 1902, [1190] vol. cxxix, Appendix to the General Report p. 601). See also V. Morgan & W.A. Macafee (1984) 183–5. In the district under study,
unlike others in 1851, linen was the near-exclusive branch of domestic manufacture, and local enumerators were scrupulous in designating 'linen weavers'.   **4** S. Horrell & J. Humphries (1995), 97.
Weaving households often turned exclusively to fieldwork at several points in the year — especially in autumn and in spring. This is relevant to this analysis, since the census was taken in late March
in both 1851 and 1901.

may have periodically turned at other stages in the life-cycle. The extent of changes in the weaving workforce between 1851 and 1901 can also be measured using manuscript census returns from the townland of Craigs, measuring 2,801*a.* 2*r.* 21*p.*, for which 1851 and 1901 records survive.[5] While units which formed the basis of census enumeration varied between 1851 and 1901, the townland remained stable as a unit of measurement and allows us to compare broad characteristics of the workforce over fifty years. The population of the townland shrank during that period, as figure 3.2 shows, but at a modest pace compared, as we shall see, to neighbouring districts.

3.2: Population of the townland of Craigs, 1851–1901

Census year	*Population*	*Change on previous census year*
1851	1482	—
1861	1570	5.9
1871	1352	-13.9
1881	1417	4.8
1891	1303	-8.0
1901	1231	-5.5

Sources: *Report of the commissioners of the census of Ireland, 1841* [504], HC 1843, vol. xxiv; *Census of Ireland 1851*, pt. I, Area, population, and number of houses, by townlands and electoral divisions: Co. of Antrim [1565] HC 1852–53, vol. xcii; *Census of Ireland 1861*, pt. I, Area, population, and number of houses, by townlands and electoral divisions provinces of Ulster and Connacht [3204,] HC 1863, vol. lv; *Census of Ireland 1871*, pt. I, Area, population, and number of houses; occupations, religion and education, volume III, Province of Ulster; Summary tables, indexes [C.964] HC 1874, vol. lxxiv, pt. 1; *Census of Ireland 1881*, Area, population and number of houses; occupations, religion and education, volume III, Province of Ulster [C.3204], HC 1882, vol. lxxviii; *Census of Ireland 1891*: Area, population and number of houses; occupations, religion and education, volume III, Province of Ulster [C.6626], HC 1892, vol. xcii; *Census Returns of Ireland for 1901*: giving details of the Area, houses, and population, also ages, civil or conjugal condition, occupations, birth-places, religion and education of the people, in each county and summary tables for each province: volume III: Province of Ulster [C.1123] HC 1902, vol. cxxvi.

Craigs was a site of extensive rural bleaching and industrial activity, its valuation growing from £1,870 10*s.* to £2,346 4*s.* William Morgan and Valerie Macafee,

5 In 1851 this townland was listed in the parish of Ahoghill, and thereafter in the parish of Craigs. For other studies using the 1851 returns, see T.W. Guinnane (1997); V. Morgan & W.A. Macafee (1987) and (1984).

using the 1851 returns,[6] have observed that in Craigs — a district of fine linen man-ufacture — males were more intensively engaged in the linen sector than in other areas. Ages of marriage contrasted between weaving and labouring populations on one hand, and farmers on the other. Farmers' livelihoods were influenced by access to land, which imposed restrictions on nuptuality. For weavers, access to a loom was the primary condition for weaving income. Since this could be effected with relative ease, and since weaving was organized around household systems of pro-duction, weaving supported early family-formation in households. But by the turn of the twentieth century there was little evidence of vibrant domestic handloom manufacture in this district.

Between 1851 and 1901 the most striking change in the weaving workforce in Craigs was the remarkable decline in the number of weavers. In the Lagan Valley, Brenda Collins has shown that the proportion of households with weavers in 1901 ranged from 25% in Ballygowan to 81% in Gortnacor.[7] In Craigs, however, man-uscript returns reveal that female weavers declined in number by almost 80% between 1851 and 1901 and male weavers by more than 93%. From 26% of the population in 1851, weavers fell to only 4% in 1901.[8] One explanation of differ-ences between Lagan Valley and mid-Antrim weavers lies in their specialist branches of manufacture. Lagan Valley linen weavers wove cambric handker-chiefs, diaper and damask, which, for a variety of factors explored earlier in this study, including technical limitations and the state of demand, were more resilient than the Ballymena shirting trade, which diminished decisively in scale in the 1890s.[9] During this contraction, the profile of mid-Antrim's workforce seemed to support contemporaries' claims that the shirting trade was indeed 'dying'.

An 1888 article in the *Irish Textile Journal* described handloom weavers in the Antrim village of Ahoghill as women and elderly men. This observation is con-firmed by 1851 and 1901 census data. A much greater proportion of weavers was female in 1901. This finding confirms the 'gendered re-division of weaving work' which Brenda Collins observed in the Lagan Valley, where female weavers accounted for 6% of the workforce in the 1901 census.[10] It also underscores the importance of age as an influence over labour allocation. In 1898 Clara Collet noted of the Ballymena district that 'A considerable (but not the greater) propor-tion of weavers are women. Generally speaking they do about as much work as the men, but not quite such fine work, and earn about 1*s*. a week less.'[11] In many dis-

---

6 V. Morgan & W.A. Macafee (1987) and (1984).   7 B. Collins (1997).   8 The decline in the parish population, by contrast, was approximately 17%, from 1,482 to 1,126.   9 *Factory and workshops commission*, part III, vol. II, Minutes of evidence [C.1443–I], HC 1876, vol. xxx, evidence of Dr Musgrave, certifying surgeon of Lisburn, q. 17548–53.   10 B. Collins (1997). There was an ongo-ing feminization of weaving work in most districts of Ulster throughout this period: employers of cambric weavers in Armagh and district described their labour force in 1912 as predominantly female, with young girls working in the trade until marriage (*Outworkers in Ireland*, evidence of John H. McCann, q. 976–81).   11 *Board of Trade report*, 52–3.

tricts in England after 1850, John Chartres has argued that the continuing presence of rural industrial hand production was partly due to a labour 'reserve' of such female and elderly workers.[12] Their work interacted with mechanization in complex ways throughout the UK, from the expansion of hand-work in the ready-to-wear garment trade of the north-west of Ireland to smaller-scale craft work in the Highlands of Scotland. But females' unpaid work was broadly characterized by low earnings and by casual labour. In mid-Antrim the proportion of female weavers grew from 39.1% of the 391 weavers in 1851 to 66% of the much smaller population of 47 weavers in 1901.

Because the remunerative potential of linen branches diverged greatly, several branches of linen production did not become associated with women and old men. In workshop production (more prevalent in trades such as damask and cambric than in shirting), a return to the Factory and Workshops Act Commission in 1876 showed that 61% of workshop handloom weavers were males.[13] While male weavers were said to own their looms, female weavers were described as weaving in support of their households, and 'very rarely the owners of their looms, which generally belong to their fathers, the latter drawing their daughters' wages'.[14] These sexual divisions had important consequences for the definition of craft authority in the trade, especially as men continued to dominate both the most remunerative branches and handloom trade associations through the first decade of the twentieth century. Although women became the backbone of Ulster's labour force, the public image of the skilled weaver remained resolutely male. In Lurgan, narrow goods such as napkins were mainly woven by females, who could earn wages of 8s. to 10s. weekly. By contrast, men comprised the bulk of the fine cambric workforce, and on wider goods they could earn 13s. to 15s. weekly.[15] The mid-Antrim handloom shirting trade was generally less remunerative than these branches, with a much smaller amount of fine work in the exclusive hands of men. Increasingly, rural women formed a large section of the shirting workforce as the industry contracted and as work became casualized and less remunerative.

There are a number of indicators of shirting as a 'dying trade' in 1901, including the marked increase in the average age of female and male weavers. Weaving skills transmission historically involved an informal apprenticeship through which young children progressed from winding yarn from about the age of 6, graduating to the loom by the age of 10.[16] Indeed, over half of daughters and sons weaving in

12 J. Chartres, (2000), 1103–4. **13** Workshops were defined for the purpose of this enumeration under the 1867 Factory Act. (*Factory and Workshops Act commission* [C.1443], HC 1876, vol. xxix, Appendix B). **14** *Board of Trade report*, 53. **15** *Outworkers in Ireland*, evidence of A.N. Ireland & W.R. McMurray, q. 1356. In his study of a largely cambric handloom weaving region in north-west Down, W.H. Crawford (1993) found male weavers out-numbering females in 1901 census returns. **16** 'Evidence upon the handloom weaving and hosiery manufactures in Ireland and Scotland', evidence of Amelia Cairns, q. 7, of Hane Fay, q. 8, q. 9, of William Graham, q. 10.

the 1851 census of Craigs were in households headed by a linen weaver. This apprenticeship drew younger household members into the trade and facilitated inter-generational skills transfer.[17] But by 1906, specialized winding factories were supplying manufacturers with weft wound on paper bobbins, displacing a task historically assigned to young children and the elderly, and disrupting a traditional means of household apprenticeship.[18] The introduction of compulsory education in the 1890s also discouraged the recruitment of young children into the trade. Schools drew children away from the cottage and the loom, restricting weavers' access to unpaid household labour. In the 5 to 13 year-old cohort, less than a quarter of males and females were enumerated as 'at school' in 1851, whereas fifty years later the number of 'scholars' (the term then used) had risen to over 90%.[19] Observers also claimed that emigration and a resistance to 'bringing children up in the trade' greatly reduced the number of young weavers apprenticing in the trade. When the trade began a brief period of revival in 1895, manufacturers of Ballymenas found that they could no longer find workers. Local weavers had gravitated to factory and full-time field work.[20] An assistant commissioner for the Royal Commission on Labour noted in 1893 that spinning mills and factories offered extensive employment in the district, especially for women, who constituted 700 of the Braidwater Flax Spinning Co.'s workforce of 1,100, and also three-quarters of the workers in two local weaving companies.[21] Again in 1900, when a long period of depression gave way to high demand and improved wages for Ballymena handloom goods, there were few weavers remaining in the district. The *Irish Textile Journal* noted that the protracted downturn had discouraged younger hands from taking up the trade, and that the ageing workforce was diminishing 'year by year'.[22] 'More wages', one observer noted, 'can be earned in powerloom factories or on the Clyde.'[23] By 1912, a few linen looms around Ballymena, and particularly in the Ahoghill area, had been converted to produce hand-woven tweeds, with factories in the area giving out yarn.[24] Woollen firms aiming to capitalize on weavers' skills found the local linen trade all but extinct.

---

17 In 1841, Census Commissioners noted that in restricting their occupational survey to those over fifteen, they were not able to account for labour of children of 'the Tailor, the Weaver, or the Shoemaker [who] may employ the young members of his own family in assisting him'. See *Report of the commissioners on the census of Ireland*, 1841 [504], HC 1843, vol. xxiv, xx.   **18** *Irish Textile Journal*, 10 July 1906; W.R. McMurray, 'Handloom linen, cambric and damask weaving, and linen embroidery', in W.T. Macartney-Filgate (ed.), *Irish rural life and industry, with suggestions for the future* (1907), 166.   **19** In 1851 enumerators were asked to record 'if a Child, whether attending School'. Census enumerators also received specific instructions in 1901 to record as scholars 'children or young persons attending a school, or receiving regular instructions at home' as scholars. *General Report, Census of Ireland for the year 1901* [1190], HC 1902, vol. cxxix, 600.   **20** *Irish Textile Journal*, 15 November 1895.   **21** *R. McCrea report*, 86.   **22** *Irish Textile Journal*, 15 February 1900.   **23** *Irish Textile Journal*, 15 July 1896.   **24** *Outworkers in Ireland*, evidence of W.T. Macartney-Filgate, q. 342–43. See also a discussion of efforts to convert linen looms for the production of other cloth in *Irish Textile Journal*, 15 December 1901 and 15 January 1902, in which 'Mr Bankhead' of Ahoghill is cited as superintending such efforts.

As unpaid juvenile labour was displaced, many ageing workers continued to weave. Commenting on the decline of handloom wages from £220,000 in 1893 to £55,000 in 1910, for instance, the linen baron Sir William Crawford suggested that the introduction of Old Age Pensions had reduced dependence on the handloom for income in old age.[25] Older workers, male and female, had few income alternatives to remaining at the loom and the enumerated workforce, especially its male element, aged considerably between 1851 and 1901. The average age of female weavers rose from 22 to 29; that of male weavers increased from 28 to 39.

As late as the 1890s, families were still weaving in cottages around Ballymena, but, as we have seen, changes in *who* was weaving within households were striking as older weavers and females came to predominate in the shirting trade.[26] We can learn more about them by examining the household status of weavers. The census provides information on the relationship of household residents to an individual defined as the 'head' — often a 'productive' adult male married member of the household, but designated in detailed, albeit ambiguous, instructions to enumerators in 1841 as the person in the 'highest social position'.[27] This implied a degree of social, cultural and economic authority over other household members, and in census enumeration it included responsibility for completing household returns.[28]

3.3 Household status of Craigs weavers, 1851 and 1901

Position	1851 (No.)	1851 (%)	1901 (No.)	1901 (%)
Head Male	99	25.3	8	17.0
Female	5	1.3	2	4.3
Son/Stepson	97	24.8	8	17.0
Daughter/Stepdaughter	84	21.5	24	51.1
Servant Male	16	4.1	0	0.0
Female	20	5.1	0	0.0
Wife	32	8.2	4	8.5
Brother	8	2.0	0	0.0
Other/Unclear	30	7.7	1	2.1

Sources: Manuscript census returns, *Census of Ireland, 1851*, PRONI, Belfast, MIC/5A/15, 16; *Census of Ireland for 1901*, PRONI, Belfast, MIC/354/1/18.

25 W. Crawford (1910), 12–13. **26** In W.E. Coe (1969), 68. **27** *Report of the commissioners on the census of Ireland*, 1841 [504], HC 1843, vol. xxiv, xi. **28** Census instructions in 1851 directed the head to fill, or 'cause to be filled', when competent to do so, the enumeration form for his 'fam-

Comparing the household status of weavers in 1851 and 1901, we see from figure 3.3 that the number of 'heads' who wove fell by 92%, while the overall number of weavers fell by 88%. Wives constituted over 8% of weavers in the two census years: their enumerated work was linked very closely to that of their husbands. Indeed in 1851, all but one of the 32 weaving wives lived in households headed by a male weaver; of the 4 recorded in 1901, one each was married to a weaver, labourer, general labourer and agricultural labourer. The remnant of the handloom workforce in 1901 was largely female: daughters were over half of the weavers. Compared to males, more females in 1901 may have used skills acquired in childhood as a source of income; male weavers left the trade altogether if they were able to find better-paid work, leaving an ageing workforce. By 1901 the daughters who formed more than half the enumerated weaving workforce were drawn largely from households whose male heads were engaged in other waged labour: 6 were agricultural labourers, 6 general labourers, 3 male linen weavers, and one each a carpenter, a surfaceman, a 'retired linen weaver and pensioner' and farmer.

In nearby farming districts weavers were drawn from the same social stratum: most were from households headed not by a farmer, but rather by a waged worker, including general labourers, agricultural labourers and weavers. Ballylummin townland in Ahoghill Parish, measuring 1,139a. 2r. 20p., comprised a population of 385 in 1901, of whom 50 were weavers.[29] Its valuation had increased marginally over fifty years from £727 to £876 10s., but its population had decreased dramatically, as figure 3.4 illustrates. Population loss was especially heavy between 1891 and 1901, due, according to the 1901 census, to 'emigration and removals'.

Agricultural work dominated the townland's occupational structure: among males aged 14 and over, 24.8% were enumerated as the relatives of farmers, 24.1% as farmers and 22.1% as agricultural labourers; 12.4% were recorded as weavers. Among females 14 and over, 26.1% had no occupation recorded, 20.3% were linen weavers, 19.6% were relatives of farmers and 13.7% were listed in some form of domestic service employment.[30] Yet a closer inspection of the weavers and their households confirms many of the observations made in Craigs, including the preponderance of women (62%) and a gap between the average age of male weavers (56) and females (39). Average ages obscure two distinct groups who accounted for 26 of the 31 weavers enumerated in the townland: 8 were widows or spinsters engaged in weaving as a form of continuous employment (whose average age was 52), and 16 were daughters in households headed by male linen weavers and agricultural labourers (their average age was 29). Marriage may

ily', as well as for visitors and servants within that family's abode. See *Census of Ireland, 1851*: pt. VI: *General Report* [2134], HC 1856, vol. xxxi, vi, cix.   **29** Manuscript returns from the *Census of Ireland for 1901*, PRONI, Belfast, MIC/354/1/18.   **30** 'Housekeeper' is an ambiguous designation, but here is considered an occupational title denoting domestic service.

3.4 Population of Ballylummin townland, 1851–1901

Census year	Population	Change on previous census year
1851	731	—
1861	773	5.7
1871	725	-6.2
1881	678	-6.5
1891	554	-18.3
1901	385	-30.5

Sources: *Report of the commissioners of the census of Ireland, 1841* [504], HC 1843, vol. xxiv; *Census of Ireland 1851*, pt. I, Area, population, and number of houses, by townlands and electoral divisions: Co. of Antrim [1565] HC 1852–53, vol. xcii; *Census of Ireland 1861*, pt. I, Area, population, and number of houses, by townlands and electoral divisions provinces of Ulster and Connacht [3204,] HC 1863, vol. lv; *Census of Ireland 1871*, pt. I, Area, population, and number of houses; occupations, religion and education, volume III, Province of Ulster; Summary tables, indexes [C.964] HC 1874, vol. lxxiv, pt. 1; *Census of Ireland 1881*, Area, population and number of houses; occupations, religion and education, volume III, Province of Ulster [C.3204], HC 1882, vol. lxxviii; *Census of Ireland 1891*: Area, population and number of houses; occupations, religion and education, volume III, Province of Ulster [C.6626], HC 1892, vol. xcii; *Census Returns of Ireland for 1901*; giving details of the Area, houses, and population, also ages, civil or conjugal condition, occupations, birth-places, religion and education of the people, in each county and summary tables for each province: volume III: Province of Ulster [C.1123] HC 1902, vol. cxxvi.

have ended their work at the loom: in 1912, for instance, employers of handloom weavers in Cos. Down and Armagh claimed that daughters generally gave up the trade after marriage.[31] Joanna Bourke has also argued that as unpaid household work became more narrowly defined as a mother's preserve, daughters focused on regular, paid, productive labour.[32] But marriage also imposed new constraints on the enumeration of women's work. Women retained weaving skills and may have woven cloth occasionally, perhaps seasonally, in adulthood: their work, because of its more casual character, escaped census enumeration.[33] Widowed and spinster heads of households engaged in more continuous weaving to support themselves and any dependents; as their primary means of support, it was more likely to be enumerated in the census. This broad trend towards feminization of

31 *Outworkers in Ireland*, evidence of John H. McCann, q. 972–7.   32 J. Bourke (1993) and (1991a).   33 J. MacPherson (2001).

the workforce is also suggested by other sources: in 1912, it was reported by the Handloom Weavers' Society that only about 1,100 of Ireland's 3,000 handloom weavers, mostly in cambric and damask trades, were heads of families. The majority were 'children and wives' engaged in weaving work.[34] The weavers made another bold assertion that coupled gender and skill: 'lower classes' of work, they insisted, were generally woven by casual, female labour.

CASUALIZATION

For decades, weaving and farm work had been intertwined in mid-Antrim. This labour strategy continued, in several forms, in the later-nineteenth century. An 1882 select committee heard that mid-Antrim's population was 'thick in conse-quence of weaving', and that its weavers were seasonal agricultural workers who saw 'themselves as labourers' since they held cottages under the same terms — often in return for work in the field.[35] Indeed, in 1885 R.H. Reade testified that 'nearly all' of Ulster's handloom weavers were cottiers, living on small plots of land of 2 to 3 acres and regularly undertaking agricultural work.[36] In elevated parts of Ballymena's poor law union, relatively poor soil encouraged pastoral farming, but in rural districts around populous towns and villages, the district's gravelly loam and clay supported a mixed agricultural economy, with tillage focused on oats, flax, turnips and potatoes, and modern ploughs in very limited use.[37] Within this mixed agricultural system weavers found a range of complementary work in both agriculture and rural industry. But demand for field labour declined from the 1850s, as the acreage under crops diminished in the district and as figures 3.5 and 3.6 show, the conversion to pastoral agriculture intensified.[38]

Links between agricultural systems and rural industry have been asserted in many studies of dispersed rural textile production.[39] According to proto-industrial theory, for instance, a shift to pastoralism was a determinant of rural industrial development, because it released labour to industrial work. Although most studies have discredited it as a sole determinant of cottage industry, in mid-Antrim it seems to have played a role in hastening rural depopulation, as the shift from arable agriculture to pastoral activity, especially after 1871, reduced demand for labour on farms and in fields. The cottiers who were the backbone of the rural textile workforce responded to worsening conditions by

34 *Outworkers in Ireland*, evidence of James Wood, q. 405–10.   **35** *Select committee of the House of Lords on land law*, evidence of John Young, q. 3095, 3170.   **36** *Select committee on industries (Ireland)*, evidence of R.H. Reade, q. 11,665–6.   **37** *R. McCrea report*, 85.   **38** For a wider dis-cussion of these changes in Ireland as a whole, see H.D. Gribbon (1996).   **39** N. Verdon (2002) also emphasizes the need to analyze rural domestic hand-production within the context of the labour structure of local agriculture. See especially chapter 5, 'Alternative employment opportunities: domestic industries', 132–63.

3.5 Numbers of selected stock in Ballymena poor law union, 1851–1901

Stock	1851	1861	1871	1881	1891	1901	Change, 1851–1901 (%)
Cattle	30,558	30,660	39,258	32,424	38,707	38,050	24.5
Sheep	7,152	9,632	16,918	9,166	21,878	18,405	157.3
Pigs	8,317	9,504	17,700	10,707	15,843	14,190	70.6
Poultry	51,747	63,278	83,951	109,267	136,312	193,855	274.6

Sources: *Agricultural statistics of Ireland for the year 1861* [3156], HC 1863, vol. lxix; *Agricultural statistics of Ireland for the year 1871* [C.762], HC 1873, vol. lxix; *Agricultural statistics of Ireland for the year 1881* [C.3332], HC 1882, vol. lxxiv; *Agricultural statistics of Ireland for the year 1891* [C.6777], HC 1892, vol. lxxxviii; *Agricultural statistics of Ireland for the year 1901* [Cd.1170], HC 1902, vol. cxvi.

3.6 Acres of selected crops in Ballymena Poor Law Union, 1861–1901

Crop	1861	1871	1881	1891	1901
Wheat	380	798	167	116	167
Oats	18,895	23,521	16,093	14,526	13,785
Potatoes	15,357	15,717	12,021	11,392	9,975
Turnips	677	927	958	944	1,412
Flax	4,379	3,410	7,302	5,836	4,574

Sources: *Agricultural statistics of Ireland for the year 1861* [3156], HC 1863, vol. lxix; *Agricultural statistics of Ireland for the year 1871* [C.762], HC 1873, vol. lxix; *Agricultural statistics of Ireland for the year 1881* [C.3332], HC 1882, vol. lxxiv; *Agricultural statistics of Ireland for the year 1891* [C.6777], HC 1892, vol. lxxxviii; *Agricultural statistics of Ireland for the year 1901* [Cd.1170], HC 1902, vol. cxvi.

leaving the district.[40] The 1886 annual *Report of the chief inspector of factories and workshops*, for instance, found that Ulster's weavers were 'gradually falling away through emigration, and those at present engaged not bringing up their children to the trade'.[41]

> Since I reported last year on the handloom weaving trade, I regret that there has been no improvement in the prices the weavers can earn, which average between 6*s.* and 8*s.* a week for 12 to 14 hours' work a day. These weavers are a most industrious class of persons, and are very numerous in the province of Ulster. They chiefly make fine linens and Irish cambric handkerchiefs. The masters tell me they have a greater demand for the cheaper handkerchiefs made by the powerloom; hence the small prices these poor weavers are able to earn.[42]

Rural depopulation in many linen weaving districts accelerated in the last two decades of the century. George Henry Bassett wrote in 1888 that 'Many men emigrate in order to be saved from the necessity of bringing up their children to the [handloom] trade.'[43] In 1897 government commissioners also identified emigration as a key cause of the handloom workforce's decline.[44] Indeed, rural mid-Antrim's population decreased markedly after 1861. While the population of Ballymena poor law union decreased at a relatively steady level of 3–5% each decade between 1841 and 1881, with a brief upturn of 4.3% between 1851 and 1861, the census recorded a decline of over 13% between 1881 and 1891, and almost 10% in the subsequent decade. The Union's population, which was 74,109 in 1841, stood at 53,082 by the turn of the twentieth century. It was affected by the Famine, but the decade which saw the most significant population loss came more than thirty years later, as agricultural and linen sectors of the economy experienced accelerating transformations — the

---

40 *Linen Trade Circular*, 19 January 1884.   **41** *Report of the chief inspector of factories and workshops to Her Majesty's principal secretary of state for the Home Department for the year ending 31st October 1886*, HC 1887 [C.5002], vol. xvii, 10.   **42** Ibid., *for the year ending 31st October 1887*, HC 1888 [C.5328], vol. xxvi, 24.   **43** G.H. Bassett (1888a), 281.   **44** Employers of handloom weavers in Armagh declared in 1912 that the trade was 'dying' and that emigration was a response to the ongoing displacement of the handloom (*Outworkers in Ireland*, evidence of John H. McCann, q. 892–899). This age profile corresponds to that of the immiserated Scottish weaving labour force from the 1840s, when 'natural wastage' reduced their number and left a small group of aged handloom weavers with few other employment alternatives to labouring at the loom (N. Murray [1978]). **45** The extensive employment of male labour on the Belfast to Ballymena Railway line, for instance, which gave work to some 4,000 men in 1846, indicates both the extent of available hands and the development of strategies to mitigate their distress. See the statement of the number of men who may be employed in the Belfast and Ballymena Railway in the summer of 1846, C. Lanyon, July 7th 1847, NAI, Dublin, RLFC/3/1/481. Newspaper reports during the period also emphasized the extent of local suffering and in some rural areas the population declined. See, for instance, the *Belfast Protestant Journal*, 14 November 1846.

former shifting more decisively towards pastoral agriculture, while rural hand manufacture declined. The cottier population from which both sectors drew contracted.

For shirting weavers in the 1880s, seasonal paid agricultural labour and textile labour continued to be intertwined. This work pattern corresponds with textile labour strategies in other areas of Europe.[46] But the reallocation of weaving within the household requires particular attention, as households adjusted to low earnings in the handloom trade. Men's and women's relative earnings in agriculture and weaving were especially important in decisions surrounding the sexual division of work. Rural households and individual members devised strategies, bounded by prevailing ideologies of gender that Bourke has described, to maximize the productive capacity of each member. Often this meant that women turned to seasonal or occasional paid work.

Our insight into household labour allocation strategies is partial. By and large, our understanding of rural women's agricultural work in Ireland, as in Britain, has been undermined by an historiographical preoccupation with men's waged labour.[47] But there is considerable evidence of significant male-female wage gaps in the Irish agricultural sector, and that the gendering of work in agriculture was as pronounced as in rural industry.[48] Earning differentials in the field were historically stark in Co. Antrim (where an allowance for food was often a component of wages). Average weekly rates of pay in 1860, for instance, were 8s. 3½d. for men, 4s. 6d. for women and 3s. 3½d. for children under 16.[49] Figure 3.7 shows marked differences in 1870, too.

The weekly earnings of agricultural labourers in Co. Antrim, as laid out in A.L. Bowley's 1899 study and listed below,[50] increased in the 1870s and diminished in the 1880s, but their income was still considerably higher than the 7s. earned by most of Ballymena's handloom weavers in the century's final decade. Even with the effect of cheaper retail prices, which increased real wages,[51] handloom earnings compared unfavourably with those in paid agricultural work.[52]

46 F. Hendrickx (1997) and (1993); G. Gullickson (1986).   **47** For an excellent study that attempts to redress this imbalance, see N. Verdon (2002).   **48** For England, see P. Sharpe (1996).   **49** Return of average rate of weekly earnings of agricultural labourers in Ireland, July–December 1860 (2), HC 1862, vol. lx. Weekly earnings by task and job work were 10s. for men, 5s 6½d. for women and 3s. 9d. for children under 16, in addition to allowances for food and drink. At harvest time men's earnings rose to 12s. 8½d. Around that period, the *Ballymena Observer* noted that a weaver 'toiling to midnight, was unable to earn more than 4s. a week, and in many cases not more than 3s. 6d.' See *Observer*, 20 December 1862. Thomas Shillington, Jr. of Altavilla, Portadown, declared that earnings at the loom varied widely, but were 'very low', while agricultural labour was valued at 9s. to 10s. on average (*Working of Landlord and Tenant Act*, evidence of Thomas Shillington, 5398, 5407–10).   **50** J. Mokyr (1983) points out many deficiencies in the source-base for Bowley's estimates.   **51** H.D. Gribbon (1996), 315–17.   **52** Ibid., 319.

3.7 Agricultural wages in selected poor law unions in Ulster, 1870

Union	Increase in weekly wages in the last 20 years	Weekly	Daily	By the half-year with board and lodging
Antrim	3s. to 5s. (said to be 50%)	8s. to 12s.	1s. 4d. to 2s.	£5 to £7
Ballymoney	about 5s. (said to be 100%)	about 10s.	1s. 8d.	£5 to £7
Banbridge	2s. 6d. to 3s.	7s. to 9s.	1s. 4d. to 1s. 6d.	£5 to £7
Ballycastle	about 4s.	8s. to 9s.	1s. 4d. to 1s. 6d.	£5 to £8
Ballymena	about 3s. (said to be 60–70%)	10s.	1s. 8d.	£5 to £8
Belfast	about 3s. 6d.	10s. to 14s.	1s. 8d. to 2s. 0d.	£6 to £10
Cookstown	about 5s.	10s. to 12s.	1s. 8d. to 2s. 0d.	£5 to £7
Coleraine	about 5s.	about 9s.	1s. 6d.	£7 to £9
Dungannon	about 4s. (said to be 50%)	about 8s.	1s. 4d.	£5 to £6
Downpatrick	about 4s.	8s. to 9s.	1s. 4d. to 1s. 6d.	£6 to £7
Larne	about 3s. 6d.	8s. to 10s.	1s. 4d. to 1s. 8d.	£6 to £9
Lisburn	about 5s.	9s. to 10s.	1s. 6d. to 1s. 8d.	£5 to £7
Lurgan	about 3s.	9s. to 12s.	1s. 6d. to 2s. 0d.	£5 to £7
Magherafelt	about 2s. 6d.	about 8s.	1s. 4d.	£5 to £6
Newtownards	about 3s.	about 9s.	1s. 6d.	£5 to £7
Newtown -limavady	about 3s. 6d. (said to be 75%)	about 9s.	1s. 6d.	£4 to £7

Source: *Reports from poor law inspectors on wages of agricultural labour in Ireland*, HC 1870 [CC.35], vol. xiv, Dr Knox's Report, 5.

Agricultural work, like textile work, was characterized by deep and durable sexual divisions of labour. Women and children largely participated on a seasonal basis in such work as sowing, harvesting and potato planting, both on their own land and on other holdings.[53] Earnings differentials in agricultural labour partly account for weaving's feminization, given the relatively lower levels of female agricultural earnings, which reduced the 'opportunity cost' for rural women to

53 Women's work in agriculture did not always attract pay, but their unpaid labour was an important contribution. In 1905, for instance, it was reported that 'Except where there are market gardens

3.8 Average weekly earnings of ordinary day labourers
in Co. Antrim and Ulster in selected years, 1777–1894

Year	Antrim	Ulster	Year	Antrim	Ulster
1777	3s. 6d.	3s. 3d.	1870	11s. 0d.	8s. 3d.
1801–10	6s. 0d.	5s. 7d.	1880	—	10s. 0d.
1829	6s. 0d.	5s. 7d.	1881	11s. 0d.	—
1833–40	6s.0d.	5s. 4d.	1886	11s. 0d.	9s.10d.
1845	6s. 0d.	5s. 3d.	1893	11s. 0d.	9s.10d.
1850	7s 0d.	5s. 1d.	1894	13s. 6d.	11s. 0d.
1862	9s. 6d.	7s. 5d.			

Source: A.L. Bowley, 'The statistics of wages in the United Kingdom during the last hundred years' (1899) 395–404. This information appears on pages 400–1.

work at the loom. Young females participated in paid seasonal fieldwork and extensive unpaid work on holdings. It was noted in 1898, for instance, that 'Handloom goods become scarce in this district at certain seasons, as both men and women go to field work during harvest time, or hay time, or potato planting, &c. Girls at such work earn about 1s. 6d. a day, a higher rate than can be made by hand weaving.'[54] While reports to the Royal Commission on Labour on the Ballymena district recorded that there was a 'growing indisposition on the part of females to field labour, except on their own holdings', suggesting a withdrawal from paid agricultural labour, it may be more accurate to describe this pattern as markedly casual or seasonal participation in paid work. Women's weekly earnings during the local flax and grain harvest could be as high as 2s. daily.[55] Casual male labour during harvest and haytime earned even higher rates of pay — 3s.

near large towns', women were not often engaged in out-door work for wages, though 'wives and daughters' of small farmers assisted on the farm. In some districts, however, women were engaged, generally by the day, in such work as haymaking and harvest, weeding and hoeing, turnip lifting, potato picking, and flax pulling. Girls were also said to be 'engaged in the farmhouses for farmhouse work' (*Second report on the wages, earnings and conditions of employment of agricultural labourers in the United Kingdom*', [2376] HC 1905, vol. xcvii, 118. For a discussion on family agricultural labour, see also D. Fitzpatrick (1980). **54** *Board of Trade report*, 53. Among features of the sexual division of labour was the designation of potato-harvesting as female work. As well, at harvest time, many members of local households engaged in waged agricultural labour. See J. Bell (1979). **55** *Royal commission on labour*, The Agricultural Labourer, vol. IV, Ireland, Part V, Indexes (analytical and general) to the reports of the assistant agricultural commissioners contained in volume IV. Parts I to IV [C.6894–XXII], HC 1893–94, vol. xxxvii, pt. 1 (hereafter '*Royal Commission on Labour*'), 25, 47.

daily.[56] In Co. Antrim and in Lurgan throughout the 1880s and 1890s, the *Irish Textile Journal* described regular diminutions in handloom production during harvest time as male and female household members turned to fieldwork for several weeks.[57] Occasionally, potato-planting was contracted out by large farms, but on most holdings it was assigned to family members. By the 1890s, women mainly participated as paid workers in seasonal planting and harvesting, while able males engaged in lucrative, continuous farm work, their weekly wages considerably above those of women.[58] Women in turn contributed to the household economy through unpaid work in the field and in the home, as well as in paid industrial work that endorsed the idea of the home as women's space and her primary duty as its stewardship.[59] Handloom weaving continued on a much smaller scale than fifty years before, but for rural women, and especially daughters, it was an important element in work strategies that encompassed a multitude of tasks, paid and unpaid, centred on the domestic setting.

GENDER, WORK AND RURAL INDUSTRY

In addition to weaving, many women and girls in rural townlands such as Craigs engaged in 'making-up' industries, involving hemstitching, embroidery and finishing of articles, which drew a large pool of rural female labour into the low-paid outwork sector.[60] Representative earnings are listed in figure 3.9.

3.9 Rates of females' wages in the manufacture of handkerchiefs in Cos. Armagh, Antrim and Down, at 1 October 1886

Occupation	No.	Average weekly rate of wages
Handloom weavers (outdoor)	402	7s. 8d.
Embroiders, hemstitchers and winders (outdoor)	1,470	4s. 8d.
Hemstitchers, Machine	110	8s. 9d.

Source: *Return of wages in minor textile trades* [C.6161], HC 1890, vol. lxviii.

56 *Royal commission on labour*, 40.   57 See, for instance, *Irish Textile Journal*, 15 September 1893. 58 The rate was 9s. to 10s. 'wet and dry' for ordinary labourers with a cottage, with casual labourers earning 6s. and food in winter (*Royal commission on labour*, 37).   59 J. Bourke (1999) also makes the point that men assumed a number of domestic duties connected with the 'upkeep' of the home which challenge the rhetorical binary between male and female space.   60 R.L. Patterson (1903), 144.

In 1900, even as the *Irish Textile Journal* reported that it was hard to have hand embroidery done in the Ballymena district since earnings had been depressed by power-driven Swiss embroidery machinery, Messrs Raphael and Co. and Messrs Wolsley and Co. continued to have a 'small army of employees stretching all over the country' engaged in embroidery and the making-up of linen.[61] Shirt-manufacture, which incorporated both homework and factory stages of production, also expanded in mid-Antrim to such an extent that by the end of the 1870s Tillie and Henderson, the pre-eminent Londonderry firm, was advertising for agents in the Ballymena area.[62] In most of these domestic industries, earnings were lower than in handloom weaving; they tended to involve routinized tasks considered suitable for 'nimble' female hands. But they paralleled handloom weaving by endorsing the home as women's workspace, and resembled it in their seasonality. While the small handloom workforce was clearly drawn from households engaged in agricultural labour, those involved in other rural industries came from households in which male members, including husbands and sons, were engaged in such waged industrial work as bleaching, which had expanded throughout the last half of the century. By 1901, 95 males in Craigs townland had an occupational title related to bleaching — more than the 70 listed as farmers. By contrast, only 3 females were recorded as being employed specifically in bleaching.

The bleaching industry starkly illustrates powerful constraints imposed by gender ideologies and divisions of labour on female employment in rural textile work. Bleaching and finishing activity intensified in rural townlands between the 1850s and the turn of the century: by the 1890s, the Lisnafillan works located beside Ballymena had a workforce of 200.[63] In the townlands of Kildrum and Lisnawhiggle, dye and finishing works owned by John Hanna covered many acres of land, and were enlarged in 1885–6.[64] In contrast with other areas, mid-Antrim's bleachgreens — historic centres of rural industry — drew heavily on male labour. Like handloom weaving, the gendering of bleaching work varied by locality, and ultimately by the types of cloth being finished on the greens.[65] The differentiated bleaching workforces in Ulster were illuminated by the 1854–5 report of a commissioner charged with exploring whether the Factory Acts should be extended to bleaching and finishing concerns. Female workers in bleaching and finishing firms were mainly employed in stove-fired drying rooms most common in districts of handkerchief manufacture where cambric and other similar cloth was finished. Messrs Richardson and Co., of the Lambeg Bleach-Works in Lisburn, for instance, employed 136 females out of a total workforce of 300 — and most of them in stove rooms where handkerchiefs were finished.[66] In a small Lurgan

61 *Irish Textile Journal*, 15 January 1900.   **62** J.A. Grew (1987), 191.   **63** *R. McCrea report*, 86.   **64** G.H. Bassett (1888a), 287.   **65** The salience of sexually differentiated work alternatives is underscored by G. Gullickson (1981) and (1986).   **66** *Report of the commissioner appointed to inquire how far it may be advisable to extend the provisions of the acts for the better regulation of mills and fac-*

concern which was dedicated solely to the bleaching and finishing of cambric cloth, 39 of 63 employees were females.[67] In such concerns, the proportion of female labour was considerably higher than in places where other linen cloth was bleached and finished. In areas where the technology of the stoves was not used, males dominated almost all work on the bleachgreen — with women usually engaged only in folding and a few other tasks. In mid-Antrim far fewer females were employed in the bleaching sector, which siphoned off male hands from rural industrial households and encouraged female members to look for paid alternatives to weaving, such as outwork, in rural industrial areas. As we have seen previously in this chapter, these rural areas were not major local weaving centres in mid-Antrim by 1901.

Local employment in bleaching increased dramatically between 1851 and 1901, despite the overall decrease in the population of Craigs townland. In 1900, it was reported that the Lisnafillan Bleaching, Dyeing and Finishing Co., located on Ballymena's borders, employed some 200 hands — double the level of twenty years previously.[68] Local bleaching concerns such as the Hillmount Bleach Green, outside Cullybackey, also expanded in the last quarter of the century. Hillmount had originally largely bleached Ballymenas, but by 1888 its work was chiefly on fine damask cloth, sheetings and household linens, with an average weekly turnout in that year of 2,000 pieces by the firm's 200 employees.[69] The nearby Lisnafillan Bleaching concern turned out some 3,000 pieces weekly, including Ballymenas, but also plain linen-cambrics and cottons and woven bordered handkerchiefs.[70] Located near the key transportation hub of Ballymena, they serviced the province's linen sector and provided extensive local employment — mostly to men in rural industrial districts such as Craigs, where population loss was not as dramatic as in some farming districts, where handloom weaving activity had declined markedly, and where the remnant of the handloom workforce was a small group of adult daughters resident with one or more parents, and an elderly cohort of male weavers.

CONTOURS OF A LONG DECLINE: WOMEN, WEAVING AND WORK

In complex work strategies, rural women undertook housework and tended to their households' holdings, but they also engaged in seasonal paid agricultural

tories to bleaching works established in certain parts of the United Kingdom of Great Britain and Ireland [1943], Minutes of evidence, HC 1854–55, vol. xviii, evidence of Messrs Richardson and Co., Lambeg, Bleach-Works, Lisburn, q. 904–5.   67 Ibid., evidence of Mr Henry Martin, manager, Messrs Thomas and Charles Richardson, Springfield, Lurgan, q. 966.   68 *Irish Textile Journal*, 15 January 1900, 12.   69 *Irish Textile Journal*, 15 December 1888, 139–40   70 Ibid. Other concerns discussed in this article are the Moorfields Dyeing and Finishing Co., which specialized in the dyeing and finishing of cotton goods, and Arthur and Co., Greenfield, Kells, which specialised in linen and union

labour, and occasionally wove cloth.[71] Combining paid and unpaid labour, and work in industry and in agriculture, they contributed to household livelihood strategies that also expressed durable sexual divisions of labour in a variety of work. However between 1851 and 1901 the most marked feature of the weaving trade in mid-Antrim was its diminishing size, and the persistence of pockets of weavers, especially in farming districts. They were mainly aged men and daughters of rural waged labourers. This survey of mid-Antrim's weaving workforce in the second half of the nineteenth century illustrates the extent of rural social differentiation, feminization and casualization in the shirting trade, as well as the broad contours of its decline. As the weaving population in the district changed, becoming centred on a cottier class, and the status of shirting weaving declined, masculine claims to skills proprietorship and the public representation of weaving craftsmanship in Ulster were constructed in opposition to casual, female-dominated weaving, with skill denoting masculine expertise.

goods for the Belfast trade.   **71** *Royal commission on labour*, 22, 28. See also A. O' Dowd (1994).

4

Labour and craft in post-Famine Ulster

By the last decades of the nineteenth century the image of the independent weaver-farmer, lauded as the emblem of the linen trade's 'golden age', had dissolved. Two stark types had emerged as the face of handloom weaving: the casual 'secondary' female weaver working in low-paid branches of manufacture and the skilled male weaver in more regular, remunerative employment. Although there were other handloom workers, including aged men, these two categories provided poles around which discourses of handloom skill were formulated. The content of handloom skill varied, but two ideas lay at its core — that skilled weaving was an especially complex technical process; and that male practitioners of the craft enjoyed relative autonomy and authority over production. Contests over these two elements of handloom skill were important expositions on gender. Outside Ireland, the politics of Europe's rural industrial workers, including handloom weavers, lie at the heart of research into nineteenth-century social and labour history, which explores the mobilization of artisans, especially males, in large-scale movements later in the century.[1] In contrast, the putatively early eclipse of textile hand production in the United Kingdom, a corollary to the UK's precocious industrialization, has largely removed the British and Irish handloom weavers from such inquiries, constructing instead a narrative of their early nineteenth-century proletarianization, involving fitful but fruitless acts of resistance against the advent of new organizational systems and deskilling technologies.[2] In Ireland, a focus on agrarian politics and on urban textile labour has also contributed to the construction of two poles of scholarly investigation — the rural agricultural and urban industrial worlds — largely neglecting rural handloom weavers who straddled them in the second half of the nineteenth century.[3] The most ambitious structural synthesis of the linen sector and Ulster politics after 1850, Peter Gibbon's *Origins of Ulster Unionism*, is premised on the eclipse of the rural handloom and the development of urban systems of industrial produc-

---

1 See, for instance, the work of G. Crossick & H-G. Haupt (1995) and (1984); J.H. Quataert (1987). **2** The classic expression of this view is E.P. Thompson (1963). **3** Early explorations of the social base of Irish nationalism focused on farmer and rural labourers, largely excluding rural industrial hand producers: see S. Clark (1979); P. Bew (1978). Within Irish labour history, the focus has tended to be on urban trades: see, for instance, E. O'Connor (1992) and J.W. Boyle (1988). In Ulster the focus has clearly been on the position of labour within large-scale urban production in particular, as previous chapters have shown. A useful study analyzing artisnal labour in the nineteenth century is Maura Cronin (1994).

tion. It offers no analysis of rural weavers after the 1850s.[4] Gibbon also argues that processes of capitalist development eroded the autonomous handloom weaving 'interest' in Ulster's linen trade by mid-century. The diversity of the weaving workforce undermines the idea of a monolithic interest, and the gendered public representation of handloom skill casts another of Gibbon's claims in doubt. Weavers' voices in the late-nineteenth century expressed neither the homogenizing experience of proletarianization nor definitive eclipse; instead they revealed pronounced cleavages within the workforce, centred on sex and skill.

While the relationship between sectarianism and skill lies at the core of industrial labour history in Ireland, sexual divisions of labour demand closer attention in the analysis of the handloom trade. This chapter explores strategies through which weavers formulated claims to skill in the late-nineteenth and early-twentieth centuries, and the influence of gender over these claims. In the 1870s and 1880s, in mid-Antrim and elsewhere, contests over the putative diminution of craft authority centred on workers' claims that customary rights were eroding. The scope of their political activity expanded considerably with the extension of the franchise and the incorporation of male weavers within electoral politics. They embarked upon a concerted campaign, articulated through trade associations, to assert proprietorship over handloom skill. Sometimes observers regarded these efforts as reflexive responses to new technology — in 1907 one writer dismissed them by claiming that 'We all know that steam power has been steadily supplanting the primitive forces of manual labour for a couple of generations, and that it has generally been met with the most stern hostility on the part of those who were engaged in the old methods.'[5] But weavers achieved notable successes in securing legislative protection and wider social validation of handloom craftsmanship, endorsing claims to skill which were also expositions on status and gender.

HANDLOOM WEAVING AFTER 1870: THE COMMERCIAL TERRAIN

Sexual divisions of labour in the cambric, damask and shirting branches evolved as the trade changed. By the late 1860s and the early 1870s, competition, protectionism and variable demand for linen products transformed the commercial environment in which the Irish trade operated. During the 1870s, the value and quantity of yarn exports fell, as figure 4.1 illustrates. By the 1880s European com-

---

4 Studies of urban Ulster and Irish labour have tended, through their almost exclusive focus on the urban and factory setting, to overlook rural textile production after 1850. For urban history, see A.C. Hepburn (1996); for politics, see C. Hirst (2002); P. Gibbon (1975); H. Patterson (1980a). In F. Wright (1996), regions outside Belfast are explored in some depth (383–431) — a welcome corrective, especially in his engagement of smaller urban centres. In Irish labour history, key studies have focused on the factory setting: see, for instance, Emmet O'Connor (1992), 35–7; M. Greiff (1997); B. Messenger (1978); M. Cohen (1997). 5 *Irish Textile Journal*, 15 October 1907.

petitors undercut Irish yarn abroad and increased their share of the UK yarn market. Irish yarn exports declined precipitously after 1875, only stabilizing around 1880 at levels considerably below those of the 1860s. Irish spindle capacity also reached a high of 924,817 in 1875, diminishing only slightly thereafter. Indeed, though in 1900 the number of spindles stood at 843,934, the relatively small diminution belied the fact that many more spindles and mills sat idle as trade bodies such as the Power-Spinners' Association organized industry-wide responses to slumping demand by reducing yarn output.[6]

While the quantity and value of linen yarn exports fell in the 1870s, cloth piece rates also declined. The Irish industry faced mounting competition from continental countries that adopted mechanized production methods. It also encountered stiff tariff barriers in major export markets and intensifying competition from cheaper cotton fabrics.[7] All of these factors conspired against the Irish industry's expansion, and its experience of growth and high profits, buoyed by strong demand in the early- and mid-1860s, was a distant memory by the middle of the next decade.

Facing foreign competition, protectionism and over-supply, commercial practices that governed the export trade to America in the 1860s — cash payments in ten days or one month, with a 5% or 6% trade discount, respectively — also changed. They were lengthened by the early-1870s to sixty days and to four months, with a 5% discount for payment in thirty days, 4% for sixty days, 3% for ninety days and 2% for four months.[8] Additionally, some American purchasers were able to demand a lengthening of the date of payment and a *de facto* 5% discount on four months' payment. Facing these challenges, manufacturers lobbied the government for legal instruments to increase their authority over hand producers and, through them, over systems of cloth supply. They met fierce resistance from weavers who believed that such changes undermined customary relations, challenged the formulation of handloom skill which privileged craft autonomy, and threatened their livelihoods.

Weavers encountered the fluctuating commercial climate in a variety of ways. The Ballymena shirting trade, by the century's end, was very much in decline, as the previous chapter outlined. Indeed, when the *Irish Textile Journal*'s Ballymena correspondent surveyed the locality in January 1900, and remarked favourably on a renewed demand for linen cloth, he lamented that in the handloom trade, 'production is not by any means up to what it should be owing to the very bad

---

6 Sir R.L Patterson, 'The British flax and linen industry' (1903), 126.   7 France, Brazil, Austria, Denmark and Sweden all levied tariffs of around 25% on the value of linen imports. In August 1870, the rate of tariffs in the largest market for Irish linen exports, the United States, stood at 30 to 40%, depending on the class of good. Exports to American markets had declined considerably, with the United States taking just over a third of exports in 1867 and 1868, down from almost half in 1866 (Robert Donnell, 'The linen trade and the customs duties', *Journal of the Statistical and Social Inquiry Society of Ireland* 5 [1870], 196–212, especially 197).   8 *Irish Textile Journal*, 15 May 1887.

4.1 Quantity and value of selected classes of linen goods exported from the United Kingdom, 1868–86

Year	Plain linen (bleached or unbleached)			Linen (printed, checked or dyed and damask)		
	Quantities (yards)	Value (£)	Value per yard (d.)	Quantities (yards)	Value (£)	Value per yard (d.)
1868	197,635,508	6,173,898	7.50	8,887,854	344,902	9.31
1869	204,658,286	6,022,230	7.06	7,131,957	268,211	9.03
1870	210,405,228	6,271,734	7.15	12,405,841	421,178	8.15
1871	207,041,820	6,377,010	7.39	9,296,124	311,538	8.04
1872	233,838,338	7,241,338	7.43	7,397,940	233,736	7.58
1873	195,404,195	6,204,800	7.62	8,197,598	260,639	7.63
1874	180,926,285	5,876,864	7.79	8,987,132	287,754	7.68
1875	186,763,770	5,904,958	7.59	13,742,124	470,295	8.21
1876	146,666,075	4,365,072	7.14	13,181,129	449,918	8.19
1877	159,274,650	4,597,665	6.92	14,411,156	471,982	7.86
1878	147,499,700	4,423,879	7.20	9,719,600	299,204	7.39
1879	149,661,000	4,140,302	7.08	6,559,700	200,396	7.33
1880	156,689,600	4,818,841	7.38	4,987,600	150,182	7.23
1881	165,217,600	4,838,664	7.03	5,487,100	161,023	7.04
1882	165,899,200	4,761,271	6.89	6,952,400	234,948	8.11
1883	152,163,000	4,408,454	6.95	6,576,600	213,616	7.80
1884	143,672,800	3,961,692	6.62	6,983,200	188,115	6.47
1885	138,186,600	3,653,817	6.34	7,219,200	206,584	6.87
1886	152,314,800	3,795,333	5.98	8,368,000	218,789	6.27

Source: *Flax Supply Association annual report for 1886* (1887), 58.

conditions of trade which so long prevailed in this end'.[9] Prices had been so depressed that weavers had turned to other pursuits, 'and now when prices have improved the result is that handloom fabrics cannot be produced at the present time with the rapidity required, or with even the same degree of efficiency as formerly'. Yet in other districts and branches, conditions favoured handloom production for a longer time. In damask, for instance, the prohibitive costs of mechanization militated against the adoption of powerlooms and led to distinctive systems of industrial organization. It was estimated in 1910 that powerlooms to produce light and narrow linens cost between £40 and £50, while those required for making wide damasks or sheetings could cost £100 to £200 per loom.[10] Indeed, Lurgan handloom manufacturers in 1912 claimed that there was no difference between handloom and powerloom articles in some ends of the damask trade, except that they lacked the 'very considerable amount of capital' required to move production to machines.[11] Handloom production was now centred on these classes of goods, often in workshops, where manufacturers provided weavers with looms.[12] In 1902, the *Irish Textile Journal* declared:

> The time-honoured handloom has not yet become as silent as the proverbial 'Sythestone at Christmas,' for, notwithstanding the strides of modern thought in its application to textile production, all old persons who adhere to cambric and damask weaving according to the methods of half a century ago, can find employment still. The powerloom is, none the less, pressing on to its inevitable monopoly.[13]

Insulated to varying degrees from mechanization, the fine cambric and damask branches' fortunes fluctuated through the first decade of the century, though handloom cambric was frequently described as a trade in which 'the expiring generation only' was engaged. Observers' remarks on cambric's ageing, low-waged workforce echoed their earlier comments in the last years of the Ballymena shirting trade.[14] By the turn of the twentieth century, the damask trade was the main preserve of handloom labour — and the main arena for the negotiation of skill. It remained buoyant in the first years of the new century, which coincided with the decisive end of the shirting trade in Ballymena. While cambric handloom weavers were described in

---

9 *Irish Textile Journal*, 15 January 1900.   **10** Sir W. Crawford, *Irish linen and some features of its production* (1910), 10.   **11** *Report of the departmental committee with regard to the application of the National Insurance Act to outworkers in Ireland*, vol. II, Minutes of evidence and appendices [Cd. 7686], HC 1914–16, vol. xxxi [hereafter '*Outworkers in Ireland*'], evidence of A.N. Ireland and W.R. McMurray, q. 1373 and 1386.   **12** Handlooms were also expensive and beyond the reach of some weavers. In 1912 representatives of the Handloom Weavers' Association reported that less than one-half of weavers rented their looms from their employers. (*Outworkers in Ireland*, evidence of James Wood, q. 420–421).   **13** *Irish Textile Journal*, 15 May 1902.   **14** *Irish Textile Journal*, 15 August 1906. See also *Irish Textile Journal*, 15 February 1907.

1903 as 'old weavers located in the rural districts' engaged in a trade which the *Irish Textile Journal* believed would soon 'be a thing of the past',[15] in damask the situation was described as 'very different'. At the turn of the twentieth century, cambric production was based in the Co. Armagh districts of the Lurgan poor law union on both sides of the Bann, while the Co. Down divisions of the Union were primarily regions of damask production.[16] In the damask districts, the *Irish Textile Journal* reported that the trade was 'expected to survive the advance of power competition for a long time to come'; conversely, in cambric districts, handloom weaving was 'dying out' at a rapid pace.[17] Wages in damask and cambric weaving differed, as did the organizational systems under which weavers worked. Cambric weavers usually worked for a number of agents on the outwork system, while damask weavers often worked exclusively for one manufacturer, being unable to afford expensive damask looms on their own accounts. The cambric workforce was sexually mixed: one Lurgan agent claimed that his workforce of 60 weavers comprised 35 women. It also displayed the internal, sexual work divisions characteristic of other handloom branches, with 'highly-skilled' weavers earning 12*s.* weekly, and others, principally 'girls', earning 7*s.* in the years before the Great War.[18] While W.H. Crawford has identified a number of women recorded as damask weavers in several townlands in Co. Down in 1901, more than two-thirds were male, compared to less than half of those identified as cambric weavers or weavers of undefined cloth.[19] Clearly there was dissonance between the public representation of damask labour and the composition of the labour force; male damask weavers sought to resolve these contradictions through discourses of skill. The home industries revival, so effectively harnessed by male damask weavers celebrated highly-gendered 'craft trades', whether lacemaking (female), tweed-weaving (male) or many other small-scale domestic activities. The wider programme of home industries revival, with its explicit gendering of craft skill, seemed at odds with a handloom trade in which the workforce had been sexually-mixed for decades. Yet male weavers dominated handloom trade associations, placing them in a powerful position to shape the public discourses on skill, and to construct male weaving as a handicraft industry. The Handloom Weavers' Society, which was based near Lurgan in Waringstown, Co. Down, had a male membership of 700 to 800 in 1912, more than three-quarters of whom were weavers of damask cloth. Far fewer cambric weavers were involved, damask weavers claimed, because they could not afford membership in the Society.[20] This trade body also gave expression to sexual divisions in the workforce and a highly gendered evaluation of skill. It limited its

15 *Irish Textile Journal*, 16 March 1903. **16** *Irish Textile Journal*, 15 February 1900. **17** Ibid. **18** *Outworkers in Ireland*, evidence of R.G. Lonnsdale, q. 1778–9. See also the evidence of James Wood, who gave as daily damask wages 2*s.* 6*d.*, in contrast with 1*s.* 6*d.* for cambric (q. 430). **19** W.H. Crawford (1993), 6. **20** *Outworkers in Ireland*, evidence of representatives of the Handloom Weavers' Association, q. 395–406; 12*s.* to 18*s.* could be earned weekly at the damask loom, 10*s.* to

membership to male 'heads of families', claiming to speak, through them, for their 'children and wives'.[21] This restriction had implications for how handloom skill was formulated and defended by the Society.

In the damask district embracing Lurgan, Waringstown, Donacloney, Bleary and Dollingstown, as well as in Lisburn, Banbridge and Ardoyne, the *Irish Textile Journal* estimated that some 1,200 looms were at work in 1910.[22] Portadown's (largely male) handloom weavers were a significant component of this labour force, even if by 1888 their numbers had fallen by 1,500 to 2,500. Commenting on that district, G.H. Bassett remarked that 'The young people are not following the occupation of their fathers to an appreciable extent, and a great many of the families have emigrated. The powerloom has been resisted as long as possible, but it has latterly been coming into fashion here with a rush.'[23] Continuing use of the handloom two decades later belied this claim, but the extent of handloom activity had certainly diminished. A local government board inspector, commenting on the handloom trade, contrasted Lurgan and Ballymena, where the trade 'was dying out and had almost ceased to exist'.[24] And in a December 1901 report on the 'Decay of the Handloom', the *Irish Textile Journal*, predicting that there would always be some work in branches for which the powerloom was ill-suited, called upon the Department of Agriculture and Technical Instruction to aid in the modernization of handlooms by replacing the 'old-fashioned, cumbersome affairs that have been in the family of the weaver for generations'.[25] The *Irish Textile Journal* sounded a cautionary note in 1907, however, observing that 'The damask has withstood the inroads of mechanical development about fifty years longer than the plain [cloth]; but the handloom must give way as it is displaced by the powerloom in the damask trade as well as in the plain.'[26] Endorsing this view, W.T. Macartney-Filgate, an official in the Department of Agriculture and Technical Instruction, declared in 1912 that:

> powerloom materials, as my samples prove, have largely supplanted handwoven. The following is an instance of the competition between power

12*s*. for cambric weaving and 5*s*. to 8*s*. for coarser classes of goods (*Outworkers in Ireland*, evidence of W.T. Macartney-Filgate, q. 258a, 259, 260).   **21** *Outworkers in Ireland*, evidence of James Wood, q. 404–8.   **22** *Irish Textile Journal*, 15 February 1910.   **23** In other districts, co-extensive hand and powerloom production was evident in the second half of the nineteenth century. In Donacloney, Co. Armagh, Messrs William Liddell and Sons owned an extensive powerloom factory, but also engaged a large pool of handloom weavers to supplement mechanized production. Elsewhere, Messrs John S. Brown and Sons operated a powerloom factory in St Ellen's, Co. Down, but also engaged 1,500 handloom weavers in Ulster and 3,000 'wives and daughters of small farmers at hand embroidery' (G. H. Bassett, *Book of County Armagh* (1888b), 277).   **24** *Irish Textile Journal*, 15 March 1901. **25** *Irish Textile Journal*, 15 December 1901.   **26** *Irish Textile Journal*, 15 October 1907. It was also reported in 1912 that damask handloom weavers were entering powerloom factories and abandoning their trade (*Outworkers in Ireland*, evidence of representatives of the Handloom Weavers' Association, q. 411).

and hand in the damask trade. Within the last 10 years a certain regular order to special design for table-cloths and napkins was executed entirely on the handloom. A powerloom manufacturer tendered and secured the order. Tenders were called again for this year, and the original makers, not wishing to lose the custom, tendered for a powerloom article and again secured the work, but it is lost for ever to the handloom.[27]

Still, damask weavers remained the highest-paid workers in a dramatically reduced workforce that, numbering only a few thousand, was by the early-twentieth century, smaller than in the 1870s and 80s. Mobilized by trade associations, weavers attempted to claim influence over the management of the trade and construct an alternative discourse to that of displacement by machinery. Their efforts to win recognition of the handloom as an instrument of craft work, however, were premised on a narrow definition of industrial skill.

HANDLOOM WEAVING AFTER 1870: THE LEGAL TERRAIN

Throughout the 1860s, the putting-out trade was regulated by what one legal commentator described as a 'small code of laws', building on statutes that governed the sector following the Board of Trustees' dissolution in 1828.[28] Most special laws passed before 1840 regulated open-market activity, while later legislation focused on the putting-out trade, addressing such problems as embezzlement.[29] Throughout the 1870s, manufacturers complained that the law was weak and did not confer on them, or on legal officers, sufficient authority to monitor production in a dispersed workforce. These debates elevated to the national stage conflicts over the trade which had developed in local markets. As in mid-Antrim, most handloom weavers in Ulster worked for more than one manufacturer; fewer wove in urban workshops or exclusively for one employer. Henry Cinnamon, a manufacturer who organized handloom handkerchief cloth production in Portadown, complained before the 1864 Children's Employment Commission that '[t]he greatest difficulty with a handloom manufacturer is the not getting his webs returned, because most weavers weave for four or five different offices, and so keep back the work of one to do some for another. I have webs out now that have been out 12 months, but what good should I get by such measures? So it is best to save trouble and expense. I have been speaking of not only this place but the district for some miles round.'[30]

27 *Outworkers in Ireland*, evidence of W.T. Macartney-Filgate, q. 260. 28 A.H. Bates, 'Irish linen laws and proposed amendments thereof', *Journal of the Statistical and Social Inquiry Society of Ireland* 8 (1881), 203. 29 Ibid., 206–7. 30 *Royal commission on the employment of children in trades and manufactories not regulated by law* (3414), HC 1864, vol. xxiv; Evidence upon the handloom weaving and hosiery manufactures in Ireland and Scotland, collected by Mr J.E. White, evidence of Henry Cinnamon, q. 3.

Manufacturers such as Cinnamon demanded more powerful legal instruments to enforce weaving contracts as trading conditions worsened and as new legislation circumscribed the old linen code by incorporating common law provisions from which it had historically been exempted. Weavers, for their part, characterized these efforts as broad attacks on customary relations.

In 1875 the Masters' and Servants' Act changed the Expiring Laws Continuance Acts which had been passed to continue main linen trade legislation. Important provisions of the 1840 legislation were excised, including the authority of justices of the peace to convict weavers under summary jurisdiction if they kept a web after eight days (with a penalty of forfeiture and £5), as well as the reciprocal rights of weavers to seek summary remedies against manufacturers who failed to supply them with yarn to complete their work. The absence of these provisions from the Continuance Act of 1876 met with strong protests from the Linen Merchants' Association.[31] That year, after an abortive effort by the chief secretary, Sir Michael Hicks-Beach, to introduce new, revised main linen legislation, a committee of weavers and manufacturers met in Lurgan to advise on a bill. Under John Hancock, chairman of the town commissioners, a large meeting was held in the town on 11 October 1876. Hancock hoped that a new bill would place the trade on a sound legal footing: he recommended that remnants of the seal-master system, now in abeyance, be abolished, in light of the near-universal prevalence of putting-out and workshop weaving.[32] Thomas Carleton, a solicitor retained by local weavers, agreed that the ticketing system (which set contracts between weavers and manufacturers) required reform. But he insisted that the time given to weavers to produce cloth was often unreasonably short, and reminded manufacturers that weavers enjoyed no rights to interim payments as they worked. When William Liddell, a manufacturer and JP, disputed this claim, a local weaver, John Henry, asserted that they paid between £20 and £30 to equip themselves for the trade. A committee comprising four manufacturers and four weavers (two of cambric and two of damask cloth, and all male) was struck to address these various questions, under Hancock's chairmanship.

By the time the committee presented its findings in December, its members had reached broad agreement that elements of two earlier acts governing the trade be retained, and that special legislation which denied weavers and manufacturers provisions in common law be abandoned. Lurgan's handloom workforce numbered

---

31 *News Letter,* 15 November 1878. The Linen Merchants' Association in Belfast was established by fifty-two subscribing firms to advance the interests of the trade through 'the regulation and protection of the trade: the settlement of disputes by arbitration: the bringing before Parliament bills tending to further the interests of the linen business: and the carrying out of all projects likely to promote the advancement and prosperity of the Staple Manufacture'.   **32** He also characterized existing contracts between weavers and manufacturers as unnecessarily 'minute', and held that the 'rise and fall of prices' was a matter for negotiation between weavers and manufacturers, rather than legislation (*Portadown and Lurgan News and Co. Armagh Advertiser*, 14 October 1876).

in the thousands, and had demonstrated its strength in crippling strikes a few years earlier, when weavers held back their work. Manufacturers pointed to this agitation as an example of why harsher provisions were required to deter embezzlement.[33] No doubt cognizant of this earlier conflict, Major Waring, JP expressed 'hope that the weavers in the present crisis would not be led away from the question by any agitation or flowery eloquence'.[34] In 1877 the Linen Merchants' Association drafted a proposal for a new act under which President John Young and Belfast mayor Sir John Preston suggested that weavers be required to give security for the completion of work and be liable for a penalty of up to £20 if it were not completed. On 15 November 1878 the *News-Letter* reported that the government was considering modified versions of these proposals. A subsequent bill was examined in a paper presented before the Linen Merchants' Association in June 1878. They praised the reintroduction of provisions for summary prosecution and higher penalties. Manufacturers from Portadown, Lurgan, Ballymena and Belfast suggested additional changes.[35] The Association also argued that stronger provisions were necessary to secure the property of manufacturers from distraint.[36]

The Association's proposed amendments won support from the Belfast Chamber of Commerce, whose representatives joined members of the Association when they met with the chief secretary later in November 1878. The linen magnate and MP William Ewart stressed the importance of the putting-out system to Ulster's economy. Indeed, he argued that its importance made stringent governance of the trade critical: 'A large part of the linen manufacture of Ireland was conducted on the old system of handloom weaving, the manufacturers giving out yarn to the weavers to be taken to their own homes. Great temptation was thus put in the way of the weavers to improperly dispose of the property.'[37] The arch-Conservative *News-Letter* agreed and opined on 15 November 1878 that 'Manufacturers in the rural districts, who have thousands of pounds worth of their property scattered through numerous country houses, and who may be heavy losers by defaulting or dishonest weavers, require stringent laws to protect their property, and ought to have a large measure of power in their hands'. Samuel Black, a leading linen merchant, estimated that handloom weavers were in possession of some £40,000 worth of manufacturers' property, making its protection a priority.[38] Proponents of new legislation argued that new provisions would also benefit manufacturers in the powerloom trade, whose workers could purloin goods.[39] But the government watched this debate cautiously from the sidelines, cognizant of the increasingly vocal protests from weavers' associations and reluctant to appear to endorse 'class legislation'.

---

33 *Irish Times*, 3 November 1880.   **34** In *Portadown and Lurgan News and Co. Armagh Advertiser*, 30 December 1876.   **35** Minutes of the Linen Merchants Association, PRONI, Belfast, D/2088/1/1, 25 June 1878.   **36** *News-Letter*, 15 November 1878.   **37** *Weekly Northern Whig*, 23 November 1878.   **38** Ibid.   **39** *News-Letter*, 15 November 1878.

The new proposals were withdrawn after the second reading in 1878, but a year later the chief secretary, James Lowther, introduced a new Bill containing many of the same provisions. Weavers holding the property of manufacturers for longer than fourteen days after having received notice in writing to return them, without a reasonable explanation, would be considered to have embezzled the articles. They could be subject to summary jurisdiction and to the forfeiture of the goods and a penalty not exceeding £10.[40] This third bill was blocked by Charles Stewart Parnell as part of his campaign of general parliamentary disruption. When he finally withdrew his opposition to the government's measures, it was set aside due to the pressures of other business.

Manufacturers and merchants continued efforts to have new legislation introduced, complaining that the absence of strict mechanisms to prosecute embezzlement imperiled the fragile putting-out system and therefore the survival of Ireland's handloom trade.[41] In a meeting with the chief secretary in 1880, for instance, a deputation of the Belfast Chamber of Commerce and the Linen Merchants' Association complained that 'dishonest, slothful, and careless' weavers had exploited the legal limbo in which the trade operated, and that a restoration of the manufacturers' right of recourse to summary jurisdiction was required.[42] The chief secretary declined to accede to their request. James N. Richardson, MP, argued before him that some £5,000,000 in capital was employed in the handloom trade, with 100,000 weavers at work in Ireland, and an average of £500,000 worth of manufacturers' goods in their hands.[43] The mid-Antrim linen merchant John Young argued that since handloom weavers were generally poor and unable to offer security on their work, the threat of stringent punishment was necessary to deter theft. But the chief secretary was reluctant to accede to Young's request to see a bill reintroduced in the Parliament.

> It seems to me the best course after all is for the employer not to employ the weaver who acts improperly. Independently of the merits of the question, all these matters are of very great and special interest to particular localities. Any bill dealing with them is not regarded as first importance before the House or Government, and such bills are very difficult to carry, especially if there is obstruction. It would be an enormous advantage if there could be some arrangement in the matter. If some gentleman connected with the trade brought in a bill which would go before a Select Committee, the Government could give its support to it.[44]

The government was wary of entering into the debate, and was concerned that any legislation to which weavers objected strongly would be seen as overtly

---

40 Ibid.　**41** *Belfast Morning News*, 3 November 1880.　**42** *Irish Times*, 3 November 1880.　**43** *Irish Times*, 3 November 1880.　**44** Ibid.

antagonistic to hand producers. Three successive bills had been introduced in the House of Commons. None had received passage.[45] By the 1880s, the chief debate within the handloom trade shifted to new questions of how the erosion of craft status could be resisted and how the dexterity and complexity demanded of skilled handloom manufacturers could be highlighted in opposition to the routines of powerloom production, especially after male weavers began to flex their muscles in electoral contests following the 1884 franchise expansion, which incorporated many of them within the electorate.

HANDLOOM WEAVING AFTER 1870: THE POLITICAL TERRAIN

If fierce debate, then stalemate, attended efforts to re-define legal relations between weavers and manufacturers, weavers found aggressive parliamentary champions for an agenda of 'trade protection' later in the 1880s. Their rhetoric no longer emphasizing the need to 'restore' weavers' customary rights, handloom workers advocated a programme premised on protecting their unique skills, castigated powerloom manufactures and tapped into a growing movement that celebrated rural industrial skill as a national craft tradition. Handloom weavers' efforts to win trade protection in the 1880s were especially vigorous after 1884, when the Franchise Act empowered male members of the highly-localized handloom workforce in Ulster — especially in Lurgan, where weavers were at the vanguard of efforts to secure expanded legislative protection for their trade.

Though Lurgan was a religiously diverse urban centre, there is limited evidence of a stable relationship between sectarian divisions and handloom skill in Ulster, compared to the strong links between sex and skill. In mid-Antrim, where in many districts the rural population was overwhelmingly Protestant,[46] the denominational complexion of the workforce largely corresponded to that of the wider population. In Lurgan, especially after 1884, there were veiled appeals to weavers 'loyalty' issued by men such as the Conservative Col. Edward Saunderson, who led the campaign for trade protection at Westminster. He assiduously courted Protestant handloom weavers in his Lurgan constituency as he attempted to incorporate them within a unionist class alliance that he envisaged as an alternative to co-operation in agrarian reform. His entreaties to the weavers were encoded in public utterances as appeals to the 'loyalty' and industry of the operative weaving class.[47] Indeed, such strategies were part of a wider programme to strengthen the

---

45 The bill introduced by Sir Michael Hicks-Beach in 1876 had been withdrawn without debate, the 1878 bill had been withdrawn after second reading, and Lowther's 1879 bill had been abandoned after first reading without debate (Bates [1881], 205). **46** In the townland of Craigs, the Protestant and the Presbyterian weaving populations were diverse: 20 of the 47 weavers were recorded as 'Presbyterian' alone. Another 10 were recorded as Reformed Presbyterian, United Free Church of Scotland and other Presbyterian denominations. Eleven were Episcopalian, 4 were 'Christian', one was listed as 'not Christian' and one entry was unclear. **47** A. Jackson (1995), 68; K.T. Hoppen (1984)

social base of what Frank Wright has characterized as a 'plebeian conservatism', and they found fertile ground in Protestant weaving areas when they were allied to an agenda of protective legislation. The position of handloom weavers within populist labour politics has largely been ignored, in favour of highlighting the activities of the urban industrial working class, especially in the shipyards of Belfast.[48] But the trade was organized outside sectarian frameworks, and made only conditional alliances with unionists, as well as representatives of Labour and other groups in Parliament. Could the handloom weavers, long seen as key generators of sectarianism in the late-eighteenth century,[49] have generated alternative discourses on labour and skill that primarily asserted the gendered, rather than sectarian, proprietorship of craft skill? The rhetoric of craftsmen's protection certainly resonated with the Labour Representation Committee in Westminister, which took up their cause in the early twentieth century, and the discourses of status and skill which they advanced were forceful expositions on gender premised on the 'natural' correspondence between masculine work and weaving skill.

The rhetoric of craft, sex and status was deployed on a public stage as male weavers participated in a network of local trade bodies and in electoral contests. They forged conditional alliances with a range of figures, from Edward Saunderson to the countess of Aberdeen to the populist unionist Thomas Sloan and independent British Labour representatives who sought to incorporate their demands within a wider programme to protect skilled 'craftsmen'. Saunderson styled himself a champion of the handloom weaving interest in Parliament — a strategy that enhanced the non-factory 'skilled' male industrial base of populist unionism to counter the threat that Sloan posed to the incorporation of working-class labour within the unionist alliance.[50] In this respect, appeals to the trade's skilled aristocracy, while not overtly sectarian, were encoded in language that was familiar to the Protestant working class — and aimed to build solidarities between Saunderson and his local handloom weaving constituents. Appeals to a gendered notion of skill, however, were much more explicit. Lurgan weavers offered Saunderson their endorsement in 1885.[51] In 1888 he introduced legislation in response to proposals by Lurgan's 'Handloom Weavers' Defence Association' which aimed to restore some of the offices and functions of the old seal-master system to enforce common commercial practices and standards of measurement in the putting-out trade. Lurgan weavers issued a manifesto in support of the bill and claimed that they otherwise would slide into a condition of exploitation which they colourfully described as the handloom 'slave trade':

331–2.   **48** H. Patterson (1980a); P. Gibbon (1975).   **49** N. Curtin (1997), D.W. Miller (1983).   **50** The mid-Antrim Tory W.R. Young, himself a self-styled friend of the weaving interest, and a key actor in the Ballymena market, broke with Saunderson over his support of protective legislation for the trade. See A. Jackson (1995), 121. On Sloan, and the debate over the movement that he led, see J. Boyle (1962) and H. Patterson (1980b).   **51** F. Wright (1996), 496–7.

> We, the handloom weavers of New Street, Lurgan, are desirous to direct
> attention to the grievance under which we suffer, and to the distressed con-
> dition in which we are placed, owing to the long lengths, low wages, and
> bad yarns. Of all this the manufacturers are well aware. Now, sir, we invite
> them to visit the homes of starvation and distress in this town, and to see
> for themselves the weavers' condition...Now, although we are not in
> Spike Island with the convicts, we are chained from 14 to 16 hours a day
> to earn one shilling per day on average; taking our winding and harness to
> keep up a loom out of that would leave us about 8*d*. per day to live on, and
> pay rent and fuel...The weavers only ask what an unskilled labourer
> makes — that is, from 10*s*. to 12*s*. per week...[52]

The Linen Merchants' Association, which represented major commercial figures in the trade, and which shared Saunderson's adamant support of the Union,
was nonetheless hostile to his handloom proposals — which many members
derided as populist posturing. The *Irish Textile Journal* reported on 15 May 1888
that an 'attempt to restrict the length of goods to a uniform standard of fifty yards
will, if carried into effect, prove most disastrous to the handloom industry'. These
provisions, the *Journal* claimed, would impede the ability of merchants and manufacturers to respond to market demand, 'and, if adopted, may result in the handloom trade passing entirely away from the district'. The Association, meeting to
consider the proposed measures, argued that while it was inclined to sympathize
with 'every wise endeavour to improve the position of the handloom weavers', it
could not support measures which would, in the end, compel buyers to look elsewhere for webs over 51 yards.[53] The proposals interfered greatly, in its view, with
'freedom of contract'.[54] Additionally, the meeting resolved:

> (b) That by this Bill handloom cloth, being circumscribed in length, would
> be placed at a disadvantage as compared with powerloom cloth. (c) That
> powerloom cloth having already a tendency to push handloom cloth out
> of the market, that tendency would be increased by this Bill. (d) That
> everything which tends to decrease the diminishing demand for handloom
> cloth has a corresponding tendency to reduce the wages thereof. (e) That
> a reduction of the length of the web to 50 yards or 51 yards would neces-
> sarily cause a corresponding reduction in wages, earned at the greater cost
> to the weaver of drawing the yarn into reeds and heddles, and carrying
> home to the employer a shorter web.[55]

52 *News-Letter*, 5 May 1888.   **53** A one-yard excess was allowable under the provisions of the bill.
54 *News-Letter*, 5 May 1888.   **55** *Irish Textile Journal*, 15 May 1888.

The merchant W.R. Young argued that the bill was most injurious to handloom weavers, promoting powerlooms in their branches and 'increasing the emigration, which they all deplored so much, in the Counties of Antrim and Down'.[56] He invoked the spectre of mechanical displacement and professed deep sympathy with the plight of weavers as he and other linen merchants claimed solidarity with the trade's dwindling members. But by the 1890s, powerloom manufacture, in which many merchants were engaged, became the central foil for weavers' claims to craft status, as they denigrated its articles as mere products of mass manufacture.

One outcome of the protracted conflicts in local markets was the expansion of trade bodies to give public expression to weavers' grievances and to mobilize them at the local and national levels. In response to manufacturers' protests, a 'Lurgan Handloom Weavers' Defence Association' convened a meeting in May 1888. Weavers unanimously adopted resolutions condemning the manufacturers' position. They also called upon counterparts in other districts to form other 'Associations for the purpose of protecting' their just rights and privileges.[57] John Hamilton, chairing the meeting, lamented the 'great weakness of the weavers in the past' in their 'want of organization', but noted that Lurgan weavers had achieved a great deal by pressing political leaders in support of Saunderson's bill through their local association.[58] The weavers' labour associations gave new focus to their agenda, and became influential in local electoral contests — providing them with leverage to extract concessions from political leaders. As late as 1900, Edward Saunderson explained that repeated efforts to secure a bill for the trade had been blocked year after year, and the *Irish Textile Journal* expressed exasperation with his repeated efforts aimed at 'tinkering' with the trade.[59] But by then trade associations had adopted strategies that aimed to differentiate handloom manufacture from that of the 'inferior' powerloom, and masculine skill from casual 'feminine' weaving work and to demonstrate their political influence in advancing this agenda.

HANDLOOM WEAVING AFTER 1870: THE CULTURAL TERRAIN

In the last decades of the nineteenth century, a new movement emerged that endowed Ireland's cottage industries with special cultural value — and offered some weavers a new framework within which they asserted rights to protection as skilled craftsmen. The home industries revival provided a foundation for their work to be conflated with the preservation of indigenous craft traditions. Late-nineteenth and early-twentieth-century initiatives to 'revive' handicraft in rural

---

56 *News-Letter*, 5 May 1888.   **57** *Weekly Northern Whig*, 19 May 1888.   **58** Ibid.   **59** *Irish Textile Journal*, 15 November 1900.

regions of Ireland were inspired by a transatlantic Arts and Crafts movement.[60] They assumed special political salience in Ireland in dialogue with the wider Celtic Revival.[61] The important intellectual influences of John Ruskin and William Morris on these initiatives has been underlined by researchers, with many contemporary sponsors of the movement inspired by Ruskin's claim that 'The Irish people cannot only design beautiful things, but can also execute them with indefatigable industry.'[62] While the focus of most research into the revival has been on major artistic figures of the period and on the infrastructure dedicated to artistic training,[63] there was an allied interest in popular rural handicraft associated with the peasantry of Ireland, including lacemaking, tweed, fine embroidery and handloom linen weaving.[64]

From her arrival in Ireland in 1886, Lady Aberdeen, wife of a lord lieutenant, staunch Liberal, and conspicuous philanthropist, became pre-eminently associated, both in Ireland and in Britain, with efforts to foster 'peasant' craft production. In her view, home industry elevated the position of rural people and contributed to their prosperity.[65] Encouraging female handicraft production buttressed pervasive views of the home as women's space where, engaged occasionally in paid work, they served the interests of the family and nation as mothers, wives and craftswomen. The movement also presented itself as an alliance between embattled gentry patrons and the Irish people during a turbulent period in Irish politics.[66] If it resulted in connecting the manufactures of the Irish peasantry to consumers in Britain and abroad, and improved the Irish countryside, it might also enhance the status of stewards of Ireland's craft revival. But the rhetoric surrounding home industries was also an important exposition on gender and work. Women's domestic crafts were regarded as distinct from those of men (who were associated with work such as tweed-weaving). In the linen trade the proprietorship of craft weaving skill was also gendered as masculine. The historic male monopoly on weaving in the period before the 1820s, restrictions on females' access to training in damask weaving and male dominance of the most remunerative handloom branches underscored this fact. A movement that celebrated handloom weaving as a craft tradition provided a framework through which male linen weavers, especially workers in the lucrative damask trade, claimed exclusive proprietorship of craft skill.

Damask weavers skillfully harnessed the handicraft revival to elevate their work as a marker of indigenous craft. Through 'the unlimited resources of the houses engaged in it' and through 'special channels of consumption' linked to

60 For an interesting continental comparator, see B. Klein (2000). **61** J. Sheehy (1980); N.G. Bowe & E. Cumming (1998); J. Helland (2002). **62** *Irish hand-woven linen damask, how and why it is distinguished* ('copyright James Wright', no place, no publisher, 1909), p. 2, in NAI G 2578/12 (Various documents related to the Handloom Merchandise Act). **63** P. Larmour (1992); N.G. Bowe (1989) and (1985); N.G. Bowe & E. Cumming (1998). **64** J. McBrinn (2002) provides an excellent case study. **65** J. Helland (2004a). **66** J. Helland (2004b); N. Harris (1992).

luxury tableware markets, damask had weathered the downturns suffered by cambric and Ballymena shirtings in the 1890s. The *Irish Textile Journal* declared in August 1902 that hundreds of damask handlooms were at work, the trade having 'nothing to fear for a long time to come'.[67] Contemporary evidence suggests that while cambric weavers could earn little more than 5*s*. weekly and were engaged in a 'dying trade', damask weaving was a 'flourishing industry which affords a comfortable existence to those who follow it'.[68] In 1907, however, the damask trade was in a depressed state. Weavers in the Waringstown district began agitating in favour of protective legislation in late February, claiming that they were defending their craft against a 'united force of modern innovation, unfair competition, and neglect', and resolving after a large meeting to appeal to the government, prominent supporters of Irish cottage industry, and to the wider public to protect what the *Irish Textile Journal* described as an 'excellent, old handicraft'.[69] They aligned themselves with labour interests in Parliament, and the MP Keir Hardie championed amendments to the Merchandise Marks Bill which would require all damask linen goods to have the words 'Irish linen damask made in Ireland' woven into the cloth. When such cloth was hand-made, an additional comment to that effect was to be added.[70] The application of the proposed inweaving to the handloom damask branch signaled the extent to which its weavers dominated trade associations and equated their work with craftsmanship. While the *Irish Textile Journal* opposed this proposal, as it had the protective legislation proposed by Saunderson in previous decades, it recommended a small hallmark guaranteeing each article be stamped on all Irish linen goods.[71] The handloom hallmarking proposals won widespread support from weavers, though some local MPs expressed concern about the impact of inweaving on the value of finished goods.[72] The *Irish Textile Journal* concurred, commenting that the protection of the handloom trade was a lost cause: even the one thousand, old weavers who remained at the handloom, it claimed, were compelled to live partly on small farms for their living. Any legislative effort to revive the trade, therefore, would be unlikely to succeed.[73] The Linen Merchants' Association also opposed the bill, favouring instead the certification of all Irish linen goods, whether produced at the hand- or powerloom, to distinguish them from cotton, union and other cheaper fabrics made up in imitation of linen.[74] Indeed, the Association wanted inspectors to police wholesale and retail ends of the trade, to prevent such cloth from being fraudulently represented as pure linen.[75] Initiatives to secure special trademark protection for handloom goods sparked debates in the pages of the *Lurgan*

---

67 *Irish Textile Journal*, 15 August 1902.   **68** *Irish Textile Journal*, 15 September 1902.   **69** *Irish Textile Journal*, 15 March 1907.   **70** *Irish Textile Journal*, 15 May 1907.   **71** *Irish Textile Journal*, 15 April 1907.   **72** *Irish Textile Journal*, 15 June 1907.   **73** *Irish Textile Journal*, 15 August 1907. **74** Minutes of the Linen Merchants Association, PRONI, Belfast, D/2088/1/6, letter of 24 November 1902, 23 July 1908, 22 September 1908, 12 October 1908, 19 October 1908.   **75** *Irish Textile Journal*, 15 October 1908 and 15 February 1909.

Mail, with Samuel Anderson, president of the Handloom Weavers' Society, and William J. McMullan, general organizing secretary, arguing that the alleged disappearance of the weaving workforce was exaggerated, and that the very suggestion that it was dying denigrated weaving skill, 'as it would be impossible for old men to work at this important and difficult trade'.[76] They asserted that the 'cloven hoof' of the 'powerloom manufacturers' interest' was seeking to obviate any preferential treatment of the handloom trade. 'What about the powerloom manufacturers getting fat and rich at the expense of the handloom damask?' they asked, charging that handloom weavers faced familiar, 'bitter opposition offered by the powerloom manufacturers and also the middle-men'.[77]

Anderson insisted that handloom damask remained distinct from powerloom manufacture, that products of hand- and powerlooms were not in direct competition, and that powerloom makes could withstand any special protection offered to handloom cloth by hallmarking proposals.[78] Indeed, he insisted that the provisions merely certified the authenticity of handloom articles, so that no other cloth, of foreign provenance or powerloom manufacture, could be falsely represented as handloom cloth. He alleged that the powerloom manufacturers had long conspired against the handloom. Handloom cloth's 'quality, fineness and durability' marked it as a distinctive branch of handicraft manufacture. This echoed the claim of the *Irish Textile Journal*'s Lurgan correspondent in 1903 that 'The powerloom is still unable to compete with the handloom in the production of table linens of advanced merit, and as handloom damask weaving is still regarded as a respectable handicraft, its disappearance from this district must be a matter of the far-distant future.'[79] By describing the handloom as a traditional instrument of craft production, Anderson and other weavers tapped into currents that gave life to the home industries movement and positioned themselves rhetorically against 'the machine' that, they alleged, wished to bring about the extinction of Irish craft generally.[80] While some weavers extended their demand for a hand-made damask hallmark to other hand-made linens,[81] the focus of their energies was on the damask trade, which was still dominated by men who claimed access to a historic, restricted skills-set in a branch long associated with technical weaving skills that had been restricted to male labour for generations. The public representation of damask weaving emphasized its weavers as masculine and able-bodied — in obvious contrast to older and female weavers associated with 'lesser-skilled' work. Observing the operation of Jacquard looms in the workshop owned by Michael Andrews in Ardoyne, for instance, Anna Maria and Samuel Carter Hall had remarked in the 1840s that:

76 *Lurgan Mail*, 5 October 1907. See also 19 October 1907.   **77** *Lurgan Mail*, 19 October 1907.
78 Anderson charged that manufacturers had promoted the powerloom by providing handloom weavers with inferior yarns to undermine their work.   **79** *Irish Textile Journal*, 16 March 1903.
80 For a discussion of the moral worth attached to 'hand-made' goods, see E. Freedgood (2003).
81 *Ulster Guardian*, 4 April 1908.

... a finer, more healthy-looking, or more intelligent set of men, it would be very difficult to find together in any factory in the kingdom. They were evidently not the mere machines which mechanics are generally represented to be; but workmen who brought to their labour reflection and thought — the result of a sound and good education, which so few of the humbler classes of 'the north' are without — vying in mental cultivation with any district of Scotland.[82]

In an 1870 edition of his history of the linen trade, Hugh McCall also insisted that in damask work, 'the patterns, the sweat of the brain was much more frequently brought into play than the sweat of the brow', in an explicit linking of putative male traits with the demands of damask manufacture.[83] Another commentator noted in a description of the trade that weaving skill passed from father to son,[84] and the 1888 *Book of Antrim* described the labour force of Messrs J. Richardson and Sons and Owden, Ltd. of Lisburn as being engaged in skilled work: 'The finest and most expensive kinds of damask table linen are produced for them by manual labour in the houses of well-to-do peasants, who have inherited a delicacy of touch and taste which cannot be imitated by machinery.'[85] The gendered evaluation of technical skill in the trade combined with positive observations of its workers and their families. Damask-weaving districts were frequently represented as housing Ireland's most prosperous weaving households: an 1897 description of Waringstown by the *Irish Homestead* asserted that its cottages were neat, and children playing 'at the cottage doors are chubby and well fed.' Indeed, 'not in the most favoured districts of rural England might one hope readily to find its rival in all outer signs of well-doing'.[86] Robinson and Cleaver, one of Ireland's pre-eminent linen houses, described their damask weavers in a similar vein, echoing other comments on the complexity and autonomy of handloom skill:

> Great skill is demanded in fine handloom damask weaving, particularly of the wider widths, and in making insertions of coats of arms, crests, and monograms, the best weavers having been occupied at this handicraft from their earliest childhood. Being entirely a cottage industry, all the members of the family can lend a helping hand — the children and the aged wind the bobbins for the woof, the young men and women weave the narrower and lighter looms, and the able-bodied men the wider, heavier,

82 Mr & Mrs C. Hall, *Ireland: its scenery and character, &c.* (1843), 96.   83 H. McCall, *Ireland and her staple manufactures* 1870), 129. See also *Some Irish industries* (1897), vi.   84 W.R. McMurray, 'Handloom linen, cambric and damask weaving, and linen embroidery', in W.T. Macartney-Filgate (ed.), *Irish rural life and industry, with suggestions for the future* (1907), 165. See also Alfred S. Moore, *Linen from the raw material to the finished product* (1914), 80–4.   85 G.H. Bassett, *Book of Antrim* (1888a) 235.   86 *Some Irish Industries* (1897), 69.

and more complicated ones. These handlooms are invariably employed to weave fabrics much finer and generally more elaborate in design than those woven by powerlooms in steam factories.[87]

The dexterity, speed and intellect demanded in the damask trade were clearly attributed to the most 'able-bodied', and were gendered as masculine traits; so too were the autonomy and authority which evoked the farmer-weaver archetype. The description of a 'typical' Waringstown weaver, for instance, echoed historic portrayals of the rugged and masculine independent weaver of linen's bygone age:

> The Waringstown weaver is somewhat like his loom — a trifle old-fashioned in his ideas; for the modern labour problems that vex the souls of men in towns concern him not.
>
> He is a sturdily independent person, who owns a garden and a pig, and has his children about him as he works. Father, son, and daughter are often found working together, and, satisfied with regular employment and regular wages which are sufficient to keep him and his in comfort in a country where all life's necessaries are at their cheapest, he does not object, not being forced thereto, to work twelve hours a-day if the light serve. 'An eight-hours day!' said a weaver, with a superior smile; 'I work just as long as I can see;' and that seems to be the general rule in the summer.[88]

Young men were represented as uniquely able to undertake the complex and taxing work associated with damask weaving — 'Handloom weaving is not easy work, and calls for a strong man as well as a skilful [sic]',[89] the publication declared, suggesting that the evaluation of damask work as skilled labour rested on its association with detailed and intellectually-taxing full-time work at elaborate and expensive looms, rather than the casual domestic weaving characteristic of workers in other handloom branches.

These expositions on the masculinity of damask craftsmanship were given concrete form in the campaign to certify the authenticity of handloom articles. At a meeting of the Ulster Operative Damask Weavers' Association and the Irish Handloom Weaver's Society in Lurgan in March 1908, the two associations jointly sponsored a motion that the inweaving of 'Irish Hand-woven Linen Damask' be required; for non-damask goods, the words 'Irish Hand-woven' would certify their provenance. But the Liberal *Ulster Guardian* reported that the assembled weavers also heard from Lurgan councillor E. Lunn, in the chair, that 'one industry above every other was responsible for making Ulster not only prosperous, but historic — namely, the handloom damask weaving'.[90] In 1908, in support of the demarcation

---

87 *Some historical notes on linen ancient and modern* (n.d.), 79–80.   **88** *Some Irish industries*, 70.
89 Ibid.   **90** *Ulster Guardian*, 4 April 1908.

of handloom damask weavers, the populist unionist Thomas Sloan proposed a bill which included cloth inweaving proposals that all damask, cambric and linen diaper goods be encompassed in protective legislation — a proposal he had trumpeted before weavers while campaigning for an independent candidate in the 1907 Down West byelection.[91] The handloom weavers of West Down and Lurgan were 'agitating in its favour' through their trade association, the Handloom Weavers' Society of Ireland, into which the Ulster Operative Damask Weavers' body had been subsumed (and in which damask weavers outnumbered cambric weavers by three to one).[92] The Society insisted that the hallmarking of damask goods was a strategy to 'protect' one of Ireland's 'cottage industries'[93] that Samuel Anderson characterized as 'an old and honourable industry' threatened with extinction.[94] Invoking the same language used to promote cottage industry elsewhere in Ireland, Anderson warned that emigration would surely follow the extinction of the trade, and that woven goods, if properly protected by a system of hallmarking, would find a ready market in America.[95] A 1909 pamphlet on the damask handloom trade, published in support of handloom damask weavers' agitations, asserted that the 'sentiment' that was attached to hand-made linen, as with any such hand-made article, had made it a highly-prized commodity in markets around the world:

> It was the handloom weavers of Ireland, who, by their untiring energy and industry, created the sentiment that surrounds Irish linen, that sentiment which always attaches to the best of any hand-produced article, whether it be rug, engraving, piece of sculpture, lace or other luxury of life.[96]

This romantic portrayal of damask craft also began by quoting Margaret Ashmun's poem 'The Technical World', in which she rhapsodized about the elevated character of hand work and male skill:

> Aye! One thing more this world demands,
> Ere labor can arrive at any goal —
>   A human force more firm than turning banks,
> And more enduring than all wheels that roll:
>   A man, with skill and patience in his hands —
> A man, with strength and courage in his soul![97]

When Lady Aberdeen, the preeminent advocate of home industries, received a delegation of male weavers in 1907, imploring her to support their efforts to

91 *Irish Textile Journal*, 15 April 1908; *Ulster Guardian*, 18 April 1908; *Northern Whig*, 30 August 1907.   92 The Society was often also referred to as the Handloom Weavers' Association.   93 *Ulster Guardian*, 1 February 1908.   94 Ibid.   95 See, for instance, *Belfast News-Letter*, 30 August 1907. See also *Ulster Guardian*, 19 June 1909.   96 *Irish hand-woven linen damask*, 13–14.   97 Ibid., 2.

hallmark Irish hand-made articles, she declared that 'The fame of handloom damask was known all over the world', and offered a robust defence of handloom weaving as an exemplar of Irish craft. Aberdeen drew explicit parallels between damask weaving and 'other home work, such as the lace industry, where the introduction of machinery had made it very difficult to continue in the prosperity they would like to see them enjoy. But there was still a definite place for these home industries so long as they are carried on with a high degree of efficiency, as she knew theirs was.'[98] Not only did she issue a ringing endorsement of the handloom weavers' programme; she also visited Waringstown in February 1908 to meet handloom weavers living in the district. There, Aberdeen heard from representatives of the Handloom Weavers' Society that 'They did not want her to fight against economic laws; they only asked that the handloom industry should be made a speciality' and that hand-made damask be hallmarked as such.[99]

The countess supported the weavers, seeing parallels between the handloom trade and other home industries, including female-dominated trades such as lace-making. Others resisted weavers' efforts to hallmark goods, regarding it as a desperate measure to revive a dying trade. T.W. Russell, the vice-president of the Department of Agriculture and Technical Instruction, for instance, remarked that while his department was charged with fostering and encouraging cottage industries, he saw little value in the hallmark proposals, which he dismissed as a 'pure piece of protection, in aid of a decaying and dying industry which no legislation will suffice to keep on foot for any very long period.'[1] But male handloom weavers now enjoyed influence in a number of parliamentary constituencies. As this debate coincided with elections in West Down, it received considerable attention. In 1908, supporting the proposals proved politically expedient for the unionist candidate, because of the strong challenge being posed by an independent Sloanite unionist Andrew Beattie (who championed the handloom weavers' cause, as he had in a 1907 byelection in which he was defeated by the Unionist candidate by the relatively small margin of 3,702 to 2,918 votes). The Unionist candidate again prevailed in 1908, but Beattie polled 2,760 votes.[2] That year, local weavers leveraged their influence to see that the provisions were eventually passed into law. In 1909, the bill received Royal Assent, extending protection to the Irish handloom.[3] It was credited by representatives of the Handloom Weavers' Society with increasing work in the trade and 're-starting' the handloom production of damask table napkins.[4] But it also signaled the success of a strate-

98 *News-Letter*, 30 August 1907.   **99** *Ulster Guardian*, 15 February 1908. For insight into the life of a factory damask weaver, see E. O'Connor & T. Parkhill (1992).   **1** T.W. Russell to James Wood, 11 May 1909, in NAI, Dublin, G 2578/12.   **2** B. Walker (1978), 343.   **3** W. Crawford (1910), 13.
4 *Outworkers in Ireland*, evidence of James Wood, q. 460–2, 494–5. W.R. McMurray, a damask handloom manufacturer, complained that the requisite statement attached to handloom products under provisions of the Trade Marks Act — 'Warranted Handloom Manufacture' — undermined the sale of articles such as handkerchiefs, which were spoiled by the marking [evidence of representa-

gy through which damask weavers sought to strengthen trade protections and raise their status by identifying their work as an authentic indigenous craft tradition, associated with highly-capable, intelligent and able-bodied men who provided for their households through the application both of their bodies and their brows. By subsuming their agenda within wider programmes of handicraft revival, weavers skillfully allied their cause to the home industries movement, and, so doing, conflated protection for handloom weaving with preservation of indigenous craft. The evaluation of handloom weaving as a handicraft rested on a clear demarcation between the craftsmanship embodied in hand production and the routinized manufacture of machinery. To this definition of handicraft skill were added distinctions between skill and semi-skilled labour, old, infirm and able-bodied labour, and men's and women's work, which damask weavers expressed with increasing forcefulness in the early twentieth century.

There remained significant structural differences between branches of handloom work, even as their number decreased by the turn of the twentieth century. In Ballymena the feminization and casualization of linen weaving explored earlier in this study reflected changing conditions in the shirting trade, the structure of the wider regional economy, and strategies through which rural households responded to them. In other regions where handloom production continued, mixed textile and agricultural activity was also common: this pattern of work was characterized as 'feminine' by male damask weavers, who held that casual production prevailed amongst lesser-skilled, female weavers. Indeed, the casualization of handloom weaving was a central feature of what they characterized as unskilled labour when they demanded protection for masculine skilled work.[5] Discourses of gender and handloom skill were expounded with greatest clarity in a debate over whether the trade should be brought under the provisions of National Insurance legislation, which excluded outworkers 'where the wages or other remuneration derived from the employment are not the principal means of livelihood of the person employed'. Male weavers and their trade association insisted that skilled weavers' work was that of craftsmen and satisfied this criterion. Their foil was causal, feminine weaving.

Similar to mid-Antrim counterparts in the 1880s, many of Lurgan's weavers worked in agriculture for the farmers from whom they rented property — this work was described in 1905 as a custom of generations.[6] But the degree to which their

tives of W.R. McMurray, q. 1516–24]. In a parliamentary debate on such legislation, it was suggested that local electoral maneuvering in West Down, and in particular the challenge posed by the Sloanite Independent Unionist to the mainline Unionist candidate in the 1907 and 1908 byelections there, had led the South Down MP to raise the position of the handloom weavers in parliament, to which he responded that 'I desire to state in the most emphatic manner that I do not take the slightest interest in the domestic differences of the Ulster Unionist deadheads.' Thomas Sloan and Captain Craig both pressed the vice-president of the Board of Agriculture in Ireland, T.W. Russell, to act on the matter (*Hansard*, 4 March 1908). **5** See S. Alexander (1984); B. Taylor (1983); A.V. John (1980). **6** *Irish Textile Journal*, 16 October 1905.

work was evaluated as unskilled, or gendered as female work, was contested. In handloom districts of Armagh, employers of handloom weavers claimed in 1912 that only 40% of weavers were 'labourers' engaged in weaving work, and another 40% were 'women and girls', with the remaining 20% small farmers whose work included the cultivation of their holdings.[7] Manufacturers claimed that male weaver-labourers also pursued 'farming, fishing and fruit-growing' in addition to their textile work.[8] In fact they challenged the putative correspondence between casual work and female labour, while male weavers insisted that there was an immutable correlation between sex, skill and work patterns, and asserted that craft status was associated with only a few branches of the trade, chiefly damask weaving. This formulation of craft skill was nourished by contemporary evaluations of the skill of the farmer-weaver of the linen trade's earlier years, who, the industrial historian Hugh McCall asserted, was 'far from being an artisan':

> Spending one portion of his time at the plough, and another at the loom, the rough toils of the field unfitted him for the higher order of skill required in the workshop, and thus was continued, year after year, one of the most formidable barriers against improvement in the art of weaving.[9]

McCall believed that full-time workshop employment greatly enhanced the skills-set of the weaver, especially after the adoption of the complex Jacquard damask loom.[10] Thomas Cochrane, a cambric weaver who was not a member of the Society, insisted that as cambric weavers' earnings were low — no more than 10s. per week — these sums would be diminished further were employers to make insurance contributions on their behalf.[11] This position contrasted with that of the damask weavers and the Handloom Weavers' Society, which favoured the inclusion of homeworkers within the provisions of the Act, even if their earnings passed the threshold that required contributions from both workers and employers. Damask weavers insisted that women were drawn away from their looms to attend to unpaid domestic work and thus specialized in less rigorous (and remunerative) branches of manufacture, since their skills were not as refined. In damask manufacture their subordinate position in production was expressed by their role in 'attending' male weavers.[12] The damask-weaver-dominated Society's representatives argued that female weavers' secondary status was also signaled by lower levels of productivity, pay and skill. They contested manufacturers' claims that many men's work was also casual, and asserted that if females were deserving of National Insurance protection, it was principally because they provided assistance to the 'head' by both 'working and assisting in the upkeep of the

---

7 *Outworkers in Ireland*, evidence of Revd W.B. Allman and James Blane, q. 909–13   8 *Outworkers in Ireland*, evidence of representatives of James Bryson, q. 957.   9 H. McCall (1870), 68.   10 Ibid., 297.   11 *Outworkers in Ireland*, evidence of Thomas Cochrane, q. 1071–81.   12 W.R. McMurray, 'Handloom linen', 164.

house'.[13] James Wood, who accompanied the Society's Secretary in giving evidence, insisted that yarn was given 'to the head of the house. The man is recognized as the head of the house.'[14] He also suggested that in the damask trade, weavers continued to draw on household labour, and that their authority over it was an extension of their wider social, economic and cultural power as skilled producers.[15] Indeed, the Society's representatives portrayed women's weaving work as an adjunct to other duties, performed in the home on a casual basis: in this formulation of industrial authority, social ideologies bore heavily on the evaluation of handloom skill. A pamphlet published in support of the hallmark initiative promised that 'if a revival of their industry can be brought about', damask weavers would be better positioned to provide their 'wives and helpers' with pin money in recognition of their unpaid work.[16] This expression of male authority was a corollary to what Brenda Collins has characterized as the 'institutional primacy' accorded to weavers in 'public representations of the family labour' when contracts between households and manufacturers were set.[17]

While James Wood acknowledged that some weavers worked as small farmers,[18] he argued that weaving by the male heads of families was similar to forms of factory employment that fell under National Insurance Act provisions. When asked to explain why wives earned from 4*s*. to 5*s*. weekly, in contrast with men's 14*s*. to 15*s*. wages, Wood insisted that males worked a 'great deal more' than women, and that a man worked ten- to eleven-hour days, while his wife 'can only afford to work for six or seven hours, because she has to look after the house'.[19] The inferior level of female skill was thus presented as a corollary to their command of other tasks, specifically those that related to 'natural' domestic roles. Such claims did not go unchallenged, especially by manufacturers who did not regard male weavers as industrial workers as described in the National Insurance legislation, and who disputed claims that they should fall under its provisions. Manufacturers such as John H. McCann, who employed cambric weavers in Co. Armagh, insisted that casual weaving was far from exclusively characteristic of female labour.[20] McCann also insisted that a 'large proportion' of weavers were women and girls, and that while the distribution of work was organized through male heads of families, their wives and children formed the backbone of the cambric workforce.[21] The Handloom Weavers' Society's assertion of the primacy of male craft authority was a clear exposition of the gendering of handloom skill and echoed W.R. McMurray's claim

13 *Outworkers in Ireland*, evidence of James Wood, q. 450   **14** Ibid., q. 445–56.   **15** W. Seccombe (1986).   **16** *Irish hand-woven linen*, 13.   **17** B. Collins (1997), 244.   **18** *Outworkers in Ireland*, evidence of James Wood, q. 503–4.   **19** Ibid., q. 520–33.   **20** *Outworkers in Ireland*, evidence of John H. McCann, Revd W.B. Allman, James Blane & James Bryson, q. 883–921. In the final analysis, the committee did not recommend bringing Irish outworkers within the provisions of the Act, principally because the Act envisioned for Ireland did not provide medical benefit, and consequently the advantages of insurance was judged to be very slight.   **21** *Outworkers in Ireland*, evidence of John H. McCall, 972–8, evidence of James Blane, q. 979–81.

in the guide to the Home Industries Section of the Irish International Exhibition in 1907 that damask skill 'appears to descend from father to son'.[22] Conflating casualization, feminization, and unskilled labour, male damask weavers presented female workers as a foil for their craftsmanship. Forging astute alliances with political representatives and rural utopians, they succeeded in placing the damask weaver within the pantheon of Irish cottage craftsman, enshrining masculine weaving as an exemplar of cottage industry skill. This was enabled by their dominance of arenas in which discourses of status and handloom skill were developed, articulated and contested, by their privileged access to skills-training, and by the currency that the handloom craft developed in the context of the home industries revival, around which an ideal of masculine skill was articulated.

22 W.R. McMurray, 'Handloom linen', 165.

Conclusion

In his pioneering history of the Irish linen trade, Conrad Gill commented that cambric and fine handloom damask weaving — which were still to be seen on occasion in Ulster — were vestiges of a system of production which once underpinned the industry.[1] The weavers who worked at these looms were among the last members of a workforce that was integral to Irish industry in the mid-nineteenth century, and that endured, on a much smaller scale, into the twentieth century. Their experiences challenge historians of Irish industrialization to explain the co-existence of powerloom and handloom production in the linen trade after the 1850s, to examine diverse organizational systems, labour forces and work experiences, and to incorporate them within wider accounts of industrial labour in Ireland. It also demands attention to ways that the handloom was represented as an instrument of traditional production, and how such rhetoric linked sexual divisions of labour with formulations of status and skill, as observers lamented the eclipse of handicraft trades and pledged to aid in their revival.

This study has not charted the steady eclipse of a monolithic workforce. Instead, it suggests the uneven persistence of hand production through many branches and areas of Ulster — enabled by a variety of social, institutional and technological factors. The adoption of powerloom technology in the booming Civil War era and in the fluctuating period that followed it was more limited than triumphalist contemporary narratives anticipated. A combination of technical factors favouring powerlooms for coarse cloth production, unstable commercial conditions and a large supply of handloom weaving labour militated against the industry's complete mechanization — even at the height of the Civil War boom. Before the powerloom era dawned, the weaving workforce had incorporated female labour and had experienced diverse forms of industrial reorganization. Female participation in handloom weaving did not inaugurate an equality of status among male and female operatives. Instead sexual divisions structured handloom labour, and divisions of sex influenced the gendering of handloom skill. As it was reconstructed in the second-half of the nineteenth century, and as the handloom trade contracted, male weavers made bold and explicit claims to the monopoly of expertise in an Irish 'home industry'. New cultural politics intermingled with formulations of craft expertise in the trade to shape a relatively narrow, gendered definition of handloom craftsmanship in the Irish linen industry.

1 C. Gill (1925), 1. See also C. Ó Gráda (1994), 289.

What can handloom weavers' experiences contribute to our wider under-standing of the linen trade — and of textile workforces generally? The factors that operated in favour of dispersed handloom production in mid-Antrim affirm the salience of regional agrarian and social contexts as enablers of dispersed rural industrial work. There is considerable evidence, too, of extensive, if seasonal, engagement by women in paid labour, including weaving. The cultural contexts within which work was performed demand equal consideration: as the male damask weaver became an icon of the handicraft revival, the rhetoric that sur-rounded his craftsmanship became an exposition on industrial skill that was unmistakably gendered. In mid-Antrim, the decaying shirting trade was not cel-ebrated as an exemplar of skilled home industry, and its practitioners, mostly females and older men, were not portrayed as custodians of traditional craft expertise, but rather regarded as curious remnants of an expiring handloom work-force. Examining how Irish linen handloom weavers, male and female, became associated, often exclusively, with branches of work and formulations of status and skill illuminates how industrial hand workers encountered new structural environments after 1815. Sexual divisions contributed to structuring the linen workforce in Ireland and gender influenced the work patterns of, and discourses about, those who remained at the loom.

Census occupational categories

Census occupational titles in 1851 and 1901 manuscript returns were classified according to the following system. These categories were developed in line with the classes used in the printed census tables. Production status was a paramount factor, but other aspects of work (site of employment, relationship to capital and other resources) were also considered. Given the wide extent of textile employment in the district, a number of sub-categories were developed for flax/linen manufacture, partly organized around the axis of material upon which the individual worked (such as flax, yarn, and cloth) and the stage of production (such as weaving or finishing). A few occupational titles, such as bleacher, present ambiguity. In such cases, the titles were sometimes interpreted within the context of the enumerated work of other household members (such as the presence of servants).

Dashes given as entries were not attributed an occupation. A 'dual occupations' category was created for those people for whom two occupations were enumerated (no more than two were enumerated for any one person in the manuscript census returns under examination). In analyses of specific occupational cohorts, such people were included in both relevant groups. The 'other category' comprises occupational titles which could not be classified, as well as various entries that were not specifically indicative of occupation. While original spellings, which varied slightly for a few occupations, were preserved in all versions of the coding, here they are standardized. Unclear entries were not included in the analysis.

In order to provide for a consistent methodology when comparing 1851 and 1901 returns, only those household members recorded as present during the 1851 enumeration were included in this analysis.

Females, 1851

Domestic servant
cook
house mistress
house servant
housekeeper
housemaid
washwoman

Farmer
farmer

Textile merchant
linen merchant

Flax worker
flax dresser

Linen spinner
linen spinner
spinner
spinning linen
spinning linen yarn

Linen yarn winder
winding spools
winding yarn
yarn winder

Linen weaver
l weaver
linen weaver
weaver
weaving linen

Apprentice in weaving
learning weaver

Worker in textile finishing
bleacher

Linen worker (ancillary processes)
filling yarn

Worker in clothing manufacture
bonnet maker
dressmaker
knit
knitter
needlework
seamster
seamstress

sewer
sewing

Retailer/dealer
dealer
grocer

Labourer (general or undefined)
labourer

Scholar
at school
at school occasionally
attending school

Dual occupations
knit and sew
knitter and sewer
sew and knit

Other
annuitant
not at school
not attend school
not attending school
parochial mistress
Presbyterian
spinster

Males, 1851

Clergyman
clergy man rector

Teacher
schoolmaster

Watchman
watchman

Domestic servant
butler
house servant
servant

Labourer in agriculture and on land
agriculturalist
hurd
nurseryman
ploughman
plowing labourer
stable servant

Farmer
farm
farmer

Industrial tradesman
blacksmith
engineman
miller
millwright
tin smith
wheelwright

Building tradesman
house carpenter
carpenter
carpenter to trade
stone mason

Worker in transportation/conveyance
bread cart driver

Textile merchant
cloth merchant
linen merchant

Linen yarn winder
winding yarn

Linen weaver
l weaver
linen weaver
weaver

Worker in textile finishing
bleacher
bleaching
foreman bleacher

linen bleacher
loftman linen cloth
Linen worker (ancillary processes)
filling bobbins

Worker in clothing manufacture
shoemaker

Labourer (general or undefined)
labourer

Labourer (other)
drainage labourer

Scholar
at school
attending school
in college

Dual occupations
bleacher and weaver
engineman and weaver
watchman and weaver

Other
linen
farm
not at school
not attend school
not attending school
pensioner
Presbyterian

Females, 1901

Worker in postal services
post girl

Worker in medicine
nurse in hospital

Teacher
n.s. teacher
national school teacher
teacher

Clerk
clerkess

Domestic servant
2nd housemaid domestic servant
assistant housekeeper
cook domestic servant
domestic general servant
domestic servant cook
domestic servant general

general domestic servant
general servant
general servant domestic
governess
house woman
house work
housekeeper
house-maid
housemaid domestic servant
kitchen maid domestic servant
ladies maid domestic servant
lady companion
servant

Labourer in agriculture and on land
agricultural labourer
farm servant

Farmer
deriving support off farm
farmer

Relative of farmer
farmer's daughter
farmer's sister
farmer's wife

Yarn winder
linen yarn winder
winder of linen yarn
yarn winder
yarn winder (linen)

Linen weaver
linen weaver
weaver (linen)
weaver linen
weaver of linen

Worker in textile finishing
linen marker
marker in bleachworks
marking cloth in bleach green

Worker in clothing manufacture
dressmaker
dressmaking
milliner
seamstress

Retailer/dealer
egg merchant
grocer
saleswoman
shopkeeper

Scholar
at school
scholar

Retired
retired linen weaver

Other
cost mistress
graduate of R.U.I.
housewife
mistress of house
not at school
no profession
spinster
wife of chemical manager

Males, 1901

Soldier/policeman
army pensioner
sergeant

Clergyman
clergyman-rector of Craigs

Teacher
national school teacher
national schoolmaster
national teacher
nat'l school teacher

Domestic servant
butler domestic servant
coachman
coachman domestic servant
domestic servant
general servant
groom domestic servant

Clerk
clerk
commercial clerk
clerk-bleachworks

Watchman
night watchman in bleach works

Land agent
land agent

Labourer in agriculture and on land
agricultural labourer
assistant gardener
farm labourer
farmer servant
farmer's servant
gardener-domestic servant
gardener
landsteward

Farmer
farmer

Relative of farmer
farmer's brother
farmer's servant
farmer's son

Industrial tradesman
blacksmith
millwright

Building tradesman
carpenter
joiner
master carpenter

Apprentice in building trades
apprentice carpenter

Tradesman (unspecified)
artisan

Textile merchant
linen merchant

Flax worker
ruffer in flax mill

Linen weaver
linen weaver

Linen factory worker
stoker in linen factory

Worker in textile finishing
beetler
bleacher
bleaching labourer
bluer
calendar man in linen bleachworks
cotton beetler
crisper

crisper of cottons
dyer
general labourer for linen bleach works
general labourer in bleachwork
general labourer in bleachworks
general labourer in dyeworks
general labourer in linen bleachworks
labourer in bleachworks
labourer in dye works
labourer in linen bleachworks
linen beetler
linen bleacher
linen finisher
loft man in bleach works
loftman
wet works in bleach green
worker in bleachgreen

Apprentice in textile finishing
beetler linen apprentice

Labourer (linen, unspecified)
linen labourer

Worker in clothing manufacture
tailor

Retailer/dealer
cattle dealer
grocer
grocer's assistant

Worker in roadmaking
stone breaker on roads
surface labourer
surface labourer on road
surfaceman

Worker in yards (unspecified)
yardman

Labourer (general or undefined)
general labourer
labourer
labourer general

Scholar
at school
medical student
scholar
theological student
undergraduate Dublin university

Dual occupations
farmer and artisan
land registrar and land agent
linen merchant and bleacher

Retired
retired farmer
retired from work
retired general labourer
retired linen weaver and pensioner RA

Other
engines
better
not at school
traveller
unemployed

Bibliography

Contemporary works are signalled by an asterisk.

BOOKS AND ARTICLES

Aalen, F.H.A., Kevin Whelan, & Matthew Stout. *Atlas of the rural Irish landscape*. Toronto, University of Toronto Press, 1997.

*'Address delivered at the opening of the eighth session of the society, by Jonathan Pim, Esquire, one of the vice-presidents'. *Journal of the Dublin Statistical Society* 1, pt. 1 (1855), 6–25.

Akenson, Donald Harman, & W.H. Crawford. *Local poets and social history: James Orr, Bard of Ballycarry*. Belfast: PRONI, 1977.

Albert, Alice J. 'Fit work for women: sweated home-workers in Glasgow, *c*.1875–1914'. In Breitenbach & Gordon (eds), *The world is ill-divided*, 158–77, 1990.

Alexander, Sally. 'Women, class and sexual differences in the 1830's and 1840's: some reflections on the writing of a feminist history'. *History Workshop Journal* 17 (1984), 125–49.

——. *Women's work in nineteenth-century London: a study of the years 1820–50*. London: Journeyman Press, 1983.

Almquist, Eric L. 'Pre-Famine Ireland and the theory of European proto-industrialization: evidence from the 1841 census'. *Journal of Economic History* 39, 3 (1979), 699–718.

Anderson, Michael. 'What can the mid-Victorian censuses tell us about variations in married women's employment?' *Local Population Studies* 62 (1999), 9–30.

Ashley, W.J. (ed.). *British industries*. London: Longmans, Green, 1903.

*Bassett, George Henry. *The Book of Antrim*. Dublin: Sealy, Bryers and Walker, 1888a.

*——. *The Book of County Armagh*. Dublin: Sealy, Bryers and Walker, 1888b.

*Bastable, C.F. 'Some economic conditions of industrial development, with special reference to the case of Ireland'. *Journal of the Statistical and Social Inquiry Society of Ireland* 8 (1884), 461–73.

*Bates, Arthur Henry. 'Irish linen laws and proposed amendments thereof'. *Journal of the Statistical and Social Inquiry Society of Ireland* 8 (1881), 203–16.

Beechey, Veronica. 'On patriarchy'. *Feminist Review* 3, 3 (1979), 66–82.

Belfast and Province of Ulster Directory for 1852. Belfast: *News-Letter* Office, 1852, vol. 1.

Bell, Jonathan. 'Hiring fairs in Ulster'. *Ulster Folklife* 25 (1979), 67–78.

Berg, Maxine (ed.). *Markets and manufacture in early industrial Europe*. London: Routledge, 1991.

——. 'What difference did women's work make to the Industrial Revolution?' *History Workshop Journal* 35 (1993), 22–44.

— —. 'Women's work, mechanisation and the early phases of industrialisation in England'. In Joyce (ed.). *The historical meanings of work*, 65–98. 1987.

— —. *The age of manufactures: industry, innovation and work in Britain, 1700–1820*. London: Fontana, 1985.

Bew, Paul. *Land and the national question in Ireland, 1858–82*. Dublin: Gill and Macmillan, 1978.

Bielenberg, Andy. 'British competition and the vicissitudes of the Irish woollen industry, 1785–1923'. *Textile History* 31, 2 (2000), 202–21.

Blau, Francine, & Carol Jusenius. 'Economists' approaches to sex segregation in the labor market: an appraisal'. *Signs* 1, 3, pt. 2 (1976), 181–99.

Blaxall, Martha & Barbara Reagan (eds). *Women and the workplace: the implications of occupational segregation*. Chicago: University of Chicago Press, 1976.

*Booth, Charles. 'Occupations of the people of the United Kingdom, 1801–81'. *Journal of the Statistical Society* 49, 2 (1886), 314–444.

Bourke, Joanna. 'The ideal man: Irish masculinity and the home, 1880–1914'. In Cohen & Curtin (eds), *Reclaiming gender*, 93–106, 1999.

' "I was always fond of my pillow": the handmade lace industry in the United Kingdom, 1870–1914'. *Rural History* 5, 2 (1994), 155–69

— —. *Husbandry to housewifery: women, economic change, and housework in Ireland, 1890–1914*. Oxford: Clarendon Press, 1993.

— —. ' "The best of all home rulers": the economic power of women in Ireland, 1880–1914'. *Irish Economic and Social History* 18 (1991a), 34–47.

— —. 'Working women: the domestic labour market in rural Ireland, 1890–1914'. *Journal of Interdisciplinary History* 21, 3 (1991b), 479–99.

Bowe, Nicola Gordon. 'Two early twentieth-century Irish Arts and Crafts workshops in context: An Túr Gloine and the Dun Emer Guild and Industries'. *Journal of Design History* 2, 2–3 (1989), 193–206

— —. 'The Arts and Crafts Society of Ireland (1894–1925) with particular reference to Harry Clark'. *Journal of the Decorative Arts Society* 9 (1985), 29–40.

— — & Elizabeth Cumming, *The Arts and Crafts movements in Dublin & Edinburgh, 1885–1925*. Dublin: Irish Academic Press, 1998.

*Bowley, A.L. 'The statistics of wages in the United Kingdom during the last hundred years, part iii, agricultural wages'. *Journal of the Royal Statistical Society* 62, 2 (1899), 395–404.

Boyle, Elizabeth. *The Irish flowerers*. Belfast: Institute of Irish Studies, 1971.

Boyle, Emily. 'Vertical integration and deintegration in the Irish linen industry, 1830–1913'. In Cohen (ed.). *The warp of Ulster's past*, 211–27, 1997b.

Boyle, J.W. *The Irish labor movement in the nineteenth century*. Washington: Catholic University of America Press, 1988.

— —. 'The Belfast Protestant Association and the Independent Orange Order, 1901–10'. *Irish Historical Studies* 13, 50 (1962), 117–52.

Bradley, Harriet, 'Frames of reference: skill, gender and new technology in the hosiery industry'. In de Groot & Schrover (eds), *Women workers and technological change in Europe in the nineteenth and twentieth centuries*, 17–34, 1995.

Breitenbach, E, & E. Gordon (eds). *The world is ill-divided: women's work in Scotland in the nineteenth and twentieth centuries.* Edinburgh: Edinburgh UP, 1990.

Braverman, Harry. *Labor and monopoly capital: the degradation of work in the twentieth century.* New York: Monthly Review Press, 1974.

Brown, Martin, & Peter Philips. 'The historical origin of job ladders in the U.S. canning industry and their effects on the gender division of labour'. *Cambridge Journal of Economics* 10, 2 (1986), 129–45.

Buckley, Cheryl. ' "The noblesse of the banks": craft hierarchies, gender divisions, and the roles of women paintresses and designers in the British pottery industry, 1890–1939'. *Journal of Design History* 2, 4 (1989), 257–73

Burnette, Joyce. 'An investigation into the female-male wage gap during the Industrial Revolution in Britain'. *Economic History Review* 50, 2 (1997), 257–81.

Bythell, Duncan. 'Women in the workforce'. In Patrick O'Brien & Roland Quinault (eds), *The Industrial Revolution and British society*, 31–53. Cambridge: Cambridge UP, 1993.

— —. *The sweated trades: outwork in nineteenth-century Britain.* London: Batsford, 1978.

— —. *The handloom weavers: a study in the English cotton industry during the Industrial Revolution.* Cambridge: Cambridge UP, 1969.

Chapman, S.D. *The early factory masters: the transition to the factory system in the Midlands textile industry.* London: David and Charles, 1967.

*Charley, William. *Flax and its products in Ireland.* London: Bell and Daldy, 1862.

Chartres, John. 'Rural industry and manufacturing'. In Collins (ed.). *The agrarian history of England and Wales,* 7, 1850–1814 (pt II), 1101–49, 2000.

Clapham, J. H. *An economic history of modern Britain: free trade and steel.* Cambridge: Cambridge UP, 1963.

Clark, Alice. *Working life of women in the seventeenth century.* London: G. Routledge and Sons, 1919.

Clark, Anna. *The struggle for the breeches: gender and the making of the British working class.* Berkeley: University of California Press, 1995.

Clark, Samuel. *Social origins of the Irish land war.* Princeton: Princeton UP, 1979.

— — & James S. Donnelly, Jr. (eds). *Irish peasants: violence and political unrest, 1780–1914.* Madison: University of Wisconsin Press, 1983.

Clarke, Tony & Tony Dickson. 'Class and class consciousness in early industrial capitalism: Paisley, 1770–1850'. In Dickson (ed.). *Capital and class in Scotland,* 8–60, 1982.

Clarkson, Leslie A. 'The environment and dynamic of pre-factory industry in Northern Ireland'. In Hudson (ed.). *Regions and industries,* 252–70, 1989a.

— —. 'The Carrick-on-Suir woollen industry in the eighteenth century'. *Irish Economic and Social History* 16 (1989b), 23–41.

Cockburn, Cynthia. *Machinery of dominance: women, men and technical know-how.* London: Pluto, 1985.

— —. *Brothers: male dominance and technological change.* London: Pluto, 1983.

Coe, W.E. *The engineering industry of the north of Ireland.* New York: Augustus M. Kelley, 1969.

Cohen, Marilyn. *Linen, family and community in Tullylish, County Down, 1690–1914.* Dublin: Four Courts Press, 1997a.

— —. 'Peasant differentiation and proto-industrialisation in the Ulster countryside: Tullylish 1690–1825'. *Journal of Peasant Studies* 17, 3 (1990), 413–32.

— —. 'Working conditions and experiences of work in the linen industry: Tullylish, County Down'. *Ulster Folklife* 30 (1984), 1–21.

— —. (ed.). *The warp of Ulster's past: interdisciplinary perspectives on the Irish linen industry, 1700–1920.* New York: Saint Martin's Press, 1997b.

— — & Nancy J. Curtin (eds). *Reclaiming gender: transgressive identities in modern Ireland.* New York: Saint Martin's Press, 1999.

Coleman, Peter J. 'Rhode Island cotton manufacturing: a study in economic conservatism'. *Rhode Island History* 23 (1964), 65–81.

Collins, Brenda. 'The loom, the land, and the marketplace: women weavers and the family economy in late-nineteenth and early-twentieth-century Ireland'. In Cohen (ed.). *The warp of Ulster's past,* 229–52, 1997b.

— —. 'The organization of sewing outwork in late nineteenth-century Ulster'. In Berg (ed.). *Markets and manufacture,* 139–56, 1991.

— —. 'Sewing and social structure: the flowerers of Scotland and Ireland'. In Mitchison & Roebuck (eds). *Economy and society in Scotland and Ireland, 1500–1939,* 242–54, 1988.

— — & Philip Ollerenshaw (eds). *The European linen industry in historical perspective.* Oxford: Oxford UP, 2003.

Collins, E.J.T. (ed.). *The agrarian history of England and Wales,* vol. 7: 1850–1814 (pt II). Cambridge: Cambridge UP, 2000.

Comerford, R.V. 'Ireland, 1850–70: post-Famine and mid-Victorian'. Chapter 20 in Vaughan (ed.). *A new history of Ireland,* vol. 5, 372–95, 1989.

Crafts, F.N.R., & C. Knick Harley. 'Output growth and the British Industrial Revolution: a restatement of the Crafts-Harley view'. *Economic History Review* 45, 4 (1992), 703–30.

*Crawford, Sir William. *Irish linen and some features of its production: a lecture delivered on 14th February, 1910.* Belfast: Mayne, 1910.

Crawford, W.H. 'A handloom weaving community in County Down'. *Ulster Folklife* 39 (1993), 1–14.

— —. 'Women in the domestic linen industry'. In MacCurtain & O'Dowd (eds), *Women in early modern Ireland,* 255–64, 1991.

— —. 'The evolution of the linen trade in Ulster before industrialization'. *Irish Economic and Social History* 15 (1988), 32–53.

— —. 'Drapers and bleachers in the early Ulster linen industry'. In Cullen & Butel (eds), *Négoce et industrie en France et en Irlande aux XVIIIe et XIXe siècles,* 113–19, 1980.

— —. 'The market book of Thomas Greer, a Dungannon linendraper, 1758–59'. *Ulster Folklife* 13 (1967), 54–60.

Cronin, Maura. *Country, class or craft? The politicisation of the skilled artisan in nineteenth-century Cork.* Cork: Cork UP, 1994.

Crossick, Geoffrey, & Heinz-Gerhard Haupt. *The petite bourgeoisie in Europe, 1780–1914: enterprise, family, and independence.* London: Routledge, 1995.

——. *Shopkeepers and master artisans in nineteenth-century Europe*. London: Methuen, 1984.

Cullen, L.M. *An economic history of Ireland since 1660*. London: B.T. Batsford, 1972.

—— & T.C. Smout (eds). *Comparative aspects of Scottish and Irish economic and social history, 1600–1900*. Edinburgh: John Donald, 1977.

—— & P. Butel (eds). *Négoce et industrie en France et en Irlande aux XVIIIe et XIXe siè-cles*. Editions du Centre National de la Recherche Scientifique, 1980.

Cullen, Mary. 'Breadwinners and providers: women in the household economy of labour-ing families, 1835–6'. In Luddy & Murphy (eds), *Women surviving: studies in Irish women's history*, 85–116, 1990.

Currie, J. R. L. *The Northern Counties Railway,* vol. 1, *beginnings and development, 1845–1903*. Newton Abbot: David and Charles, 1973.

Curtin, Nancy J. 'Ideology and materialism: politicization and Ulster weavers in the 1790s'. In Cohen (ed.). *The warp of Ulster's past*, 111–38, 1997b.

Daly, Mary. *Women and work in Ireland*. Dublin: Economic and Social History Society of Ireland, 1997.

——. 'Women in the Irish workforce from pre-industrial to modern times', *Saothar* 7 (1981), 74–82.

Daunton, M.J. *Progress and poverty: an economic and social history of Britain, 1700–1850*. Oxford: Oxford UP, 1995.

*Day, Angélique, Patrick McWilliams, & Nórín Dobson (eds). *Ordnance survey memoirs of Ireland*, vol. 23, *parishes of County Antrim VII, 1831–5, 1837–8: Ballymena and West Antrim*. Belfast: Institute of Irish Studies, 1993.

*Day, Angélique, & Patrick McWilliams (eds). *Ordnance survey memoirs of Ireland*, vol. 39, *parishes of County Donegal II, 1835–6: Mid- West and South Donegal*. Belfast, Institute of Irish Studies, 1997.

de Groot, Gertjan & Marlou Schrover (eds). *Women workers and technological change in Europe in the nineteenth and twentieth centuries*. 'General Introduction', 1–16. Lon-don: Taylor and Francis, 1995.

Dickson, David. 'Aspects of the rise and decline of the Irish cotton industry'. In Cullen & Smout (eds), *Comparative aspects of Scottish and Irish economic social history, 1600–1900*, 100–15, 1977.

Dickson, Tony et al. *Scottish capitalism: class, state and nation from before the Union to the present*. London: Lawrence and Wishart, 1980.

—— (ed.). *Capital and class in Scotland*. Edinburgh: John Donald, 1982.

*Dobbs, Conway E. 'Some observations on the tenant right of Ulster'. *Transactions of the Dublin Statistical Society* 1 (1849), 3–13.

*Donnell, Robert. 'The linen trade and the customs duties'. *Journal of the Statistical and Social Inquiry Society of Ireland* 5 (1870), 196–212.

*Dubourdieu, John. *Statistical survey of the County of Antrim*. Dublin: Graisbery and Campbell, 1812.

Drake, Michael. 'Aspects of domestic service in Great Britain and Ireland, 1841–1911'. *Family & Community History* 2, 2 (1999), 119–28.

Durie, A.J. 'Government policy and the Scottish linen industry before c.1840'. In Collins & Ollerenshaw (eds), *The European linen industry in historical perspective*, 229–44, 2003.

——. *The Scottish linen industry in the eighteenth century*. Edinburgh: John Donald, 1979.

Edelstein, T. J. (ed.). *Imagining an Irish past: the Celtic Revival, 1840–1940*. Chicago: the David and Alfred Smart Museum of Art, 1992.

England, Paula. 'The failure of human capital theory to explain occupational sex segregation'. *Journal of Human Resources* 17, 3 (1982), 358–70.

Evans, Nesta. *The East Anglian linen industry: rural industry and local economy, 1500–1850*. Aldershot: Gower, 1985.

Farnie, D.A. 'Part I: the textile industry: woven fabrics'. In Singer et al. (eds), *A history of technology*, 5, 569–94. 1958.

Fitzpatrick, David. 'The disappearance of the Irish agricultural labourer, 1841–1912'. *Irish Economic and Social History* 7 (1980), 66–92.

Foster, John. *Class struggle and the Industrial Revolution: early industrial capitalism in three English towns*. London: Weidenfeld and Nicolson, 1974.

Freedgood, Elaine. ' "Fine fingers": Victorian handmade lace and utopian consumption.' *Victorian Studies* 45, 4 (2003), 625–47.

Freifeld, Mary. 'Technological change and the "self-acting" mule: a study of skill and the sexual division of labour'. *Social History* 11, 3 (1986), 319–43.

Geary, Frank. 'Puzzles in the economic institutions of capitalism: production coordination, contracting and work organisation in the Irish linen trade, 1750–1850'. *Cambridge Journal of Economics* 29, 4 (2005), 559–76.

——. 'Regional industrial structure and labour force decline in Ireland between 1841 and 1851'. *Irish Historical Studies* 30, 118 (1996), 167–94.

——. 'The Belfast cotton industry revisited'. *Irish Historical Studies* 26, 103 (1989), 250–67.

——. 'The rise and fall of the Belfast cotton industry: some problems'. *Irish Economic and Social History* 8 (1981), 30–49.

—— & Tom Stark. 'Trends in real wages during the Industrial Revolution: a view from across the Irish Sea.' *Economic History Review* 57, 2 (2004), 362–395.

Gibbon, Peter. *The origins of Ulster Unionism: the formation of popular protestant politics and ideology in nineteenth-century Ireland*. Manchester: Manchester UP, 1975.

Gillespie, Raymond. *Colonial Ulster: the settlement of east Ulster 1600–1641*. Cork: Cork UP, 1985.

Gill, Conrad. *The rise of the Irish linen industry*. Oxford: Clarendon Press, 1925.

Gray, Jane. *Spinning the threads of uneven development: gender and industrialization in Ireland during the long eighteenth century*. Lanham, MD: Lexington Books, 2005.

——. 'The Irish, Scottish and Flemish linen industries during the long eighteenth century'. In Collins & Ollerenshaw, *The European linen industry*, 159–86, 2003.

——. 'Spinners and spinning in the political economy of pre-Famine Ireland: evidence from County Cavan'. In Cohen & Curtin (eds), *Reclaiming gender*, 161–84, 1999.

——. 'Gender and plebian culture in Ireland'. *Journal of Interdisciplinary History* 24, 2 (1993a), 251–70.

——. 'Folk poetry and working class identity in Ulster: an analysis of James Orr's "The Penitent"'. *Journal of Historical Sociology* 6, 3 (1993b), 249–75.

——. 'Rural industry and uneven development: the significance of gender in the Irish linen industry'. *Journal of Peasant Studies* 20, 4 (1993c), 590–611.

Gray, Robert Q. *The labour aristocracy in Victorian Edinburgh*. Oxford: Clarendon Press, 1976.

Green, E.R.R. *The Lagan Valley, 1800–1850: a local history of the Industrial Revolution*. London: Faber and Faber, 1949.

— —. 'The cotton hand-loom weavers in the north-east of Ireland'. *Ulster Journal of Archaeology* 3 Ser. 7 (1944), 30–41.

Greiff, Mats. '"Marching through the streets singing and shouting": industrial struggle and trade unions among female linen workers in Belfast and Lurgan, 1872–1910'. *Saothar* 22 (1997), 29–44.

Gribbon, H.D. 'Economic and social history, 1850–1921'. In Vaughan (ed.). *A new history of Ireland*, vol. 6, 260–356, 1996.

— —. 'The Irish Linen Board, 1711–1828'. In Cullen & Smout, *Comparative aspects,*, 77–87, 1977.

— —. *The history of water power in Ulster*. Newton Abbot: David and Charles, 1969.

Guinnane, Timothy W. *The vanishing Irish: households, migration, and the rural economy in Ireland, 1850–1914*. Princeton: Princeton UP, 1997.

Gullickson, Gay L. *Spinners and weavers of Auffay: rural industry and the sexual division of labor in a French village, 1750–1850*. Cambridge: Cambridge UP, 1986.

— —. 'Agriculture and cottage industry: redefining the causes of proto-industrialization'. *Journal of Economic History* 43, 3 (1983), 831–50.

— —. 'Proto-industrialization, demographic behaviour and the sexual division of labor in Auffay, France, 1750–1850'. *Peasant Studies* 9, 2 (1982), 106–18.

— —. 'The sexual division of labor in cottage industry and agriculture in the Pays de Caux: Auffay, 1750–1850'. *French Historical Studies* 12, 2 (1981), 177–99.

Hafter, Daryl M. (ed.). *European women and preindustrial craft*. Bloomington, IN: Indiana UP, 1995.

*Hall, Mr, & Mrs C. *Ireland: its scenery, character, &c.*, vol. 3. London: Jeremiah How, 1843.

Hall, Catherine. 'The home turned upside down? The working-class family in cotton textiles, 1780–1850,' in Whitelegg et al. (eds), *The changing experience of women*, 17–29, 1982.

Hamill, Jonathan. 'Childcare arrangements within the Belfast linen community, 1890–1930'. In Whelan (ed.). *Women and paid work in Ireland, 1500–1930*, 120–32, 2000.

Hammond, J.L., & B. *The skilled labourer, 1760–1832,* London: Longmans, Green, 1919.

*Hancock, W. Nelson. 'The differences between the English and Irish Poor Laws, as to the treatment of women and unemployed workers'. *Journal of the Statistical and Social Inquiry Society of Ireland* 3 (1862), 217–35.

Harris, Neil. 'Selling national culture: Ireland at the World's Columbian Exposition'. In Edelstein (ed.). *Imagining an Irish past*, 82–105, 1992.

Harte, N.B. 'The rise of protection and the English linen trade, 1690–1790'. In Harte & Ponting (eds), *Textile history and economic history*, 74–112, 1973.

— — & K.G. Ponting (eds). *Textile history and economic history: essays in honour of Miss Julia de Lacy Mann*. Manchester: Manchester UP, 1973.

Hartmann, Heidi. 'The unhappy marriage of Marxism and feminism: towards a more progressive union'. *Capital and Class* 8 (1979), 1–33.

———. 'Capitalism, patriarchy, and job segregation by sex'. In Blaxall & Reagan (eds), *Women and the workplace*, 137–69, 1976.

*Haughton, James. 'The application of machinery to manufacture, beneficial to the working classes'. *Transactions of the Dublin Statistical Society* 2 (1851), 3–12.

Helland, Janice. 'Embroidered spectacle: Celtic revival as aristocratic display'. In Taylor Fitzsimon & Murphy (eds), *The Irish Revival reappraised*, 94–105, 2004a.

———. 'Exhibiting Ireland: the Donegal Industrial Fund in London and Chicago'. *RACAR* 29, 1–2 (2004b), 28–46.

———. 'Rural women and urban extravagance in late nineteenth-century Britain'. *Rural History* 13, 2 (2002), 179–97.

Hendrickx, F.M.M. *'In order not to fall into poverty': production and reproduction in the transition from proto-industry to factory industry in Borne and Wierden (the Netherlands), 1800–1900*. Amsterdam: I.I.S.G., 1997.

———. 'From weavers to workers: demographic implications of an economic transformation in Twente (The Netherlands) in the nineteenth century'. *Continuity and Change* 8, 2 (1993), 321–55.

Hepburn, A.C. *A past apart: studies in the history of Catholic Belfast, 1850–1950*. Belfast: Ulster Historical Foundation, 1996.

Hewitt, John, (ed.). *Rhyming weavers and other country poets of Antrim and Down*. Belfast: Blackstaff, *c*.1974.

Higgs, Edward. 'Household and work in the nineteenth-century censuses of England and Wales'. *Journal of the Society of Archivists* 11, 3 (1990), 73–7.

———. 'Women, occupations and work in the nineteenth century'. *History Workshop Journal* 23 (1987), 59–80

Hill, Bridget. 'Women, work and the census: a problem for historians of women'. *History Workshop Journal* 35 (1993), 78–94.

Hirst, Catherine. *Religion, politics and violence in nineteenth-century Belfast: the Pound and Sandy Row*. Dublin: Four Courts, 2002.

Holmes, Janice & Diane Urquhart (eds). *Coming into the light: the work, politics and religion of women in Ulster, 1840–1940*. Belfast: Institute of Irish Studies, 1994.

Honeyman, Katrina. *Well suited: a history of the Leeds clothing industry, 1850–1990*. Oxford: Oxford UP, 2000a.

———. *Women, gender and industrialisation in England, 1700–1870*. Hampshire: Macmillan Press, 2000b.

Hoppen, K. Theodore. *Elections, politics, and society in Ireland, 1832–1885*. Oxford: Clarendon Press, 1984.

Horner, John. *The linen trade of Europe during the spinning-wheel period*. Belfast: McCaw, Stevenson and Orr, 1920.

Horrell, Sara, & Jane Humphries. 'The origins and expansion of the male breadwinner family: the case of nineteenth-century Britain'. *International Review of Social History* 42 (Supplement 5) (1997), 25–64.

———. 'Women's labour force participation and the transition to the male-breadwinner family, 1790–1865'. *Economic History Review* 48, 1 (1995), 89–117.

Howe, Anthony. *The cotton masters, 1830–1860*. Oxford: Clarendon Press, 1984.

Hudson, Pat. *The genesis of industrial capital: a study of the West Riding wool textile industry, c.1750–1850*. Cambridge: Cambridge UP, 1986.

— — (ed.). *Regions and industries: a perspective on the Industrial Revolution in Britain*. Cambridge: Cambridge UP, 1989.

— —. 'Proto-industrialisation: the case of the West Riding wool textile industry in the eighteenth and early nineteenth centuries'. *History Workshop Journal* 12 (1981), 34–61.

Humphries, Jane. "Lurking in the wings ...": women in the historiography of the Industrial Revolution'. *Business and Economic History* 20 (1991), 32–44

Hutton, Séan & Paul Stewart (eds). *Ireland's histories: aspects of state, society and ideology*. London: Routledge, 1991.

Jackson, Alvin. *Colonel Edward Saunderson: land and loyalty in Victorian Ireland*. Oxford: Clarendon Press, 1995.

Jenkins, David (ed.). *The Cambridge history of western textiles*, vol. 2. Cambridge: Cambridge UP, 2003.

Jenkins, D.T., & K.G. Ponting. *The British wool textile industry, 1770–1914*. London: Heinemann Educational Books, 1982.

John, Angela V. *By the sweat of their brow: women workers at Victorian coal mines*. London: Croom Helm, 1980.

— — (ed.). *Unequal opportunities: women's employment in England, 1800–1918*. Oxford: Basil Blackwell, 1986.

John Gallagher's 'Old Ballymena'. Ballymena: Mid-Antrim Historical Group, 1995

Johnson, David S., & Liam Kennedy. 'Nationalist historiography and the decline of the Irish economy: George O'Brien revisited'. In Hutton & Stewart (eds), *Ireland's histories*, 11–35, 1991.

Joyce, Patrick (ed.). *The historical meanings of work*. Cambridge: Cambridge UP, 1987.

— —. *Visions of the people: industrial England and the question of class, 1848–1914*. Cambridge: Cambridge UP, 1991.

Kennedy, Líam, & Philip Ollerenshaw (eds). *An economic history of Ulster, 1820–1940*. Manchester: Manchester UP, 1985.

Kennedy, Líam. 'The rural economy'. In Kennedy & Ollerenshaw (eds), *An economic history of Ulster, 1820–1940*, 1–61, 1985.

Klein, Barbro. 'The moral content of tradition: homecraft, ethnology, and Swedish Life in the twentieth century'. *Western Folklore* 59, 2 (2000), 171–95.

Kriedte, Peter, Hans Medick, & Jürgen Schlumbohm. 'Proto-industrialization revisited: demography, social structure, and modern domestic industry'. *Continuity and Change* 8, 2 (1993), 217–52.

Larmour, Paul. *The Arts and Crafts movement in Ireland*. Belfast: Friar's Bush Press, 1992.

Lazonick, William. 'Industrial relations and technical change: the case of the self-acting mule'. *Cambridge Journal of Economics* 3, 3 (1979), 231–62.

Levine, David. 'Industrialization and the proletarian family in England'. *Past & Present* 107 (1985), 168–203.

Littlewood, Barbara. *Feminist perspectives on sociology*. Harlow: Pearson Education, 2004.

Lloyd-Jones, Roger. *Manchester and the age of the factory: the business structure of Cottonopolis in the Industrial Revolution*. London: Croom Helm, 1988.

Lown, Judy. *Women and industrialization: gender at work in nineteenth-century England*. Cambridge: Polity Press, 1990.

Lyons, John S. 'Family response to economic decline: handloom weavers in early nineteenth century Lancashire'. *Research in Economic History* 12 (1989), 45–91.

Lyons, Laura. 'The state of gender in Irish studies: a review essay'. *Éire-Ireland* 32–3 (1997/98), 236–60.

Luddy, Maria. 'Women and work in nineteenth- and early-twentieth-century Ireland: an overview'. In Whelan, *Women and paid work in Ireland*, 44–56, 2000.

— — & Cliona Murphy (eds). *Women surviving: studies in Irish women's history*. Swords: Poolbeg, 1990.

— —. *Women and philanthropy in nineteenth-century Ireland*. Cambridge: Cambridge UP, 1995.

*MacAdam, James. 'On schools of design in Ireland', *Transactions of the Dublin Statistical Society* 1 (1849), 3–11.

Macartney-Filgate, W.T. (ed.). *Irish rural life and industry, with suggestions for the future*. Dublin: Hely's, 1907.

MacCurtain, Margaret, & Mary O'Dowd (eds). *Women in early modern Ireland*. Edinburgh: Edinburgh UP, 1991.

MacCurtain, Margaret, et al. 'An agenda for women's history in Ireland, 1500–1900'. *Irish Historical Studies* 28 (1992), 1–37.

Mackey, Brian. 'Overseeing the foundation of the Irish linen industry: the rise and fall of the Crommelin legend'. In Collins & Ollerenshaw, *The European linen industry*, 99–122, 2003.

MacPherson, James. ' "Ireland begins in the home": women, Irish national identity, and the domestic sphere in the *Irish Homestead*, 1896–1912'. *Éire-Ireland* 36, 3–4 (2001), 131–52.

Mager, Wolfgang. 'Proto-industrialization and proto-industry: the uses and drawbacks of two concepts'. *Continuity and Change* 8, 2 (1993), 181–215.

*Malcolm, A.G. 'The influence of factory life on the health of the operatives, as founded upon the medical statistics of this class at Belfast'. *Journal of the Statistical Society of London* 19, 2 (1856), 170–81.

*Marx, Karl. *Capital: a critique of political economy*. New York: Modern Library, 1906.

Mathias, Peter. *The first industrial nation*. 1969, reprinted in London by Routledge, 2001.

Matthaei, J.A. *An economic history of women in America: women's work, the sexual division of labor, and the development of capitalism*. Brighton: Harvester, 1982.

McBrinn, Joseph. 'The peasant and folk art revival in Ireland, 1890–1920: with special reference to Ulster'. *Ulster Folklife* 48 (2002), 14–61.

*McCall, Hugh. *Ireland and her staple manufactures, being sketches of the history and progress of the linen and cotton trades, as well as other details connected with the northern province*, 3rd edition. Belfast: Henry Greer, 1870.

McCutcheon, W.A. *The industrial archaeology of Northern Ireland*. Rutherford: Fairleigh Dickinson UP, 1984.

McKernan, Anne. 'War, gender and industrial innovation: recruiting women weavers in early nineteenth-century Ireland'. *Journal of Social History* 28, 1 (1994), 109–24.

McLennan, Gregor. ' "The labour aristocracy" and "incorporation": notes on some terms in the social history of the working class'. *Social History* 6, 1 (1981), 71–81.

*McMurray, W.R. 'Hand loom linen, cambric and damask weaving, and linen embroidery'. In Macartney-Filgate (ed.). *Irish rural life and industry*, 162–7, 1907.

Mendels, Franklin. 'Proto-industrialization: theory and reality. General report'. In *'A' themes: eighth international economic history congress, Budapest, 1982*, 69–107. Budapest: Akadémiai Kiadó, 1982.

— —. 'Proto-industrialization: the first phase of the industrialization process'. *Journal of Economic History* 32, 1 (1972), 241–61.

Messenger, Betty. *Picking up the linen threads: a study in industrial folklore*. Austin: University of Texas Press, 1978.

Miller, David W. 'The Armagh troubles, 1784–95'. In Clark & Donnelly (eds), *Irish peasants,* 155–91, 1983.

Mincer, Jacob, & Solomon W. Polachek, 'Family investments in human capital: earnings of women'. *Journal of Political Economy* 82, 2 (1974), s76–s108.

Minutes of the Trustees of the Linen and Hempen Manufactures of Ireland containing the reports of their secretary, on a tour of inspection through the province of Ulster, in October, November, and December, 1816. Dublin: W. Folds and Sons, 1817.

Mitchison, Rosalind, & Peter Roebuck (eds). *Economy and society in Scotland and Ireland, 1500–1939*. Edinburgh: John Donald, 1988.

Mokyr, Joel, & Cormac Ó Gráda. 'Poor and getting poorer? Living standards in Ireland before the Famine'. *Economic History Review*, 2nd series, 41, 2 (1988), 209–35.

Mokyr, Joel. *Why Ireland starved: a quantitative and analytical history of the Irish economy, 1800–1850*. London: Allen and Unwin, 1983.

Monaghan, Amy. 'An eighteenth-century family linen business: the Faulkners of Wellbrook, Cookstown, Co. Tyrone'. *Ulster Folklife* 9 (1963), 30–45.

*Moore, Alfred S. *Linen from the raw material to the finished product*. London: Pitman, 1914.

Moorhouse, H.F. 'The Marxist theory of labour aristocracy'. *Social History* 3, 1 (1978), 61–82.

More, Charles. 'The end of the labour aristocracy?' *Labour History Review* 60, 1 (1995), 61–4.

Morgan, Carol E. *Women workers and gender identities, 1835–1913: the cotton and metal industries in England*. London: Routledge, 2001.

Morgan, V., & W.A. Macafee. 'Household and family size and structure in County Antrim in the mid-nineteenth century'. *Continuity and Change* 2, 3 (1987), 455–76.

— —. 'Population in Ulster, 1660–1760'. In Roebuck (ed.). *Plantation to partition*, 46–63, 1981.

— —. 'Irish population in the pre-Famine period: evidence from County Antrim'. *Economic History Review*, New Series, 37, 2 (1984), 182–97.

Morris, Jenny. 'The characteristics of sweating: the late nineteenth-century London and Leeds Tailoring Trades'. In John (ed.). *Unequal opportunities*, 94–121, 1986.

Murray, Norman. *The Scottish hand loom weavers, 1790–1850: a social history*. Edinburgh: John Donald, 1978.

Nardinelli, Clark. 'Technology and unemployment: the case of the handloom weavers'. *Southern Economic Journal* 53, 1 (1986), 87–94.

*National Commercial Directory of Ireland. Manchester: I. Slater, 1856.

Neill, Margaret. 'Homeworkers in Ulster, 1850–1911'. In Holmes & Urquhart (eds), *Coming into the light*, 2–32, 1994.

O'Brien, George. *The economic history of Ireland from the Union to the Famine*. London: Longmans, Green, 1921.

O'Connor, Emmet. *A labour history of Ireland, 1824–1960*. Dublin: Gill and Macmillan, 1992.

— — & Trevor Parkhill, (eds). *A life in Linenopolis: the memoirs of William Topping, Belfast damask weaver, 1903–56*. Belfast: Ulster Historical Foundation, 1992

O' Dowd, Anne. 'Women in rural Ireland in the nineteenth and early-twentieth centuries: how the daughters, wives and sisters of small farmers and landless labourers fared'. *Rural History* 5, 2 (1994), 171–83.

O'Dowd, Mary. *A history of women in Ireland, 1500–1800*. Harlow: Pearson Education, 2005.

Ogilvie, Sheilagh C., & Markus Cerman. *European proto-industrialization*. Cambridge: Cambridge UP, 1996.

Ó Gráda, Cormac. *Ireland: a new economic history, 1780–1939*. Oxford: Oxford UP, 1994.

O'Hearn, Denis. 'Irish linen: a peripheral industry'. In Cohen, *The warp of Ulster's past*, 161–90, 1997b.

Ollerenshaw, Philip. 'Stagnation, war and depression: the UK linen industry, 1900–1930'. In Collins & Ollerenshaw, *The European linen industry*, 285–307, 2003.

— —. 'Problems of the European linen industry, 1870–1914'. In Cohen, *The warp of Ulster's past*, 191–210, 1997b.

— —. *Banking in nineteenth century Ireland: the Belfast banks, 1825–1914*. Manchester: Manchester UP, 1987.

— —. 'Industry, 1820–1914'. In Kennedy & Ollerenshaw, *An economic history of Ulster*, 62–108, 1985.

Osterud, Nancy Grey. 'Gender division and the organisation of work in the Leicester hosiery industry'. In John, *Unequal opportunities*, 45–68. 1986.

Parr, Joy. 'Disaggregating the sexual division of labour: a transatlantic case study'. *Comparative Studies in Society and History* 30, 3 (1988), 511–33.

Patterson, Henry. *Class conflict and sectarianism: the Protestant working class and the Belfast labour movement, 1868–1920*. Belfast: Blackstaff Press, 1980a.

— —. 'Independent Orangeism and class conflict in Edwardian Belfast: a reinterpretation'. *Proceedings of the Royal Irish Academy* 80, Section C (1980b), 1–27.

**Patterson, Sir R. Lloyd. 'The British flax and linen industry, with special reference to its position in Ireland'. In Ashley (ed.). *British industries*, 120–49, 1903.

Perceval-Maxwell, M. *The Scottish migration to Ulster in the reign of James I*. London: Routledge and Kegan Paul, 1973.

Phillips, A., & B. Taylor. 'Sex and skill: notes towards a feminist economics'. *Feminist Review* 6 (1980), 79–88.

*Pigot and Company's City of Dublin and Hibernian Provincial Directory. London: J. Pigot, 1824.

Pinchbeck, Ivy. *Women workers and the Industrial Revolution, 1750–1850.* London: Routledge, 1930.

*Porter G.R. 'Examination of the recent statistics of the cotton trade in Great Britain'. *Journal of the Statistical Society of London* 13, 4 (1850), 305–12.

Prest, John. *The Industrial Revolution in Coventry.* Oxford: Oxford UP, 1960.

Prus, Mark J. 'Mechanisation and the gender-based division of labour in the U.S. cigar industry'. *Cambridge Journal of Economics* 14, 1 (1990), 63–79.

Quataert, Jean H. 'Survival strategies in a Saxon textile district during the early phases of industrialisation, 1780–1860'. In Hafter (ed.). *European women and preindustrial craft*, 153–78, 1995.

— —. 'A new view of industrialization: "protoindustry" or the role of small-scale, labour-intensive manufacture in the capitalist environment'. *International Labor and Working-Class History* 33 (1988), 3–22.

— —. 'The politics of rural industrialization: class, gender, and collective protest in the Saxon Oberlausitz of the late nineteenth century', *Central European History* 20, 2 (1987), 91–124

— —. 'Combining agrarian and industrial livelihood: rural households in the Saxon Oberlausitz in the nineteenth century'. *Journal of Family History* 10, 2 (1985), 145–62.

Raaschou-Nielsen, Agnete. 'The organisational history of the firm: the putting-out system in Denmark around 1900'. *Scandinavian Economic History Review* 41, 1 (1993), 3–17.

Rendall, Jane. *Women in an industrializing society: England, 1750–1880.* Oxford: Basil Blackwell, 1990.

Rhodes, Rita M. *Women and the family in post-Famine Ireland: status and opportunity in a patriarchal society.* New York: Garland, 1992.

Richards, Paul. 'The state and early industrial capitalism: the case of the handloom weavers'. *Past & Present* 83 (1979), 91–115.

Rimmer, W.G. *Marshalls of Leeds, flax-spinners, 1788–1886.* Cambridge: Cambridge UP, 1960.

Roebuck, Peter (ed.). *Plantation to partition: essays in Ulster history in honour of J. L. McCracken.* Belfast: Blackstaff Press, 1981.

Royle, S.A. 'The Lisburn by-elections of 1863'. *Irish Historical Studies* 25, 99 (1987), 277–92.

Rose, Mary B. *The Gregs of Quarry Bank Mill: the rise and decline of a family firm, 1750–1914.* Cambridge: Cambridge UP, 1986.

Rose, Sonya O. 'Respectable men, disorderly others: the language of gender and the Lancashire weavers' strike of 1878 in Britain'. *Gender & History* 5, 3 (1993), 382–97.

— —. *Limited livelihoods: gender and class in nineteenth-century England.* Berkeley: University of California Press, 1992.

— —. Gender antagonism and class conflict: exclusionary strategies of male trade unionists in nineteenth-century Britain'. *Social History* 13, 2 (1988), 191–208.

— —. 'Gender segregation in the transition to the factory: the English hosiery industry, 1850–1910'. *Feminist Studies* 13, 1 (1987), 163–84.

— —. '"Gender at work": sex, class and industrial capitalism'. *History Workshop Journal* 21 (1986), 113–31.

— — & Laura L. Frader. *Gender and class in modern Europe*. Ithaca: Cornell UP, 1996.

Rule, John. 'The property of skill in the period of manufacture'. In Joyce, (ed.). *The historical meanings of work*, 99–118, 1987.

Sabel, Charles F. *Work and politics: the division of labour in industry*. Cambridge: Cambridge UP, 1982.

— — & Jonathan Zeitlin. 'Historical alternatives to mass production: politics, markets and technology in nineteenth-century industrialization'. *Past & Present* 108 (1985), 133–76.

Samuel, Raphael. 'The workshop of the world: steam power and hand technology in mid-Victorian Britain'. *History Workshop Journal* 2 (1977), 6–72.

Schmiechen, James A. *Sweated industries and sweated labor: the London clothing trades, 1860–1914*. Urbana: University of Illinois Press, 1984.

Schwarzkopf, Jutta. 'Gender and technology: inverting established patterns. The Lancashire cotton weaving industry at the start of the twentieth century'. In Walsh (ed.). *Working out gender*, 151–66, 1999.

Searby, Peter. 'The relief of the poor in Coventry, 1830–1863'. *Historical Journal* 20, 2 (1977), 345–61.

Seccombe, Wally. 'Patriarchy stabilized: the construction of the male breadwinner wage norm in nineteenth century Britain'. *Social History* 11, 1 (1986), 53–76.

Sharpe, Pamela. *Adapting to capitalism: women working in the English economy, 1700–1850*. Houndsmills, Hants.: Macmillan Press, 1996.

— — & Stanley D. Chapman. 'Women's employment and industrial organisation: commercial lace embroidery in early nineteenth century Ireland and England'. *Women's History Review* 5, 3 (1996), 325–51.

Sheehy, Jeanne. *The rediscovery of Ireland's past: the Celtic Revival, 1830–1930*. London: Thames and Hudson, 1980.

Simonton, Deborah. *A history of European women's work, 1700 to the present*. London: Routledge, 1998.

Singer, Charles, et al. (eds). *A history of technology*, vol. 5: *the late nineteenth century, c.1850 to c.1900*. Oxford: Clarendon Press, 1958.

*Slater's Late Pigot's Royal national commercial directory of Ireland. Manchester: I. Slater, 1870.

Smail, John. *Merchants, markets and manufacture: the English wool textile industry in the eighteenth century*. New York: Saint Martin's Press, 1999.

**Smith, F.W. *The Irish linen trade hand-book and directory*. Belfast: *Northern Whig* Office, 1876.

Smout, T.C. (ed.). *The search for wealth and stability: essays in economic and social history presented to M.W. Flinn*. London: Macmillan Press, 1979.

— —. 'The strange intervention of Edward Twistleton: Paisley in depression, 1841–3'. In Smout (ed.). *The search for wealth and stability*, 218–242, 1979.

Solar, Peter. 'The Irish linen trade, 1852–1914'. *Textile History* 36, 1 (2005), 46–68.

— —. 'The linen industry in the nineteenth century'. In Jenkins (ed.). *The Cambridge history of western textiles*, vol. 2, 809–823, 2003.

— —. 'The Irish linen trade, 1820–1852'. *Textile History* 21, 1 (1990), 57–85.

— —. 'A Belgian view of the Ulster linen industry in the 1840s'. *Ulster Folklife* 34 (1988), 16–25.

*Some Irish industries. Dublin: *Irish Homestead*, 1897.

*Some historical notes on linen ancient and modern. Belfast: Robinson and Cleaver, n.d.

*Sproule, John. (ed.). *The resources and manufacturing industry of Ireland, as illustrated by the exhibition of 1853*. Dublin: John Sproule, n.d..

Takei, Akihiro. 'The first Irish linen mills, 1800–1824'. *Irish Economic and Social History* 21 (1994), 28–38.

Taylor, Barbara. *Eve and the new Jerusalem: socialism and feminism in the nineteenth century*. London: Virago, 1983.

Taylor Fitzsimon, Betsey, & James H. Murphy (eds). *The Irish Revival reappraised*. Dublin: Four Courts Press, 2004a.

Thomas, Janet. 'Women and capitalism: oppression or emancipation? A review article'. *Comparative Studies in Society and History* 30, 3 (1988), 534–49.

Thomas, Morgan D. 'Economic geography and the manufacturing industry of Northern Ireland'. *Economic Geography* 32, 1 (1956), 75–86.

Thompson, E.P. *The making the English working class*. London: Penguin, 1963.

Timmins, Geoffrey. *The last shift: the decline of handloom weaving in nineteenth-century Lancashire*. Manchester: Manchester UP, 1993.

*Ure, Andrew. *Dictionary of arts, manufactures, and mines containing a clear exposition of their principles and practice by Robert Hunt, assisted by F.W. Rudler*, 7th edition. London: Longmans, 1875, vol. 3, J-Z.

*— —. *The philosophy of manufactures, or, an exposition of the scientific, moral, and commercial economy of the factory system of Great Britain by the late Andrew Ure, MD, FRS*, 3rd edition, *continued in its details to the present time, by P.L. Simmonds, FSS*. London: H.G. Bohn, 1861.

Valenze, Deborah. *The first industrial woman*. Oxford: Oxford UP, 1995.

Vallas, Steven Peter. 'The concept of skill: a critical review'. *Work and Occupations* 17, 4 (1990), 379–98

Vaughan, W.E. (ed.). *A new history of Ireland*, vol. 5, *Ireland under the Union, I, 1801–70*. Oxford: Clarendon Press, 1989, and vol. 6, *Ireland under the Union II, 1870–1921*, Oxford: Clarendon Press, 1996.

Verdon, Nicola. *Rural women workers in nineteenth-century England: gender, work and wages*. Woodbridge, Suffolk: Boydell Press, 2002.

Walby, Sylvia (ed.). *Gender segregation at work*. Milton Keynes: Open UP, 1988.

— —. 'Segregation in employment in social and economic theory'. In Walby (ed.). *Gender segregation at work*, 14–28, 1988.

Walker, Brian M. (ed.). *Parliamentary election results in Ireland, 1801–1922*. Dublin: Royal Irish Academy, 1978.

Walsh, Margaret (ed.). *Working out gender: perspectives from labour history*. Aldershot: Ashgate, 1999.

*Wakefield, Edward. *An account of Ireland, statistical and political*. London: Printed for Longman, Hurst, Rees, Orme, and Brown, 1812, vol. 1.

Whelan, Bernadette (ed.). *Women and paid work in Ireland, 1500–1930*. Dublin: Four Courts Press, 2000.

Whitelegg, Elizabeth et al. (eds). *The changing experience of women*. Oxford: Martin Robertson, 1982.

Wright, B.D. et al. (eds). *Women, work, and technology: transformations*. Ann Arbor: University of Michigan Press, 1987.

Wright, Frank. *Two lands on one soil: Ulster politics before Home Rule*. New York: St Martin's Press, 1996.

*Young, Arthur. *Tour in Ireland (1776–1779)*, edited with an introduction by Arthur Wollaston Hutton, vol. 1. London: George Bell and Sons, 1892.

UNPUBLISHED SOURCES

Boyle, Emily Joan. The economic development of the Irish linen industry, 1825–1913. Unpublished PhD dissertation, Queen's University of Belfast, 1977.

Greeves, Oliver. The effects of the American Civil War on the linen, woollen and worsted industries of the U.K. Unpublished PhD dissertation, University of Bristol, 1969.

Grew, Julie Ann. The Derry shirt making industry 1831–1913. Unpublished MPhil dissertation, University of Ulster, 1987.

Hamill, Jonathan Philip. A study of female textile operatives in the Belfast linen industry: 1890–1939. Unpublished PhD dissertation, Queen's University, Belfast, 1999.

LEGISLATION AND PARLIAMENTARY DEBATES

3 Geo. III, c. 34

21 & 22 Geo. III, c. 35.

5 & 6 William IV, c. 27.

3 & 4 Vic., c. 91.

24 & 25 Vic., c. 96.

Hansard

PARLIAMENTARY PAPERS IN ORDER OF PUBLICATION

Select committee on the laws regulating the linen trade of Ireland, Report, minutes of evidence, appendices (463), HC 1825, vol. v.

Select committee on the state of agriculture in the United Kingdom (612), Report, minutes of evidence, appendix, Index, HC 1833, vol. v.

Report of the select committee on the petitions of hand-loom weavers, with minutes of evidence and index (556) HC 1834, vol. x.

Select committee on the petitions of hand-loom weavers (341), HC 1835, vol. xiii, Analysis of the evidence taken before the *Select committee on Hand-Loom Weavers' Petitions* (1834–35).

Royal commission on the condition of the poorer classes in Ireland, Appendix C, Part I, State of the poor and charitable institutions in principal towns in Ireland [35], HC 1836, vol. xxx.

Royal commission on the condition of the poorer classes in Ireland, Appendix E, Baronial examination relative to food, cottages and cabins, clothing and furniture, pawnbroking and savings banks, drinking; Supplement [37], HC 1836, vol. xxxii.

Royal commission on handloom weavers, Assistant Commissioners' Reports, pt. III (Yorkshire, West Riding; Ireland) (43–II), HC 1840, vol. xxiii.

Report of the commissioners on the census of Ireland, 1841 [504], HC 1843, vol. xxiv.

Evidence collected by T. Martin, *Royal commission on children's employment in mines and manufactories*, 2nd Report (manufactures), with Reports and evidence from sub-commissioners, II [432], HC 1843, vol. xv.

Reports of the inspectors of factories to the secretary of state for the home department for the half-year ending 31 October 1850 [1304], HC 1851, vol. xxiii.

Census of Ireland 1851. Part II: Returns of agricultural produce [1589]. HC 1852–53, vol. xciii.

Sixth annual report of the commissioners administering the laws for relief of the poor in Ireland [1645], Report, appendices, HC 1852–53, vol. l.

Census of Ireland 1851: pt. I, Area, population, and number of houses, by townlands and electoral divisions: County of Antrim [1565] HC 1852–53, vol. xcii.

Report of the commissioner appointed to inquire how far it may be advisable to extend the provisions of the acts for the better regulation of mills and factories to bleaching works established in certain parts of the United Kingdom of Great Britain and Ireland [1943], with evidence and appendix, HC 1854–55, vol. xviii.

Royal commission to inquire into the state of fairs and markets in Ireland, Part II, Report, minutes of evidence [1910], HC 1854–55, vol. xix.

Census of Ireland, 1851: pt. VI: General Report [2134], HC 1856, vol. xxxi.

Return of average rate of weekly earnings of agricultural labourers in Ireland, July-December 1860 (2), HC 1862, vol. lx.

Reports of the inspectors of factories to the secretary of state for the home department for the half-year ending 31 October 1862 [3076], HC 1863, vol. xviii, Report of Robert Baker.

Agricultural statistics of Ireland for the year 1861 [3156], HC 1863 vol. lxix.

Census of Ireland 1861, pt. I, Area, population, and number of houses, by townlands and electoral divisions, Provinces of Ulster and Connaught [3204] HC 1863, vol. lv.

Census of Ireland, 1861: pt. IV: Reports and tables relating to religious professions, education and occupations, vol. II, Religions and occupations [3204–III], HC 1863, vol. lx.

Royal commission on the employment of children in trades not regulated by law, Second Report, with minutes of evidence [3414] HC 1864, vol. xxii.

Reports from poor law inspectors on wages of agricultural labourers in Ireland [C.35], HC 1870, vol. xiv, Dr. Knox's Report.

Agricultural statistics of Ireland for the year 1871 HC 1873 [c.762], vol. lxix.

Eighth annual report of the Registrar-General for Ireland [C.968] HC 1874, vol. xiv.

Census of Ireland for 1871, pt. I, Area, population and number of houses; occupations, religion and education, volume III, Province of Ulster; summary tables, indexes [C.964], HC 1874 vol. lxxiv, Pt I.

Factory and workshops commission, part III, vol. II, minutes of evidence [C.1443–I] HC 1876, vol. xxx.

Factory and Workshops Act commission [C.1443], HC 1876, vol. xxix, Appendices.

Report of Her Majesty's commissioners of inquiry into the working of the landlord and tenant (Ireland) Act, 1870 and the Acts amending the same, minutes of evidence, [C.2779–II], HC 1881, vol. xviii.

Eighteenth Annual Report of the Registrar-General for Ireland [C.3368], HC 1882, vol. xix.

Select committee of the House of Lords on land law (Ireland), First report, proceedings, minutes of evidence, appendix (249), HL 1882, xi.

Agricultural statistics of Ireland for the year 1881 [C.3332], HC 1882 vol. lxxiv.

Census of Ireland 1881, Area, population and number of houses; occupations, religion and education, volume III, Province of Ulster [C.3204], HC 1882, vol. lxxviii.

Select committee on industries (Ireland), Report, proceedings, minutes of evidence, appendix, index (288), HC 1885–85, vol. ix.

Report of the chief inspector of factories and workshops to Her Majesty's principal secretary of state for the home department for the year ending 31st *October 1886* [C.5002], HC 1887, vol. xvii.

Return of wages published between 1830 and 1886 (industrial workers in the United Kingdom) [C.5172], HC 1887, vol. lxxxix.

Report of the chief inspector of factories and workshops to Her Majesty's principal secretary of state for the home department for the year ending 31st *October 1887* [C.5328], HC 1888, vol. xxvi.

Return of rates of wages in the principal textile trades of the United Kingdom, with report thereon [C.5807], HC 1889, vol. lxx.

Return of the rates of wages in the minor textile trades of the United Kingdom with report thereon [C.6161], HC 1890, lxviii.

Twenty-eighth annual report of the registrar-general for Ireland [C.6787], HC 1892, vol. xxiv.

Census of Ireland 1891: Area, population and number of houses; occupations, religion and education, volume III, Province of Ulster [C.6626], HC 1892, vol. xcii.

Agricultural statistics of Ireland for the year 1891 [C.6777], HC 1892 vol. lxxxviii.

Royal commission on labour, third report (Agricultural Labour) (vol. IV, Ireland, part I)
  [C.6894–XVIII], HC 1893–94, vol. xxxvii, pt. 1., General report.

Royal commission on labour. The Agricultural labourer, vol. IV, Ireland, Part V, Indices
  (analytical and general) to the reports of the assistant agricultural commissioners contained in volume IV. Parts I to V [C.6894–XXII], HC 1893–94, vol. xxxvii, pt 1.

*Board of trade report by Miss Collet on changes in the employment of women and girls in
  industrial centres*, Part I, *flax and jute centres* [C.8794], HC 1898, vol. lxxxviii.

Agricultural statistics of Ireland for the year 1901 [Cd.1121], HC 1902, vol. Cxvi, Pt 1.

 Census of Ireland for the year 1901, General report [Cd.1190], HC 1902, vol. cxxix.

Census returns of Ireland for 1901; giving details of the area, houses, and population, also
  ages, civil or conjugal condition, occupations, birth-places, religion and education of
  the people, in each county, and summary tables for each province: vol. III: Province of
  Ulster [Cd.1123] HC 1902, vol. cxxvi, cxxvii.

*Reports by Mr. Wilson Fox on the wages, earnings and conditions of employment of agri-
  cultural labourers in the United Kingdom, with statistical tables and charts* [Cd. 2376],
  HC 1905, cxvii.

*Report of the departmental committee with regard to the application of the national insur-
  ance act to outworkers in Ireland*, vol. II, Evidence and appendices [Cd. 7686], HC
  1914–16, vol. xxxi.

NEWSPAPERS

Ballymena Observer

Banner of Ulster

Belfast Morning News

Belfast Protestant Journal

Irish Textile Journal

Irish Times

Linen Market

Ulster Guardian

Belfast Linen Trade Circular

Lurgan Mail

News-Letter

Northern Whig

*Portadown and Lurgan News and
  County Armagh Advertiser*

Textile Manufacturer

Weekly Northern Whig

ARCHIVAL MATERIAL

Public Record Office of Northern Ireland, Belfast

Elevation and plans, hotel, Ballymenagh C. Antrim' [*sic*], D/929/HA12/11/4.

Putting-out book of Edward Gribbon, D/1191/29.

Weaver's book of John Keightley, M1C/26/1.

Minutes of the Linen Merchants Association, D/2088/1.

*Report of John Greer, inspector general for Ulster, of the state of the linen markets in
  said province*, D/562/6225.

Braidwater Spinning Company machine book, D/1492/8.
Annual Report of the Linen Merchants' Association, Belfast, 1873, D/2088/11/2.
Admittance rolls from the Ballymena Union Workhouse, MIC 15F/31 and 32.
Marriage register of the First Presbyterian Church, Ballymena, MIC/1P/114/1.
Manuscript returns from the *Census of Ireland for 1901*, MIC/354/1/18.
Manuscript census returns, *Census of Ireland, 1851*, MIC/5A/15, 16.

Linen Hall Library, Belfast
Flax Supply Association, Annual Report, for the Year 1886. Belfast: Adair's Steam
    Printing Works, 1887.
Annual Report of the Flax Supply Association for 1894. Belfast: Hugh Adair, 1895.
Flax Supply Association Annual Report for 1895. Belfast: Hugh Adair, 1896.
Annual Report of the Flax Supply Association for 1905. Belfast: Hugh Adair, 1906.

National Archives of Ireland, Dublin
Statement of the number of men who may be employed in the Belfast and Ballymena
    Railway in the summer of 1846, C. Lanyon, July 7th 1847, RLFC/3/1/481.
CSO RP 1873
G 2578/12 (Various documents related to the Hand Loom Merchandise Act).

Rensselaer County Historical Society, Troy, New York
Cluett, Coon and Company Collection.

Deputy-Registrar's Office, Ballymena
Craigs Parish register of marriages, Books 1 and 2.

Index

Aberdeen, countess of, 126, 129, 134–5

Adair, William, 43

agricultural labourers, earnings of, compared with handloom weavers, 46, 60; earnings of, 107–10

Ahoghill, linen industry in, 27; weavers in, 98, 100

America, Civil War and cotton prices, 68, 77; Civil War and effects on linen trade with Ireland, 67–74, 76–8, 82; collar and cuff industry in, 82, 88–9; linen export markets in, 30, 52, 63–4, 69, 71, 82; protectionist measures in, 88; terms of commerce in, 70, 116

Anderson, Samuel, 131, 134

Antrim, Co., linen industry in, 53, 58 — *see also* individual place names

Ardee, Co. Louth, linen market in, 25

Armagh, Co., linen industry in, 53, 58, 89 — *see also* individual place names

Armagh, town, linen market in, 22, 26, 37, 44

Arvagh, Co. Cavan, linen market in, 28

assistant handloom commissioners — *see also* 'C.G. Otway' and 'R.M. Muggeridge', 16, 23, 42, 45, 84

Australia, linen export markets in, 62

Austria, linen export markets in, 62

Ballylummin townland, 102–3

Ballymena, Co. Antrim, intergenerational transmission of handloom skill, 99–100; agitations by weavers in, 93–6; bleaching industry, 43, 45, 111–12; casualization of handloom weaving in, 104–10; cloth prices, 89, 116–18; cloth specialization, 27–8, 80–2; feminization of weaving workforce in, 95, 96–104, 108–10; First Presbyterian Church, 91–3; handloom trade associations — *see also* (Hand-

loom) Weavers' Defence Association (Ballymena); handloom weavers, earnings of, 83, 88, 93, 98–9; handloom weavers, intergenerational social mobility of, 91–2; handloom weavers, literacy, compared to other occupations, 91; handlooms used for shirting manufacture, 82; linen market in, 27, 43–4,49, 50–1, 56, 77, 80, 95; location, physical description of, 42–3; market institutions in, 43; *Observer*, 93–4; population of Ballymena poor law union, 106; railway line, 44–5; yarn spinning in, 28

Ballymenas — *see also* shirtings

Ballymoney, Co. Antrim, linen market in, 27, 49

Ballynagh, Co. Cavan, linen market in, 28

Banbridge, Co. Down, linen industry and market in, 22, 26, 44, 48, 52–3, 54, 56, 77

Barnsley, England, linen industry in, 55

Bastable, C.F., 58

Belfast, cotton industry in, 53; earnings of cotton handloom weavers in, 30–1; linen market in, 26, 37, 44; linen workforce in, 53–4, 58, 62, 77; yarn spinning industry in, 35; Belfast Chamber of Commerce, 85, 123, 124; Belfast Linen Trade Committee, 50; *News-Letter*, 123

Belgium, linen export markets in, 62; linen handloom weavers in, 50

Bessbrook, Co. Armagh, linen industry in, 64

bleachers, 24–5

bleaching industry, 24–5, 111–13

Board of Trustees of Linen and Hempen Manufacture, dissolution of, 23, 52, 121; establishment and mandate of, 20–1; and market regulations, 21–2, 55.

Bourke, Joanna, 10, 107